Knowledge Mobilization and Educational Research

How can educational research have more impact? What processes of knowledge exchange are most effective for increasing the uses of research results? How can research-produced knowledge be better 'mobilized' among users such as practising educators, policy-makers and the public communities?

These sorts of questions are commanding urgent attention in global educational discourses and research policies. This attention has been translated into powerful material that shapes what is now considered to be worthwhile research. It directly affects how research is funded, recognized and assessed. Yet precisely what activities constitute effective knowledge mobilization, or even what is meant by 'moving knowledge', remains unclear. *Knowledge Mobilization and Educational Research* explores:

- what politics are at play in determining knowledge 'impact' across radically different contexts;
- who determines what counts as impact, and for what purposes;
- how 'results' of educational research are separated from its participants and processes;
- how languages are used in the construction of knowledge, the enactment of policy processes and the ways in which research unfolds.

This volume is unique in bringing together these wide-ranging issues of knowledge mobilization in education. The volume editors critically analyse these complex issues and also describe various efforts of knowledge mobilization and their effects. The contributors in *Knowledge Mobilization and Educational Research* speak from diverse occupational and theoretical locations. Leading scholars in Canada, the USA, the UK and Australia bring disciplinary perspectives from law, digital media studies, museum studies, journalism and policy-making, as well as fields of education. Some speak from Anglo-'Western' perspectives, but others are able to give perspectives from Asian, indigenous and diasporic locations.

Tara Fenwick is Professor of Education at the School of Education, University of Stirling in Scotland.

Lesley Farrell is Professor and Associate Dean of Research and Development in the Faculty of Arts and Social Sciences, University of Technology, Sydney, Australia.

Knowledge Mobilization and Educational Research

Politics, languages and responsibilities

Edited by
Tara Fenwick and
Lesley Farrell

Routledge
Taylor & Francis Group

LONDON AND NEW YORK

First published 2012
by Routledge
2 Park Square, Milton Park, Abingdon, Oxon OX14 4RN

Simultaneously published in the USA and Canada
by Routledge
711 Third Avenue, New York, NY 10017

Routledge is an imprint of the Taylor & Francis Group, an informa business

British Library Cataloguing in Publication Data
A catalogue record for this book is available from the British
Library

Library of Congress Cataloging in Publication Data
Knowledge mobilization and educational research: politics,
    languages and responsibilities/[edited by] Tara Fenwick,
    Lesley Farrell.
    p. cm.
    1. Education—Research. 2. Access to knowledge movement.
    I. Fenwick, Tara J. II. Farrell, Lesley.
    LB1028.K54 2011
    370.72—dc22   2011008760

ISBN: 978-0-415-61464-1 (hbk)
ISBN: 978-0-415-61465-8 (pbk)
ISBN: 978-0-203-81746-9 (ebk)

Typeset in Galliard and GillSans
by Florence Production Ltd, Stoodleigh, Devon

MIX
Paper from
responsible sources
FSC
www.fsc.org   FSC® C004839

Printed and bound in Great Britain by
TJ International Ltd, Padstow, Cornwall

Contents

Illustrations

Notes on contributors

Chris Chesher is Senior Lecturer in Digital Cultures in the Faculty of Arts, University of Sydney, Australia. His research draws on media studies and technology studies to examine the politics and epistemic implications of technical artefacts as they mediate and reconfigure cultural practices.

Amanda Cooper, a former secondary school teacher, is a doctoral candidate at the Ontario Institute for Studies in Education, University of Toronto, Canada. Her interests professionally and academically revolve around improving research use in education. Her doctoral research compares efforts made by KM intermediaries in Education.

Ian Dyck (PhD, University of Alberta, Canada, 1976) is an emeritus Curator at the Canadian Museum of Civilization in Quebec, Canada, where he was responsible for Prairies archaeology from 1989 to 2010. In addition to doing archaeological science and exhibitions, he has written about the histories of museums and archaeology.

Anne Edwards is a Professor of Education and Director of the Department of Education at the University of Oxford, UK. Her most recent work has been on the relational turn in expertise required for collaboration across the boundaries between practices.

Lesley Farrell is Professor and Associate Dean, Research and Development, in the Faculty of Arts and Social Sciences, University of Technology, Sydney, Australia, researching language and social change in globalizing workplaces and the policy dimensions of workforce development more generally.

Tara Fenwick is Professor of Education at the School of Education, University of Stirling in Scotland. Her research and teaching focus on professional practice and learning, with particular interest in professionals' knowledge sources and strategies in complexity, and the changing nature of professional responsibility.

Michael Fraser, AM, FAICD, is Professor of Law and Director of the Communications Law Centre, University of Technology, Sydney, Australia.

A founder and former CEO of Copyright Agency Limited (CAL) for 21 years, he influences change in copyright, media and communications in the public interest.

Ian Hardy is Lecturer in Educational Studies at the School of Education, The University of Queensland, Brisbane, Australia. Ian teaches and researches education policy and practice, including in the areas of teacher professional development and initial teacher education. He also researches the nature of teachers' and academics' work under current conditions. He has published widely in these areas.

Stephen Heimans is a full-time PhD student in the School of Education at The University of Queensland, Brisbane, Australia. His PhD research is concerned with the processes of production and enactment of education policy and is informed by critical approaches to material-discursive practices. This research focuses on the articulation of policy into and through the state and its progress into and around a public Vocational Education and Training Institute.

Sarah Howard is a Lecturer in Information and Communication Technologies in the Faculty of Education, University of Wollongong, Australia. Her research considers how knowledge practices, in teaching, change with the use of technology and how educational cultures impact on these changes.

Deirdre M. Kelly is a Professor of Sociology of Education in the Department of Educational Studies at the University of British Columbia, Vancouver, Canada. Her research interests include teaching for social justice and democracy, gender and youth studies, and news and entertainment media as public policy pedagogy.

Ben Levin is a Professor and Canada Research Chair in Education Leadership and Policy at the Ontario Institute for Studies in Education, University of Toronto, Canada, where he leads the 'knowledge mobilization research team' (www.oise.utoronto.ca/rspe).

Bob Lingard is Professor in the School of Education and is also affiliated with the Institute for Social Science Research at The University of Queensland, Brisbane, Australia. His most recent book, co-authored with Fazal Rizvi, is *Globalizing Education Policy* (Routledge, 2010). He currently has three Australian Research Council grants dealing with globalization and the national testing and curriculum, rich accountabilities for schools, and performance indicators as technologies of governance across health, welfare and education.

Jenny Ozga is Professor of the Sociology of Education, University of Oxford, UK. Her latest publication (with Peter Dahler-Larsen, Christina Segerholm and Hannu Simola) is *Fabricating Quality in European Education: Data and Education Governance* (Routledge 2010).

Phan Le Ha lectures in Culture and Pedagogy in the Faculty of Education, Monash University, Melbourne, Australia, and holds honorary positions at Vietnamese universities. Her teaching and research interests include knowledge mobilization, cultural sociology of education, identity studies and EIL (English as an International Language).

Andrew Pollard is a Professor of Education at the Institute of Education, University of London and at the Graduate School of Education, University of Bristol, both in the UK. He was director of the UK's Teaching and Learning Research Programme (TLRP) (https://portal.ioe.ac.uk/http/en.wikipedia.org/wiki/TLRP) and chair of the Strategic Forum for Research in Education. He is currently director of ESCalate, supporting teaching of education in higher education, and chair of a panel preparing to assess the quality of UK Educational Research.

Margaret Somerville is a Professor of Education (Learning and Development) at Monash University, Melbourne, Australia. She is interested in alternative methodologies and modes of representation in educational research and the ways in which these can be relevant and engaging for local communities.

Michelle Stack is an Associate Professor in the Department of Educational Studies, University of British Columbia, Vancouver, Canada. Her research centres on media, policy and education, media education and media–academic communication aimed at expanding public discussion and input concerning public policy, particularly education policy.

Charles Ungerleider is a Professor of the Sociology of Education at The University of British Columbia, Vancouver, Canada and managing partner at Directions Evidence and Policy Research Group. A former Deputy Minister of Education, Ungerleider teaches about educational politics, policy and governance.

Dolores van der Wey is of mixed ancestry, including the Haida and Coast Salish people of British Columbia, Canada. She is currently an Assistant Professor at Simon Fraser University, Vancouver, British Columbia. Her research and teaching passions include Aboriginal literature and pedagogy, teacher education and engaging the politics of difference.

Rui Yang has taught and researched in the Chinese mainland, Australia and Hong Kong. He received his PhD from the University of Sydney, Australia in 2001. He is now based in the Faculty of Education at the University of Hong Kong.

Abbreviations

AERA	American Educational Research Association
AMHRS	Alabin Museum of Historical and Regional Studies
ARC	Australian Research Council
BERA	British Educational Research Association
CMC	Canadian Museum of Civilization
EI	Engineering Index
ERA	Excellence in Research for Australia
ESL	English as a second language
ESRC	Economic and Social Research Council
EUR	euro
FLOSS	free/libre/open-source software
GAPP	General Administration of Press and Publications
GATT	General Agreement on Tariffs and Trade
HE	higher education
HEP	Higher Education Press
ICT	information and communication technology
IF	impact factor
ISP	internet service provider
KM	knowledge mobilization
LMS	learning management system
MDB	Murray–Darling Basin
NERF	National Educational Research Forum
NGO	non-governmental organization
NNSF	National Natural Science Foundation
NSW	New South Wales
OECD	Organisation for Economic Co-operation and Development
p.a.	per annum
PISA	Programme for International Student Assessment
PLP	personal learning plan
PR	public relations
RMB	renminbi
RQF	Research Quality Framework

RSPE	Research Supporting Practice in Education [programme]
SCI	Science Citation Index
SCI-E	Science Citation Index-Expanded
SNP	Scottish National Party
SSE	school self-evaluation
SSHRC	Social Sciences and Humanities Research Council
STEM	science, technology, engineering and mathematics
STM	scientific, technical and medical
TESOL	teaching of English to speakers of other languages
TIMMS	Trends in International Mathematics and Science Study
TLRP	Teaching and Learning Research Programme
TRIPS	Agreement on Trade-Related Aspects of Intellectual Property Rights
UNESCO	United Nations Educational, Scientific and Cultural Organization
USD	US dollar
WIPO	World Intellectual Property Organization
WTO	World Trade Organization

Introduction: Knowledge mobilization

The new research imperative

Tara Fenwick and Lesley Farrell

How can educational research have more impact? How do we know the depth and scope of the impact it has? What processes of knowledge exchange are most effective for increasing the uses of research results? How can research-produced knowledge be better 'mobilized' among users such as practising educators, policy-makers and the public communities?

These sorts of questions, despite their many embedded definitional, philosophical and pragmatic problems, are commanding urgent attention in educational discourses and research policies now circulating in the UK and Europe, Canada and the USA and Australia and other parts of the world. This attention has been translated into powerful material exercises that shape what is considered to be worthwhile research and how research is funded, recognized and assessed. Granting agencies request knowledge mobilization or knowledge exchange plans and offer special funds for these purposes. Researchers and universities are explicitly directed, in research design and accountability, to emphasize knowledge exchange or mobilization – announced by one funding council as a core priority (SSHRC 2008, 2010).

Yet precisely what activities constitute effective knowledge mobilization, or even what is meant by 'moving knowledge', remains unclear. Equally puzzling is why a predominant focus on applied research – with linear associations of knowledge being piped from one site to another – has become a desirable aim for educational research. What *politics* are at play in determining knowledge 'impact' across radically different contexts, each comprising unique needs and diffuse educational processes where multiple influences are entangled? What activities, exactly, enact effective knowledge mobilization according to different audiences? Who determines what counts as impact, and for what purposes? How are 'results' of educational research separated from its participants and processes? What are the consequences of distinguishing users from producers in educational knowledge and research, and who benefits from such distinctions?

Knowledge mobilization in educational research also invokes debates about the *languages* through which knowledge is constructed, policy processes are enacted and research unfolds. A panoply of terms that signify very different processes and interests are often used synonymously: knowledge mobilization, exchange, transfer and use; research results, processes and impact; research, inquiry, knowledge and evidence. Knowledge mobilization in some formulations is portrayed as a linear and rational matter of designing more-targeted and appealing dissemination, but it is entangled in social processes and contradictory influences. The worlds of research and of policy (Ungerleider, this volume), for example, function with very different rhythms, orientations, risks and accountabilities, and knowledge-sharing among their languages is a fraught endeavour at best. Certainly, as research and its texts move around the globe, problematics emerge about what is valued as scholarship as it is mediated and made visible or invisible through particular dominant languages and relations of research, as argued in this volume's final chapter (Lingard, Hardy and Heimans).

Indeed, in any relationships among researchers and the communities they serve, there exist conflicts over the value, purpose and ultimately the *responsibilities* of knowledge mobilization: different systems often attempt to shape educational research to meet their own needs (Edwards, Sebba and Rickinson 2007: 653). Increasing concern, for instance, has been voiced about researchers' responsibilities in approaching unique epistemologies such as Indigenous knowledges, which have historically been colonized by dominant forms of educational research (L.T. Smith 1999). Negotiating these diverse expectations may require special knowledge about communicating and building relationships (Nutley *et al.* 2007), about knowledge politics and about the material-discursive processes through which knowledge is enacted. As today's knowledge scapes are being reconfigured through Web 2.0 worlds of interconnectivity and blurrings of user/producer, public/private, it is increasingly difficult to trace knowledge production and movement. Issues of ownership and rights of access to knowledge have prompted debates about scholarly responsibility to circulate knowledge freely (Willinsky 2005). Some iterations suggest that researchers bear responsibility for creative knowledge design, pedagogic and civic enactments in diverse communities, as well as relational bridge-building. And yet, as Edwards *et al.* (2007) point out, while educational researchers are even now making huge efforts to engage with professionals in schools as well as with policy-makers, the perception continues that they are not engaged much at all.

This book explores these three issues of knowledge mobilization – politics, language and responsibilities – through the voices of 21 authors based in the UK, Canada, Hong Kong and Australia, speaking from disciplinary perspectives based in law, digital media studies, museum studies, journalism and policy-making as well as in fields of education.

Perspectives of 'mobility' in contexts of knowledge

Generally, knowledge mobilization seems to be about active engagement of diverse public users of research results – engagement that extends beyond 'traditional' forums of academic dissemination such as journal articles directed towards academic readers. Outcomes of this engagement should then mobilize the public to become research users, and mobilize impact or visible change among these research users. In health care research, 'knowledge-to-action' is the term suggested by Graham *et al.* (2006) in their survey of 33 research-funding agencies in nine countries: the intent underpinning most terms for knowledge mobilization or exchange is, they show, often focused on involving users from the beginning of the knowledge-creation process and throughout activities of moving and sustaining applications of the knowledge.

But – what is knowledge when it moves? Increasingly, knowledge is reified and mobilized as language. Texts make knowledge portable. In many respects knowledge seems, or used to seem, unambiguously situated – in the practices of disciplines, professions, industries, times, places, histories, cultures and so on. The textual dimension of knowledge was secondary. The contemporary domination of communications technologies, and especially Web 2.0 technologies, has challenged and transformed the practices associated with specific forms of knowledge, re-emphasizing the textual character of knowledge.

D. Smith (1999) argues that it is the textual character of knowledge that allows it to move from one domain to another and it is the textual character of knowledge, its apparent immutability and objective 'truth', that gives it its coercive force in locations that are remote from its origins. The words and images that instantiate knowledge as they move across temporal, spatial and disciplinary boundaries appear to be stripped of their place and their time when they are constituted as texts to be circulated. But, words cannot avoid 'dragging their pasts behind them' (Bakhtin 1981) and they are inevitably, as Appadurai (2000) argues, reconstituted with differently inflected meanings as they circulate through new locations. So knowledge is, paradoxically, both fixed and mutated as it is mobilized across boundaries.

What is implied by references to knowledge mobilization is that the boundaries of different knowledges are distinct and that they can move about across different domains to (re)organize thought, space and practices. However, knowledge that moves is itself embedded in material practice. Knowledge is inscribed within objects such as texts, tools, technologies and bodies. It emerges in new ways as these objects circulate among different activities, making/dissolving connections with one another, making/dissolving their own boundaries, and mutating as they themselves are mediated in local practices. Among the important questions to ask may be those about which objects become most visible and through what material processes, which material practices become most durable, and what linkages and labour hold them in place. Some education analysts have argued that these are not questions of mobilizing new perspectives or interpretation, as when an object such as a curriculum guide is interpreted differently in different classrooms, but that, in effect, different worlds can be mobilized through the same object (e.g. Fenwick 2010; Mulcahy 2010; Verran 2001). We see some of these flows in the meeting of art, research and Indigenous and scientific knowledge (Somerville, this volume).

Education itself is both a technology and a catalyst of knowledge mobilization, at the same time as education's dynamics (its premises, purposes and processes) are an outcome of knowledge mobilization. In considering the mobilities and connections of objects, we need also to consider carefully just what might be the role of educational researchers in the textual, social and material practices that enact knowledge mobilization.

Issues in 'knowledge mobilization' in educational research

While this book is organized around three broad themes of politics, languages and responsibilities in knowledge mobilization, more issues trickle across these themes. Four are outlined below to provide some background for the chapter discussions.

Heterogeneity of understandings

Levin (2008) has pointed to three main problems of hetereogeneity in writings about knowledge mobilization: (1) a lack of agreement on terminology; (2) multiple conceptual frames and lack of agreement on main issues; and (3) working across disciplines. Heterogeneity emerges in diverse views and traditions of different disciplines regarding the relationship between researchers and society. It also becomes evident across national research strategies. For example, in comparing such strategies in the UK, Canada and Australia, one can discern different priorities and responsibilities envisioned for the state and state-funded granting agencies with respect to enabling links of researchers and the communities that might benefit from their studies.

The term 'knowledge mobilization' itself is particularly prominent in Canadian research policy discourses, where it is generally understood to refer to 'the flow of knowledge among multiple agents leading to intellectual, social and/or economic impact' (SSHRC 2010: 4). The Social Sciences and Humanities Research Council of Canada characterizes knowledge mobilization as a 'co-constructed' process distinct from linear, one-way knowledge dissemination or knowledge transfer. The Council's 2009–11 strategic plan for knowledge mobilization (SSHRC 2010: 2) places strong value on accessibility and impact of research for 'knowledge users'. The responsibility for SSHRC is largely limited to fostering 'connections' and the sharing of information. This leaves ambiguous questions of exactly where responsibility lies for engaging non-researchers in knowledge production and use, configuring research findings in formats and forums that are truly accessible and attractive to users, and conducting research processes in ways that users might value as impact.

In the UK's Economic and Social Research Council (ESRC 2010a: para.1) the more prevalent term is 'knowledge exchange', defined as 'exchanging good ideas, research results, experiences and skills between universities, other research organizations, business, Government, the third sector and the wider community to enable innovative new products, services and policies to be developed'. Knowledge transfer, incidentally, is defined exactly the same way. Here the emphasis is on 'conversation' (ESRC 2010b: para.2), with responsibilities listed for both 'those carrying out research' and 'those using research'. The ESRC presents its own role as mostly promoting this knowledge exchange and, more influentially, placing increasing weight on exchange activities and their projected impact in the assessment of new research bids.

In Australia, the Research Quality Framework (RQF) of the conservative Howard government controversially proposed to measure research 'impact' in ways that would substantially influence research rankings and research funding. As it has been in the UK, this was controversial partly because the measures of impact were themselves not clearly defined and partly because considerations of 'impact', especially outside the academy, were understood to redefine the role of universities in making and mobilizing knowledge. After the defeat of the Howard government, the Rudd Labor government developed the Excellence in Research for Australia (ERA) accountability exercise and deleted 'impact' from the assessment framework, relying heavily on more traditional metrics. This too is controversial, supported by the sandstone universities, which promote research for its own sake, but opposed by the newer technological universities, which stake their reputations on the demonstrable utility of their research.

Inter/multi-disciplinarity in knowledge generation and mobilization

An increased emphasis on the utility of university research has led to an increased focus on the need for university researchers to address complex and intractable real-world problems. Such problems clearly demand interdisciplinary approaches and multidisciplinary teams, and rhetoric around university research strategies and research funding programmes endorses and advocates such approaches. They are, however, difficult to achieve. In the first place, the organization of research accountability regimes may militate against interdisciplinary work. The ERA exercise in Australia, for instance, reports and evaluates research productivity according to Field of Research (FOR) codes at the four-digit (sub-disciplinary) level. Researchers who engage in interdisciplinary projects, and publish outside their disciplinary field, may jeopardize the ranking (and ultimately the funding) of their discipline within their university. In the second place, the conduct of interdisciplinary work is itself demanding. Different disciplines have different ways of conceptualizing problems and of investigating them, and what counts as a legitimate methodological approach, with robust knowledge claims, in one discipline may be unknown, or dismissed, in another. Researchers in the field of journalism, for instance, notoriously find themselves in conflict on the matter of research ethics with social science researchers, who have different, and in some respects more stringent, constraints on interviewing behaviour than journalistic ethics impose (Richards 2009).

Access to knowledge in a capitalist economy

In a capitalist economy knowledge is also understood as a commodity to be traded on a global market. As a commodity it has value and that value has been protected through control of access and intellectual copyright laws (Fraser, this volume). An important development in the shift to knowledge mobilization has been the open access movement, whereby published work is made free to readers. The growth of open access to scholarly research has obviously been enabled by new technological tools and publishers' experimentation with online publishing. However, it has also been spurred by groups of scholars renewing commitment to the ideals of open science and the ethics of making publicly funded research available to the public, in the wake of dramatically escalating costs of accessing such research through scholarly journals whose subscription fees skyrocketed in the final decades of the twentieth century (Willinsky 2005). Debates in open access publishing focus precisely on the quality of knowledge, the forms of knowledge that can and should be made available, the avenues of availability such as archives and search engines, the costs of producing knowledge, and of course questions about ownership and property rights. Slowly, a transformation appears to be occurring in scholarly views about such issues as universities such as Harvard adopt an open access mandate to make their scholarly products available to the public, free, in open access repositories.

Willinsky, an expert on open access knowledge and director of the Public Knowledge Project http://pkp.sfu.ca, is a strong advocate of open access publishing to mobilize educational knowledge. He urges educational researchers to take more responsibility for increasing knowledge availability, such as by publishing in open access journals, sharing their data sets and archiving their published work in publicly accessible digital repositories. Provocatively, he laments what he calls the unnecessary isolation of educational research,

> within its own little corner of the academy, effectively cut off from this newly revitalized sphere by the toll-gate barriers of article and subscription costs . . . it does not make a lot of sense to watch others selectively cull aspects of this work and represent it as the whole of the relevant educational research that bears on the schools today. We need to look to the consequences of the knowledge that we seek to contribute to education . . .

> (Willinsky 2010: 9)

Recognizing and evaluating impact of knowledge mobilization

Significant emphasis on the impact of research knowledge in many quarters of research policy has prompted a number of debates reflected in this volume's chapters. Researchers wonder just what is meant by impact and what it means to consider and even measure knowledge mobilization as impact. Even when 'impact' is translated to mean something like productive outcomes, the multiplicity of variables affecting any outcome in education – or any aspect of social or natural life – prohibit a meaningful causal linkage to one particular study or to the mobilization of particular knowledge. Researchers intending to demonstrate impact, as they are required to do in ESRC-funded research in the UK, are to go beyond simply reporting outputs of a project (articles published for academics, reports given to government staff, dialogues hosted, websites or art works created) as its outcomes. Outcomes are more visible changes or effects influenced through knowledge: in scholarship, but also in policy, professional practice, products, student outcomes, or public under-standings and activities. The ESRC's impact strategy for 2008–11 defines research impact to include both economic and societal outcomes, the latter referring to effects of research on the environment, public health or quality of life, and impacts on government policy, the third sector and professional practice. In other words, researchers in education as in other fields are increas-ingly enjoined to show the direct influence of their work on the contemporary worlds around them, not the 'PR fluff' of all the information they disseminate.

The issues of identifying impact of knowledge mobilization are by now well known, following several studies of research impact since 2000. Different types of knowledge exercise influence differently. At least three different forms of impact have been proposed:

- instrumental (for example, influencing the development of policy, practice or service provision, shaping legislation, altering behaviour);
- conceptual (for example, contributing to the understanding of these and related issues, reframing debates); and
- capacity building (for example, through technical/personal skill development).

(Nutley *et al.* 2007)

The type of *environment* will affect the way in which knowledge moves and exercises influence, depending on the processes available to engage users, the willingness and availability of users to engage in this knowledge, and the perceived relevance of the knowledge. The problem of *time lag* between the completion of research and any changes that it might influence in policy and practice make impact difficult to recognize, let alone assess. There is also the problem of time lag between the production of knowledge and a particular community's need for that knowledge. It is also difficult to identify the *points of influence* throughout the complex processes whereby particular knowledge may begin to affect decisions or practices, or even the *kinds of influence* that are of most interest to users. For example, community groups often indicate that they are less interested in the actual 'findings' of particular studies, as they prefer to rely upon their own data, than in the sorts of questions that researchers help them to ask.

Taking such issues into consideration, case studies of impact in social science research were conducted by the ESRC (2010a) to identify different forms of impact, how these might be recognized and what environments and activities are most helpful to promote them. 'Key impact factors' were identified through these case studies:

- Established relationships and networks with user communities
- Involving users at all stages of the research
- Well-planned user-engagement and knowledge exchange strategies
- Portfolios of research activity that build reputations with research users
- Good infrastructure and management support
- Where appropriate, the involvement of intermediaries and knowledge brokers as translators, amplifiers, network providers.

(ESRC 2010a: 14)

In many of these iterations, however, much of the knowledge mobilization process is characterized to be organic and multi-directional, and there persists a clear division between those who produce (e.g. university-based researchers) and those who use knowledge (e.g. policy-makers, community members, industry representatives, education providers, professional practitioners, institutional managers, etc). There is also a tendency to treat knowledge as a package exchanged across domains. Here is where there is fundamental heterogeneity. Mobilizable knowledge is sometimes equated to findings, 'evidence' or 'best practice', such as when a particular protocol is developed through research and universalized for many settings of practice. Knowledge also might refer to innovation, itself a slippery term that can mean new products and services, new questions that challenge existing orthodoxies, or simply everyday improvisations. Knowledge in some inquiries may be philosophical, engaging both researchers and non-researchers in thinking differently or more broadly about their worlds. Or, what is meant by knowledge may be moved through embodied or encultured material practices. It may be more about empowering people or suggesting possibilities than solving problems or producing useful technologies. Clearly, one's understanding of knowledge in processes of mobilization is affected by how one views its purpose, and the purpose of its uses.

Acknowledging all of the heterogeneity, Levin (2008) suggests that we focus not on delineating differences, but on addressing the question: What kinds of efforts to promote knowledge mobilization have what effects under what circumstances, and what infrastructure is needed to support it? The chapters in this book each provide, in some way, a response to this question. And to do so, each has had to define, in the particular circumstances upon which it focuses, what is meant by knowledge, by mobilization and by effect.

The chapters

Ben Levin and Amanda Cooper open the book's first section 'Considering the Issues and the Players' by mapping multiple dimensions and models of research use and impact. They show why some ideas affect practice more than others – and why some practices persist in ways entirely inconsistent with strong research evidence. Research knowledge is distinct, they argue, from scientific evidence, colloquial evidence, practice-based and community knowledges and trans-national and other knowledge sources swirling through educational policy and practice. While these knowledges play important roles in communities of practice and policy, a greater use of research knowledge in education could improve educational outcomes; they present concrete strategies for ways forward in education.

Andrew Pollard, the former director of the UK's Teaching and Learning Research Programme (TLRP), describes six strategies adopted there to support impact and user engagement and offers illustrations of short-term impact. He argues that there has been a poor alignment of public aspirations for applied, relevant research and of academic incentivization for research assessment, funding and career progression. Nonetheless, he concludes that TLRP succeeded in supporting researchers in 'catching the wave' of public commitment to evidence-informed policy and practice – but, like Levin and Cooper, Pollard concurs that there is a long way to go before such practices are fully established.

Anne Edwards draws from her extensive empirical analyses of user engagement to reflect on what happens when the practices of university research come into contact with the practices of those who work in education or use educational services. This intersection can happen in ways that Edwards describes as horizontal and vertical. Her primary focus is on how practitioners outside the academy can work *in* research, alongside university-based researchers, to generate knowledge. A particularly helpful heuristic here identifies five distinct approaches to knowledge exchange among researchers and users, each underpinned by particular assumptions about knowledge. While Edwards is careful not to privilege any one of them, she emphasizes the importance of relational expertise on the part of both researchers and professional practitioners in working across the boundaries of their own knowledge communities.

Opening the second section on 'Politics in knowledge flows', Charles Ungerleider draws on his experience as a provincial Deputy Minister in Canada to contrast the different worlds of policy decision-makers and researchers. While highlighting the critical importance to decision-makers of relevant evidence, he shows the difficulties of incorporating research evidence into the fast-moving, high-stakes political environment. Decision-makers, argues Ungerleider, seek to resolve conflict and eliminate problems rapidly, need results that their voting constituencies will recognize as valuable, and draw from a wide range of evidence sources of which academic research is only one. In fact, suggests Ungerleider, the call for linking research with policy comes from the researchers, not from the policy world. He concludes that academic research would do better to focus on educational practitioners, beginning with engaging new teachers in research evidence.

In exploring the relationship between governance and knowledge 'stocks and flows', Jenny Ozga traces new governance forms of decentralization and deregulation to argue that data production and management were and are essential to governance. Knowledge and information play a pivotal role both in the pervasiveness of governance and in allowing the development of its dispersed, distributed and disaggregated form. In showing the gap between 'the fluid dream of data-based governance, and the sticky reality', her argument compares the development of data and evaluation systems in England and Scotland, with attention to the work that data do in both 'hard' and 'soft' governance through performance management and self-evaluation systems.

Margaret Somerville brings us a story of intense politics flowing across an Indigenous partner research initiative to save the Murray–Darling basin, a crisis of water shortage, competing stakeholder groups and diverse knowledges of water and water conservation. Using an arts-based research approach that she and her team refer to as 'enabling place pedagogies', the initiative seeks both to bridge these knowledges and to mobilize new knowledge. Somerville describes the overall approach as a pedagogical one, working in the space between Indigenous and non-Indigenous knowings to explore how knowledge can travel between them: 'The artworks as material objects mediate the crossing of the binaries/boundaries between bodies and places that helps the knowledge to flow'.

Individual flows are important to consider, too, in exploring the politics of knowledge and mobility. Phan Le Ha challenges the dominance of the 'global' in discussions about research-based knowledge, arguing that locality generally, and the nation state in particular, play a significant role in mobilizing knowledge across political and geographical boundaries. She uses her own biography as a Vietnamese academic working in the West to explore these ideas of nationality and transnationality, and the permeability of East/West divides in relation to knowledge. She makes a compelling case that the knowledge she produces as a researcher, while globally relevant, needs to be understood as being produced by a Vietnamese.

Ian Dyck, curator of the Canadian Museum of Civilization, opens the third section, 'Languages and Enactments of Knowledge Mobilization', with a case study of a Canada–Russia collaboration to produce a museum display on the ancient nomads of both countries. Most museums work hard on the pedagogy of their exhibits to stimulate active engagement of the public, but of course most must work within constraints of limited resources, public tastes and competition. Dyck explains the complexities of bridging languages across Russian, Canadian and Indigenous archaeological traditions, museum cultures, systems of representation and conflicts about what is the most important knowledge. His story traces the many compromises and strategies used by teams of researchers and non-researcher specialists in museum display to mobilize knowledge about ancient prairie peoples in modern museums.

Deirdre Kelly and Michelle Stack take on the issue of educational research reported in the media. Media is an influential site through which policy issues are framed and particular knowledges are recognized to wield influence among policy-makers educators, and the general public. Kelly and Stack note the relative lack of engagement of many researchers in mainstream media and argue that a key dimension here is the 'double divide' between knowledge traditions in academic research and in journalism. Each field is configured by very different knowledge structures, allegiances, values and priorities. However, far from supporting a two-solitudes approach, Kelly and Stack draw from their empirical research to offer examples of successful bridgings across this double divide, using a notion of a musical bridge providing transitions between the two 'keys' of journalism and academia. In particular, they promote the academic's role as mobilizing knowledge through the popular media in ways that can challenge problematic discourses and assumptions circulating about education and learning. Towards strengthening this role, Kelly and Stack provide a substantial list of strategies for academics to engage more fruitfully with journalists in knowledge mobilization.

Fenwick considers issues that emerge when employing art forms in knowledge mobilization. Forms such as film, visual art and drama are figuring as important means to represent research and move knowledge into active service (SSHRC 2008). While arts-based educational research has developed strong foundations and credibility as a field, the use of art by social science researchers to simply 'mobilize' knowledge is a rather more glib undertaking that raises troubling questions. These touch the tensions in combining the logics, purposes and processes of art with those of research. Fenwick tells the story of one research team's experiments in using drama to communicate their findings, an attempt whose mixed results invites reflection on the nature of knowledge, mobilities and ethics in 'using' art for knowledge mobilization.

Chris Chesher and Sarah Howard also address the question of the permeability of boundaries around knowledge, although their focus is on the tension between openness of access to knowledge and the control of intellectual property that is a central concern of contemporary universities. They are especially interested in the challenges that new technologies make to established understandings around the ownership of knowledge. They address this tension through the discussion of three ubiquitous cases: learning management systems; citation management tools; and journal databases.

Opening the final section on 'Responsibilities and Rights in Mobilizing Knowledge', Michael Fraser focuses on the issues of intellectual property in a global knowledge economy. He brings the perspective of a legal scholar to trace the legal lineage of the idea of 'intellectual property' to the foundational communication technology of the printing press and argues that this notion has made it possible to trade knowledge on a global market. He makes the argument that scholarly publishing is an anomaly in so far as universities and scholars donate their intellectual property to publishers and then buy it back from them in a business model that is already unsustainable in order to ensure that that knowledge is globally available through digital repositories.

Rui Yang takes up the question of responsibilities in scholarly publishing, focusing on the role of scholarly publishing in the Chinese mainland. He argues that scholarly publishing is viewed from within mainland China as a means of 'bringing China to the world, and the world to China'. While indigenous Chinese publishing houses are viewed as a means of breaking the domination of Western scholarly publishing, in practice it is difficult for even the best publications to challenge this domination.

Dolores van der Wey challenges educational researchers to take seriously the responsibility of repairing relations between Indigenous and non-Indigenous people by disrupting dominant Western narratives held by those who accept these as given. Her central question is, 'Whose accumulated knowledge and experience ultimately is considered most valid and worthy of knowing?' She argues for collectively building coalitions that move Indigenous knowledge more centrally into post-secondary institutions while addressing the ongoing implications of the colonial legacy for the 'broadest possible good'. Using examples from her own practices of research and pedagogy, van der Wey shows how Aboriginal literature can provide powerful tools for forming new relationships with Indigenous people.

To conclude the volume, Bob Lingard, Ian Hardy and Stephen Heimans address broadly many questions of responsibilities, as well as of politics and languages, by examining the geopolitics of mobilizing knowledge. In particular they highlight themes introduced in Somerville's, Phan's, Yang's and van der Wey's work, that existing research relations are hegemonic in reifying universal knowledge claims and suppressing, for instance, Indigenous, arts-based and non-traditional theory forms. These authors challenge the idea that theory is produced 'only in the high-status universities of the north'. They challenge this assumption through three narratives around the nature of educational policy studies, the teaching of educational policy studies and the ranking of journals for Australian Research accountability regimes. They conclude by arguing that educational knowledge needs to emerge and be supported across multiple global sites.

References

Appadurai, A. (2000) 'Grassroots globalization and the research imagination', in A. Appadurai, *Globalization*, Durham, NC: Duke University Press, 1–21.

Bakhtin, M.M. (1981) *The Dialogic Imagination*, Austin, University of Texas Press.

Edwards, A., Sebba, J., and Rickinson, M. (2007) 'Working with users: some implications for educational research', *British Educational Research Journal*, 33 (5): 647–61.

ESRC (Economic and Social Research Council) (2010a) *Taking Stock: A Summary of ESRC's Work to Evaluate the Impact of Research on Policy and Practice February 2009* (accessed on 21 October 2010 from www.esrcsocietytoday.ac.uk/takingstock).

—— (2010b) 'What is knowledge exchange?', *ESRC Society Today*, (accessed on 4 January 2011 from www.esrc.ac.uk/ESRCInfoCentre/Support/knowledge_transfer/index.aspx).

Fenwick, T. (2010) '(un)Doing standards in education with actor-network theory', *Journal of Education Policy*, 25(2), 117–33.

Graham I.D., Logan, J., Harrison, M.B., Straus, S.E. and Tetroe, J. (2006) 'Lost in knowledge translation: time for a map?', *Journal of Continuing Education in the Health Professions* 26(1): 13–24.

Levin, B. (2008) *Thinking about Knowledge Mobilization*, Toronto, ON: Canadian Council on Learning/Conseil Canadien sur l'apprentissage.

Mulcahy, D. (2010) 'Assembling the accomplished teacher: the performativity and politics of professional teaching standards', *Educational Philosophy and Theory* 43(3). Online first: doi: 10.1111/j.1469-5812.2009.00617.x.

Nutley, S., Walter, I. and Davis, H. (2007) *Using Evidence: how research can inform public services*, Bristol: Policy Press.

Richards, I. (2009) 'Uneasy bedfellows: ethics committees and journalism research', *Australian Journalism Review* 31 (2): 35–46.

Smith, D. (1999) *Writing the Social: critique, theory and investigations*, Toronto, ON: University of Toronto Press.

Smith, L. T. (1999) *Decolonizing Methodologies: research and Indigenous peoples*, London, Zed Books.

Social Sciences and Humanities Research Council (SSHRC) (2008) 'Scholarship in action: knowledge mobilization and the academic process', *Dialogue*, Summer 2008: para. 6.

—— (2010) *SSHRC's Knowledge Mobilization Strategy 2009–2011*, Ottawa, ON: Social Sciences and Humanities Research Council/CRSH.

Verran, H. (2001) *Science and an African Logic*, Chicago, IL: University of Chicago Press.

Willinsky, J. (2005) *The Access Principle: the case for open access to research and scholarship*, Cambridge, MA: MIT Press.

—— (2010) 'The new openness in educational research', in P. Hart, A. Reid and C. Russell (eds), *The Sage Companion to Educational Research*, London: Sage. Online, available: http://pkp.sfu.ca/node/1391 (accessed on 2 January 2011).

Part I

Considering the issues and the players

Chapter 1

Theory, research and practice in mobilizing research knowledge in education

Ben Levin and Amanda Cooper

Introduction

Knowledge mobilization (referred to in this chapter as KM) addresses ways in which stronger connections can be made between research, policy and practice. KM is an exploding field of interest, not only in education but in all areas of social policy (described more fully in Cooper, Levin and Campbell 2009). Although many different terms are used to refer to the issue (such as knowledge translation, knowledge management, research utilization, knowledge transfer and so on), all over the world governments, universities, school systems and various other parties are looking at new ways to find, share, understand and apply the knowledge emerging from research.

This chapter reviews the current situation around knowledge mobilization in education under the headings of theory, research and practice. The chapter addresses our growing understanding of and ideas about KM, considers some of the main issues in conducting empirical research in the field and looks at the state of activity to promote and increase KM, offering commentary and suggestions in each area. The chapter is based on the cumulative work of the Knowledge Mobilization Research Team at OISE through the Research Supporting Practice in Education (RSPE) programme (www.oise.utoronto.ca/rspe), which includes empirical work, conceptual work, practical activity and many connections with other researchers doing related work as well as fuller references to the conceptual and empirical literature informing this chapter.

Part 1 – Theory

What is 'knowledge' and what is 'mobilization'?

Much of the writing about KM remains theoretical or conceptual, focused on different ideas of what knowledge mobilization is and how it works. Both the central ideas in the concept – knowledge and its use – have multiple legitimate meanings. Much debate in the literature concerns these different ideas about knowledge and its application.

Lomas *et al.* (2005) make a useful distinction between scientific evidence (which includes research on effectiveness, implementation, organizational capacity, forecasting, economics/finance and so on) and colloquial evidence (which considers professional opinion, political judgement, values, habits and traditions, and the particular pragmatics and contingencies of the situation). Our team's primary interest is in research knowledge, defined as findings deriving from widely accepted, systematic and established formal processes of enquiry. In adopting this focus we recognize that many other kinds of knowledge are also relevant to policy and practice and that research findings alone do not provide answers to all questions of practice. Moreover, the effective use of research can – and in other professions does – enhance professional status and judgment because the findings of research must be applied in particular contexts. However, we believe that greater use of research knowledge in education has the potential to improve educational outcomes in important ways (Levin 2010), just as greater empirical knowledge has led to important improvements in other areas such as health.

KM is not synonymous with research dissemination. 'Mobilization' is more than mere 'dissemination'. In many ways, KM is what happens after dissemination – the discussions as well as the actions that occur beyond the basic requirement of sharing the research.

The knowledge emerging from research is not always correct and is subject to revision as time goes on, but it still, in our view, both provides good grounds for many practices and, just as importantly, can be a counterbalance to the emphasis on practitioner knowledge or conventional wisdom, both of which are regularly found later, based on systematic enquiry, to be incorrect or even harmful.

We also recognize that the 'use' of research has multiple dimensions. Several different typologies of research use have been proposed. The three most common uses of research from the literature are instrumental use (acting on research in specific and direct ways), conceptual use (this is more indirect; it informs our thinking) and symbolic use (to justify a pre-existing position, sometimes called political use). A fourth type of use recently emerging in the literature is imposed use, which occurs when mandates to use research evidence are applied by funders, governments or in practice settings. Nutley *et al.* (2007) provide an excellent review of this discussion and the many issues surrounding research use across public service sectors.

Clearly, research can and does have impact in varying ways, most of which do not involve direct application in a short time frame (though sometimes that too does occur). In most cases the effects of research are indirect and gradual, typically occurring over time as ideas get taken up and mediated through various social processes.

Research impact is, then, shaped by the larger social and political context. Think of the impact of research on current policy and practice in areas such as smoking, seatbelt use, exercise, recycling, energy conservation and so on. In all these cases, action came when there was sufficient consensus to prompt societal as well as individual action. In other cases, however, consensus does not arrive, and in that case research findings are typically subsumed in political conflict. The current debate over the science of climate change is an interesting example, in which there seems to be considerable scientific consensus but not enough political agreement to generate substantial action.

Differences in ideas about both 'knowledge' and 'use' create challenges in all areas of KM. Conceptually, one's stance on KM depends greatly on what kinds of knowledge are considered relevant. It is true that people's beliefs and actions are affected by various kinds of 'knowing', including knowledge of which the bearers are probably unaware. Less propositional forms of knowledge cannot be ignored if we are concerned about the realities of policy and practice. Yet if all kinds of knowledge are included, there is a danger that the discussion turns circular. The claim that practice or belief arises from knowledge of some kind seems tautological, so uninteresting. Surely what matters is the kinds of knowledge that affect what people think and do, and how those effects occur.

What are we learning about how knowledge mobilization happens?

In 2002–3, Levin was a visiting scholar at the Social Sciences and Humanities Research Council (SSHRC) helping SSHRC develop its interest in knowledge mobilization. A paper written for SSHRC (Levin 2004) developed a model of knowledge mobilization highlighting three areas where this work occurs (Figure 1.1). Six years later the model remains reasonably practical and has been used or cited by quite a few others, including Nutley *et al.* (2009) and the European Commission (Levin 2008b). The idea of contexts of research production and contexts of research use, mediated by various intermediaries and all occurring in a wider social context, seems to have lasting value as a basic conceptualization of how KM works.

Of course KM is not as simple as the diagram. The contexts of research production and use are overlapping, not separate. Similarly, the boxes in the diagram can also represent functions and processes, not necessarily structures. Arrows represent connections and varying strength of relationships (as indicated by the two-way arrows of varying thickness). KM occurs where two or more of these contexts or functions interact. Some people and organizations operate in two or even all three of the contexts. Many other research use models exist, a number of which are available on the RSPE website. Our model differs from most others in giving equal attention to the three contexts or functions that are part of knowledge mobilization. Our model also sees research use more as a function of systems and processes than of individuals.

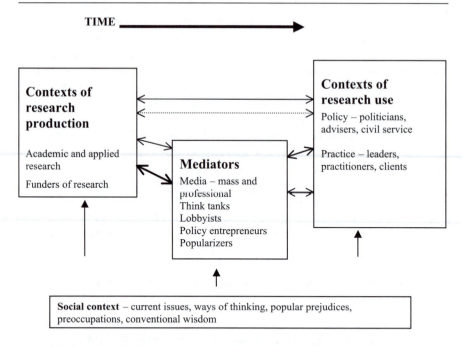

Figure 1.1 A model of research impact

Often different approaches to understanding research use are described in terms of a science push model (in which research producers try to disseminate their work more effectively), a demand pull model (in which users seek out relevant research), a dissemination model (where research is used due to the sheer amount of different formats available) and an interaction model (where research use occurs as disorderly interactions between groups, therefore both groups influence use – or lack of use) (Landry *et al.* 2001).

The simple idea that research would have direct effects on policy and practice has long been abandoned by those who study these issues, even though it may still be held by some researchers, who seem surprised or even dismayed that their work is not immediately adopted into policy or practice. However, in the last few years several other ideas about KM have become increasingly well supported from a variety of sources:

- Educators are interested in research. Although some critics attack education as a field particularly prone to valuing belief over evidence, studies (e.g. Cordingley 2009) indicate that educators express a strong interest in knowing more about research findings. They are critical of research in various ways, but they are interested. Moreover, it turns out that practice in other fields, such as medicine, also falls far short of being entirely consistent with research findings (Maynard 2007). So education is not as different from other professions as is sometimes made out, although it does lag behind health in terms of capacity and dedicated resources.

- In every field, interpersonal relationships and social contexts are the key to shaping policy and practice. People are more influenced by their own experience and by their colleagues than they are by external evidence. At the core of evidence use are interpretive processes whereby individuals and groups make meaning of evidence in ways that are profoundly shaped by their pre-existing beliefs and practices and day-to-day limits on how they direct their attention (Coburn, Honig and Stein 2009: 86). As a corollary, research products such as reports or research briefs, or even practice guidelines, while potentially valuable, do not have very much independent impact (Nutley, Percy-Smith and Solesbury 2003).

- The overall research enterprise in education remains small and weak, especially relative to the size of the sector. Most education delivery organizations, such as schools and districts, have very weak capacity to find, share, understand and apply research. Even where compelling research evidence is available, the systems for bringing it into practice are poorly developed. The same is true of many ministries of education, which seem to have weak infrastructures for inserting research into the policy process, although steps are being taken in a number of jurisdictions to improve this situation (OECD 2007).

- Many research institutions, such as universities, have rather weak knowledge mobilization efforts. Universities, the most important single source of research in education, generally do quite a poor job, especially at the institutional level, of sharing their findings or their implications. Where this work is done in universities, it is primarily the result of efforts of individual faculty members or research units. Organizations that have an explicit focus on KM, such as think tanks, tend to have much more developed processes for sharing their research.

- Significant barriers to better KM exist in both the context of research and the context of practice or policy. Barriers include skill issues (such as the ability to convey findings in plain language, or the ability to read quantitative data results), resource issues (lack of time, access to materials) and reward systems (not much push in the university to provide research relevant to educators, and not much push in the schools to read research) (for fuller discussions see Mitton *et al.* 2007). Another way to read these barriers, however, is that they indicate the lack of priority given to knowledge mobilization both in research-producing and research-consuming organizations. After all, nobody in a university or a school would suggest that we cancel classes because we don't have time to teach, or that we do not issue pay cheques because it's too complicated to calculate all the deductions. New activities are typically subject to a set of constraints that existing activities in the same organization do not have, even if the new activities are demonstrably more important or more valuable.

- Most of what people know about the evidence on education issues comes indirectly, through various third parties and mediators (hence the importance of this box in Figure 1.1). These intermediaries are important because they are often the ones adapting research for busy professionals and facilitating collaboration among different stakeholders; hence, they play a central role in KM. However, while there is increasing attention in the literature to mediators (Cooper 2010; Levin 2008a), there is still not a good sense of what this category comprises. The potential range of people and organizations who are in one way or another acting as mediators of research knowledge is huge, from individual practitioners or researchers to a whole range of think tanks, lobby groups, professional organizations and other bodies. Nor is it clear how mediators do their work, though it evidently involves a variety of practices from writing to speaking, to network building, to working with the media.
- Access to research has been dramatically changed by new technologies, primarily the internet. Almost anyone now has access to huge amounts of research information (and of course other kinds of information) on virtually any topic. Not only is the original research itself much more accessible, but the internet has also led to a proliferation of mediators, as anyone can now put up a communication of any kind on any topic, claiming to provide views informed by research. Moreover, what might be called legitimate producers and mediators of research, such as universities or non-governmental organizations (NGOs) or professional bodies, rely increasingly on the internet both as their source of material and their prime vehicle for dissemination.

If one follows the logic of the above points there is clearly cause for both optimism and concern. More research is more available in more formats than ever before. Yet, because people are chiefly influenced by their colleagues and experience, because most of their knowledge comes indirectly, and because both the sharing and applying mechanisms are weak, it is highly unlikely that we are getting the maximum benefit from research in education.

It is then entirely unsurprising to find that, although the interest in empirical evidence is considerable, there are large gaps between what that evidence tells us and common practice in schools in at least some areas. One can think of issues such as retention in grade, or student assessment practices, or student engagement, or teacher expectations, or tracking and streaming, as examples where a great deal of practice is inconsistent with a considerable and consistent body of research evidence.

The above findings represent a considerable advance on the state of knowledge even a dozen years ago. However, there is much still to learn about every aspect of KM, and in particular about what steps, if any, would increase the take-up of important research findings both in policy and practice. These issues will be discussed further in the final section of this chapter.

Part 2 – Research

As indicated earlier, interest in knowledge mobilization as a field of research has grown rapidly, not only in education but in other fields as well. A Google search using 'research practice schools' done in May 2010 for this chapter turned up more than 130 million hits, a dramatic increase from the 20 or so million generated by the same terms about 18 months earlier! The same search restricted to Canadian sites turned up 3.3 million hits. Just to give a sense of the scope, the first page of 10 hits in this search included sources as diverse as nursing, engineering, public health, school readiness, design art and mental health. A Google Scholar search with the same terms turned up 2.3 million hits. It is now impossible for any scholar to keep up even partly with the volume of work being generated.

Despite the rapid increase in scholarly work, a common concern in much of the writing about research in KM remains the methodological challenges of studying the sharing and use of research, whether in education or other fields. The challenge is rooted in part in the previously noted multiple concepts of what constitutes 'research' and what constitutes 'use'. The more one moves away from the idea of use being visible directly and immediately through behaviour, the more difficult it is to know what impact research is having on policy or practice. The more one thinks of KM as a function of organizations, or of networks of people and organizations, rather than of individuals, the harder it is to study the phenomenon.

In KM research so far researchers have often relied on self-report either of attitudes or behaviours through surveys and interviews. For example, the excellent work done by Canadian research teams headed by Landry (e.g. Belkhodja, Amara, Landry and Ouimet 2007) and Lavis (e.g. Lavis 2006) both rely primarily on surveys of researchers and research users (we have recently written a paper elaborating on some Canadian contributions to understanding knowledge mobilization – Cooper and Levin 2010).

These methods have contributed to advancing knowledge, but they have important limitations. One cannot have great confidence that self-reports of behaviour will be consistent with external observation of the same behaviour, while self-reports of beliefs are subject to considerable social desirability influences (Davies and Nutley 2008). People's behaviour can be quite different from their professed beliefs, and people may be unaware of those gaps. Even more, people often simply do not know the origins of either their beliefs or their behaviour, as readers will discover by asking themselves how they have come to 'believe' or 'know' something particular about education (or any other field). Even for a very specific belief, it is usually very difficult to trace its source and even more difficult to determine the role of empirical evidence. Our beliefs and attitudes are created through complex combinations of reading, thinking, experiencing and discussing with others.

Another approach has been to use case study methods, including quite a few recent self-reports on KM projects of various kinds (e.g. Manion *et al.* 2009; Alexanderson *et al.* 2009). Case studies have the advantage of emphasizing organizational rather than individual factors, but they have the disadvantage of small numbers and of focusing attention on specific contexts rather than common factors across settings, so it is often hard to know what lessons to take away from a case report.

Both teaching practice and education policy formation are complex activities, making the challenge of studying KM practices even greater. Real policy choices are almost always the result of some combination of education knowledge, personal experience, political considerations and the interpersonal dynamics of the organization, all of which change over time. So the task of observing or distinguishing in this *mélange* the influence of empirical research is daunting if it is even possible.

The work of teachers or school leaders also occurs as a whole, in which general ideas about instruction are affected by the larger climate of the school, by particular students and even by the time and day. A teacher might generally favour a particular instructional approach, perhaps even based on research evidence, but whether it gets used at any point is likely to be subject to this whole range of influences in ways that teachers themselves may not realize. In this fluid situation, can teachers sort out the impact on their practice of a particular piece of evidence? And if they do not know, how can researchers know?

These problems are not unique to research on knowledge mobilization: they are faced by researchers in many areas of social science. Hence the reliance in KM research on case studies, interviews and surveys of various parties – the same tools used to study many other complex social phenomena, but with the same limitations.

If better ways to manage this problem were evident, they would already have been adopted. However, some suggestions can be made and are being incorporated into our team's studies:

- Focus more on organizational processes, structures and contexts rather than individual attitudes or actions, since it appears that the former are more powerful shapers of KM than the latter:

    The conclusions from empirical research, in both education and nursing, confirm that the main barriers to knowledge use in the public sector are not at the level of individual resistance but originated in an institutionalized culture that does not foster learning.

    (Hemsley-Brown 2004: 462)

- Gather data on specific behaviours and practices rather than on generalized attitudes. While any self-report has limitations, self-reports of behaviour, especially from multiple respondents, are likely to yield a clearer picture of real practice than self-reports of general attitudes. For example, asking how often research is discussed at principals' meetings seems a more useful question than asking principals if research is important in their work. Posting such specific questions, and even observing practices, will get both easier and more effective as we learn more about KM processes.

- Work with real issues and examples. Asking people about instances where they used research, or asking about their knowledge about specific issues and then probing the role of research in those issues, seem more fruitful approaches than asking generally about research without linking it to any specific issue or occasion.
- Triangulate data by getting the perspectives of multiple parties (preferably in the same organizations) or by asking similar questions at different times as a check on validity of responses.
- Look for more opportunities to use control groups or data over time so as to have some independent verification of claims about the role of research.

These steps will not by any means eliminate the challenges; studying the causes of human behaviour will always be an uncertain activity. However, as more empirical studies are conducted with more sophisticated methods, we can expect our knowledge base to improve, yielding further improvements in methodology.

Part 3 – Practice

Governments are giving increasing attention to 'evidence-based decision-making', including establishing new policies and organizations to this end. International agencies such as the Organisation for Economic Co-operation and Develoment (OECD) or the World Bank are trying to strengthen their own use of evidence and to assist member countries in doing so. An OECD report on the issue (2007) described initiatives in a number of countries to make more use of research evidence in education. Gradually, the infrastructure to support better use of evidence in education is being built, at least in some countries.

The impact of these initiatives remains unknown but there are grounds for caution, particularly in regard to producer push approaches. A vast amount of effort is going into creating websites and virtual interaction spaces. There are now so many websites, so many discussion lists and so many competing sources of information that it is hard to see how more of them will be helpful. At the same time, we are learning about the relative ineffectiveness of products in terms of changing behaviour, suggesting that research producers should invest more in creating interpersonal connections.

One reason that research does not have more impact in education is the weak capacity of most schools and school systems to find, share and apply research. Few educational organizations dedicate time, people or resources to this end, exacerbating the tendency in the education profession to rely on tacit knowledge (Levin *et al.* 2009). Hence, even where there is strong evidence, application will tend to be weak. In a recent summary of various efforts to change practice to be more consistent with research, Nutley, Walter and Davies (2009) define five spheres of action for interventions:

- dissemination of materials and findings;
- interaction (links and collaboration between the research and policy or practice communities);
- social influence (using experts and peers to inform);
- facilitation with technical, financial, or organizational support; and
- incentives and reinforcement such as audits or financial incentives to reinforce appropriate behaviour.

Various combinations of these ideas are being used in various places, including in school systems.

Assessing the impact of these various initiatives presents another challenge to research. It is vital to learn what sorts of interventions or actions are most likely to increase the take-up of research in policy and practice settings. Here, health researchers have led the way, with many studies of different kinds of interventions intended to change the behaviour of providers such as doctors or nurses. Although many of these interventions have not yielded much of a result, the corpus of work as a whole is slowly leading to conclusions about the kinds of activities that do actually affect people's beliefs and behaviours in lasting ways. No individual intervention type is universally effective. Simply providing knowledge appears to be quite ineffective (Nutley, Percy-Smith and Solesbury 2003). However, other kinds of intervention are also limited, including incentive systems such as audits. Multiple interventions appear to be needed, sustained over time, to change practice.

Education systems have not done this work in nearly as systematic a way. For the most part, KM activity in schools, school systems and central agencies such as state education agencies is modest and low priority. Of course the same is true of the research enterprise in education, which in comparison to health is small, fragmented and disorganized.

The general conclusion, then, is that the many efforts to strengthen knowledge mobilization in education and other fields are slowly yielding evidence on their relative effectiveness, but that the goal of changing practice remains daunting.

Conclusion

This brief tour of the state of knowledge mobilization work yields several conclusions, both in general and for the education system. First, we are learning a great deal from the many initiatives underway and from the growing amount of research. Understanding has improved significantly even in the last few years, and the capacity to undertake KM of various kinds has also expanded considerably. It is no surprise that activity is running ahead of knowledge; indeed, it could hardly be otherwise.

Second, the focus of KM work and research should be on organizations and their practices more than on individual researchers, policy-makers or practitioners. KM is largely a matter of the way organizations operate, which deeply affects the way individual researchers, practitioners and policy-makers work. This view also implies more attention to interpersonal processes both within and among organizations. The central role of research mediators of various kinds needs much more exploration.

Third, research on KM requires continued improvement in terms of more sophisticated methods and also even more sharing among researchers in different fields and parts of the world. KM research must itself adopt KM principles and practices to ensure greatest impact. The necessary networks of researchers are only now being created.

Fourth, education systems need increased capacity in all spheres of research. In practice settings the challenge is the capacity in schools and school systems to find, share and apply research knowledge to a greater extent and in a more disciplined way than now exists. In research settings more focus on capacity to disseminate research in more systematic and useful ways would help. We also need better linkage mechanisms across the system, including working with third-party agencies. This need not involve great efforts or resources; modest interventions could have useful effects, and that is probably where attention should start (Levin *et al.* 2009).

There are grounds for optimism about the state of KM research and practice. The increasing effort and growing research capacity and understanding offer much promise for yielding improvements in education in ways that benefit students and are satisfying to professional educators.

References

Alexanderson, K., Beijer, E., Bengtsson, S., Hyvonen, U., Karlsson, P. and Nyman, M. (2009) 'Producing and consuming knowledge in social work practice: research and development activities in a Swedish context', *Evidence and Policy* 5(2): 127–39.

Belkhodja, O., Amara, N., Landry, R. and Ouimet, M. (2007) 'The extent and organizational determinants of research utilization in Canadian health services organizations', *Science Communication*, 28(3): 377–417.

Coburn, C., Honig, M. and Stein, M. (2009) 'What's the evidence on districts' use of evidence?' in J. Bransford, D. Stipek, N. Vye, L. Gomez and D. Lam (eds), *The Role of Research in Educational Improvement*, Cambridge, MA: Harvard Education Press, 67–87.

Cooper, A. (2010 May) 'Knowledge mobilization intermediaries in education', paper presented at the 39th Annual Canadian Society for the Study of Education Conference, Montreal, Quebec. Online, available: www.oise.utoronto.ca/rspe (accessed 29 January 2011).

Cooper, A. and Levin, B. (2010) 'Some Canadian contributions to understanding knowledge mobilization', *Evidence and Policy*, 6(3): 351–69.

Cooper, A., Levin, B. and Campbell, C. (2009) 'The growing (but still limited) importance of evidence in education policy and practice', *Journal of Educational Change*, 10(2–3): 159–71.

Cordingley, P. (2009) 'Using research and evidence as a lever for change at classroom level', paper presented to the American Educational Research Association, San Diego, CA, April.

Davies, H., and Nutley, S. (2008) *Learning More About How Research-based Knowledge Gets Used: guidance in the development of new empirical research*, New York, NY: William T. Grant Foundation.

Hemsley-Brown, J. (2004) 'Facilitating research utilization: A cross-sector review of research evidence', *International Journal of Public Sector Management*, 17(6): 534–52.

Landry, R., Amara, N. and Laamary, M. (2001) 'Utilization of social science research knowledge in Canada' *Research Policy*, 30: 333–49.

Lavis, J. (2006) 'Research, public policymaking, and knowledge-translation processes: Canadian efforts to build bridges', *Journal of Continuing Education in the Health Professions*, 26(1): 37–45.

Levin, B. (2004) 'Making research matter more', *Education Policy Analysis Archives*, 12(56). Online, available: http://epaa.asu.edu/epaa/v12n56/ (accessed 15 November 2008).

—— 2008(a) 'Thinking about knowledge mobilization', paper prepared for an invitational symposium sponsored by the Canadian Council on Learning and the Social Sciences and Humanities research Council of Canada, Vancouver. Online, available: www.oise.utoronto.ca/rspe.

—— 2008(b) 'Knowledge for action in education research and policy: What we know, what we don't know and what we need to do', in *Wissen für Handeln – Forschungsstraategien für eine evidenzbasierte Bildungspolitik*, Bonn/Berlin: Bundesministerium für Forschung, 35–44.

—— (2010) 'Leadership for evidence informed education', School Leadership and Management. Online, available: DOI: 10.1080/13632434.2010.497483.

Levin, B., Sa, C., Cooper, A. and Mascarenhas, S. (2009) *Research use and its impact in secondary schools*, CEA/OISE Collaborative Mixed Methods Research Project Interim Report. Online, available: www.oise.utoronto.ca/rspe (accessed 29 January 2011).

Lomas, J., Culyer, T., McCutcheon, C., McAuley, L. and Law, S. (2005) *Conceptualizing and Combining Evidence for Health System Guidance*, Ottawa: Canadian Health Services Research Foundation.

Manion, I., Buchanan, D., Cheng, M., Johnston, J. and Short, K. (2009) 'Embedding evidence-based practice in child and youth mental health in Ontario', *Evidence and Policy*, 5(2): 141–53.

Maynard, A. (2007) 'Translating evidence into practice: why is it so difficult?', *Public Money and Management*, 27(4): 251–56.

Mitton, C., Adair, C. E., McKenzie, E., Patten, S. B. and Perry, B. W. (2007) 'Knowledge transfer and exchange: Review and synthesis of the literature', *The Milbank Quarterly*, 85(4): 729–68.

Nutley, S., Percy-Smith, J. and Solesbury, W. (2003) *Models of Research Impact: A cross-sector review of literature and practice (Building Effective Research: 4)*, London: Learning and Skills Research Centre.

Nutley, S., Walter, I. and Davies, H. (2007) *Using Evidence: How Research can Inform Public Services*, Bristol: Policy Press.

—— (2009) 'Promoting evidence-based practice: models and mechanisms from cross-sector review', *Research on Social Work Practice*, 19 (5): 552–59.

OECD (2007) *Knowledge Management: evidence and education – linking research and practice*, Paris: OECD Publications Service.

Chapter 2

Exploring strategies for impact

Riding the wave with the TLRP

Andrew Pollard

Introduction

TLRP, the UK's Teaching and Learning Research Programme, was established, developed and concluded within specific political contexts. In its origins, it was seen as a remedial investment to strengthen what, in the late 1990s, was seen as a weak field of research. In 1999, some £9m was thus identified by the Higher Education Funding Council for England and by UK governments for a programme of research to 'improve learning outcomes across the UK'. However, by the end of the following decade, over £40m had been committed to the Programme and over 100 investments had been made involving some 700 researchers from all parts of the UK (www.tlrp.org).

The main waves that the Programme rode were those associated with the international commitment to 'evidence-based policy making'. These were strong throughout the decade and were combined with government willingness to invest in the generation of such evidence. However, like surfers when a heavy sea is running, the research community had to cope with the swell, mount the strongest waves and stay with them. To succeed as a surfer, a good sense of balance is needed, and not a little daring. And you also need to select the right board for the conditions. TLRP similarly had to find ways of combining intrinsic quality, strategic awareness and practical action.

Building on the framing of this book, the Programme had to understand and respond to the political context of the UK, to recognize and act within the diverse linguistic, social and cultural understandings of UK stakeholders and to find ways of resolving the dilemmas that exist in respect of taking responsibility for knowledge mobilization. Our response was perhaps a little naive. In essence, we simply sought to become proactive, and take the initiative.

TLRP's 2001 Communication and Impact Plan stated:

> We conceive of impact not as a simple linear flow but as a much more collaborative process: interactive, iterative, constructive, distributed and transformative. Working for impact is embedded in everything we do.
>
> (www.tlrp.org/manage/admin/caip.html)

This document was created by Charles Deforges and John Kanefsky, the first Directors of TLRP, with the backing of the Steering Committee chaired at the time by David Watson. The Communication and Impact Plan was visionary in many ways and established, in particular, the commitment to user engagement in all its forms.

In the early years, the major challenge facing TLRP was the crisis of confidence in educational research from which the Programme originated. Concerns about the relevance, quality and accessibility of research had been expressed by Ministers and MPs on both sides of the Westminster Parliament, and scepticism from senior civil servants and other staff in UK government departments and agencies was strong. Influential public lectures (e.g. Hargreaves 1996), reports (e.g. Hillage *et al.* 1998) and Ministerial speeches (e.g., Blunkett 2000) led to derision within the education media, and the teaching profession as a whole lacked confidence in what academics had to offer. There were critical questions within the House of Commons. When appointed, the TLRP Directors' Team worked to liaise with senior Westminster politicians of each of the three major parties and also with other UK governments, agencies and other users. The presentation of the Programme was designed to convey an engaged, positive message through its aims (www.tlrp.org/aims/index.html) and Identity Guidelines (www.tlrp.org/manage/admin/identity.html). The potential vulnerability of the field and Programme to the moral panic of critique was also a reason why constructive engagement was preferred to a more combative stance in relation to public policies – although the latter was in some ways encouraged by media outlets. A requirement by major funders to give 24 hours' notice of the text of all press releases, combined with the Steering Committee's wish to consider significant policy statements, made it hard to engage in the cut-and-thrust of unfolding events.

The TLRP strategy in respect of the political context was thus to engage constructively with civil servants and policy makers in the governments and agencies of the four devolved administrations that make up the UK. A TLRP Directors' Team of up to five part-time academics was deployed to facilitate such links. To recognize the diversity of stakeholder circumstances and interests, all TLRP projects were encouraged to involve users from both TLRP research sites and from associated national bodies with 'high leverage' for later impact – thus enhancing validity and eventual outreach. To tackle the question of responsibility, the TLRP stance was unequivocal: we embraced it. TLRP's research was thus explicitly intended to combine high-quality social science with high levels of user engagement and impact. This was the defining ambition of the Programme.

These decisions were not just pragmatic responses to our circumstances. Rather, we saw them in broad terms as reflecting the Enlightenment tradition of seeking to apply reason for the improvement of society. This basic, value-led perspective provided a sense of collective purpose across the Programme.

Strategies to support impact

TLRP's overall development was driven by explicit strategic commitments:

- User engagement for relevance and quality
- Knowledge generation by project teams
- Knowledge synthesis through thematic activities
- Knowledge transformation for impact
- Partnerships for sustainability
- International engagement for collaboration and comparison.

Because of the duration, scale and complexity of TLRP, these strategies were managed simultaneously. However, as the Programme matured, there was a progressive change in the balance of activity, with greater emphasis being placed on knowledge synthesis, transformation and impact, together with attempts to underpin post-Programme sustainability.

User engagement for relevance and quality
(www.tlrp.org/users)

Project teams worked closely with practitioners and others in their research sites and also linked up with key national organizations with potentially 'high leverage' for dissemination and impact activity. Such relationships were reflected in the membership of project 'Advisory Groups'. The Directors' Team maintained links with high-leverage user organizations in each educational sector and in each part of the UK. TLRP also worked directly with UK governments to maximize the use of its research and was represented on significant national bodies for the coordination of education research. TLRP led the establishment of the UK Strategic Forum on Research in Education (see www.sfre.ac.uk).

Knowledge generation by project teams
(www.tlrp.org/projects)

In 2000, TLRP started by funding four networks of projects. A second phase brought in nine larger projects and this was followed by funding of twelve more. At the same time, focused funding initiatives made specific provision for teams in Scotland, Northern Ireland and Wales – and for some high-priority topics (such as widening participation in higher education and concerning technology-enhanced learning). By the end of the Programme, funding had been provided for some 70 projects, many with teams of over a dozen researchers and budgets up to £1.5m. Some 30 small-scale fellowships were also funded. The portfolio included projects covering a wide range of theoretical and methodological perspectives and interdisciplinary collaborations.

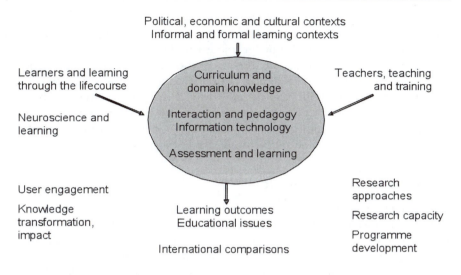

Political, economic and cultural contexts
Informal and formal learning contexts

Learners and learning
through the lifecourse

Curriculum and
domain knowledge

Teachers, teaching
and training

Neuroscience and
learning

Interaction and pedagogy
Information technology

Assessment and learning

User engagement

Research
approaches

Knowledge
transformation,
impact

Learning outcomes
Educational issues

Research capacity

Programme
development

International comparisons

Figure 2.1 TLRP's conceptual model for cross-Programme thematic analysis

Knowledge synthesis through thematic activities (www.tlrp.org/themes)

The Directors' Team provided critical friendship to project teams, encouraged collaboration, organized events and worked to build 'added value' across the projects. The main strategy for this was 'thematic development', which provided a progressive focus for collective effort as the initiative matured. The portfolio of some 20 forms of cross-Programme analysis included consultancies, thematic groups, thematic seminar series, conferences, workshops, meta-tagging of outputs and sectoral reviews. A conceptual framework (see Figure 2.1) was used to organize and integrate this work.

For example, analyses of user engagement, research warrant, capacity building, knowledge transfer and impact are results of explicit thematic investments to reflect on and understand the TLRP experience, and they thus added value to the Programme. Other cross-project analyses took place on topics such as contexts, learners, teachers, curriculum, pedagogy, assessment and learning outcomes, and such work often led to special issues of journals (see www.tlrp.org/pub/journals.html).

Knowledge transformation for impact (www.tlrp.org/publications)

TLRP's impact strategy was a multi-level one and attempts were thus made to produce research findings in forms that were tailored to specific audiences. We both produced many of our own publications and worked extensively with user bodies to maximize impact. Outputs include 'Research Briefings' (summarizing findings), 'TLRP Commentaries' (applying findings to contemporary issues), practitioner applications (classroom enquiry activities drawing on research), books (in two series with Routledge), journals (including almost 30 special issues), reports, etc. TLRP also used an electronic repository and meta-tagging system called D-space, with almost 1,600 entries. This was adopted for deposition of all project publications and significantly improved the availability of outputs via the internet and major databases. Downloads from the website considerably exceeded our expectations, with TLRP Commentaries on Teaching and Learning Principles and on Neuroscience leading the way.

Partnerships for sustainability

Despite its size, TLRP was still small in relation to the challenge and range of educational research. It was also understood that it would exist for a limited period. For such reasons, the Programme developed close working relationships with other organizations. At least five different forms of partnership can be identified. First, we sought out expertise from which we could benefit. Such partnerships existed with the British Education Index (BEI) for electronic knowledge management, the Cambridge Centre for Applied Research in Education Technology (CARET) for development of an advanced ICT infrastructure, and Routledge for book and journal publications. Second, as indicated above, we worked with key user organizations that were generous enough to promote TLRP work through their communications systems, and thus lend us some of their leverage as we attempted to maximize impact. Third, we worked with partners where cooperation enabled us to be more effective – for example, a special supplement for teachers was co-funded with the National Institute of Adult Continuing Education and the Learning and Skills Development Agency. We have also contributed to major national reviews, managed by others, on primary education, 14–19 education, work-based learning and lifelong learning. Fourth, as indicated previously, we worked where we could with the government bodies that help to form policy regarding education research within each country of the UK. For example, collaboration with the General Teaching Council for England led to distribution of a TLRP Commentary, *Professionalism and Pedagogy*, to every school in England. Finally, we worked with the British Educational Research Association (BERA) and other organizations that could take on some of the resources, assets or commitments of TLRP into the future. Indeed, one of our informal goals for many years was to 'give everything away' by the end.

International engagement for collaboration and comparison (www.tlrp.org/international)

TLRP generated a great deal of international interest throughout its existence and we had some links with researchers from every continent. For example, during 2008, TLRP represented UK research at a wide range of conferences and special events in the USA, South America, Australia, Europe and Asia. Members of the Directors' Team spoke about the Programme in ten countries, often at the request of research councils or academies. The TLRP Director served on the American Educational Research Association's (AERA's) International Advisory Committee and was appointed to the Task Force on International Exploration, which investigated the establishment of a global research association for education. TLRP provided a virtual workspace to facilitate what became the World Educational Research Association. The major links for TLRP projects continued with projects in associated educational research programmes in Finland, the Netherlands and Norway, with more informal links to projects in Canada, France, Germany, Hong Kong, Israel, New Zealand, Singapore, Spain, Sweden, Australia and the USA. Symposia, workshops and conferences were held to promote project-to-project interactions in order to facilitate mutual learning, with outcomes including publications, collaborative research design and exchange of information on methodology, data collection and data analysis. A UK coordinated study, funded as part of the European Lifelong Learning Programme, but initially supported through ESRC (Economic and Social Research Council), investigated the implications of the changing patterns of career development across Europe for continuing vocational training in the light of the Lisbon 2000 goals. TLRP was also represented on the advisory committee of the European SINCERE project that sought to establish stronger links between educational research in Europe, Latin America and South East Asia.

Outputs to support impact

To complement its strategic activity, the Programme needed to be able to represent and disseminate its findings tangibly and effectively. This was the rationale behind the 'outputs portfolio' that was developed (see Pollard 2008, and www.tlrp.org/manage/admin/outputnew.html). This comprised:

- Initial and outcomes posters
- Research Briefings
- *Improving Practice* book series
- *Improving Learning* book series
- Special issues of journals
- TLRP Commentaries
- Websites and electronic resources.

All significant TLRP investments were formally inducted into output and impact expectations and the outputs portfolio provided the major hub for templates, guidance, support and strategic papers on impact matters. Induction meetings after commissioning and the 'outputs summit meeting' with each project as it reached completion were important aspects of this, as was the foregrounding of 'key findings' in all annual reports. Specialist Media Fellows also offered journalistic expertise; members of the Directors' Team advised; and office staff offered practical and organizational help.

As a result of this targeting and supportive infrastructure, all major investments produced 'Research Briefings' providing concise summaries of project findings for use at impact events and for targeted distribution. Almost 80 were produced. Some 30 books in the TLRP *Improving Learning and Improving Practice* series have now been published by Routledge. The use of special issues of journals was an especially strong feature of TLRP, with 22 published and others in the pipeline. These became a major means for TLRP projects and thematic groups to communicate their findings. Over 450 articles were published in refereed journals. TLRP Commentaries, based on the work of Task Groups or other special initiatives, were particularly successful at bringing the expertise of researchers to bear on contemporary issues at speed and in accessible ways. Sixteen have been published at the time of writing. Two were downloaded over 200,000 times, with hard copy distribution of two others exceeding 40,000. Though more advanced technology is now available, the TLRP website as developed since 2002 was relatively sophisticated, with provision for particular audiences, news, features and advanced search tools. Hits on the website averaged over 650,000 per month during 2008 and continued to grow. They exceeded 1m for the first time in the month of April 2009. The website had *News* and *Features* sections, which were available on RSS feeds. News was also archived. A review over several years gives an excellent impression of the wide range of activities that TLRP has supported, both within the UK, internationally and across every educational sector – see: www.tlrp-archive.org/cgi-bin/tlrp/news/news_log.pl. Within the website lies an electronic repository, DSpace, for which the Programme was an advanced application. By mid-2009, total items deposited in DSpace reached almost 1,700, including 426 TLRP papers in refereed journals. These items were harvested daily by the ESRC Society Today and British Education Index online databases in automated processes. The British Education Index created a special 'TLRP Collection' of particular academic interest and, at the time of its appearance in August 2009, it contained 1,064 records. In relation to practice and policy audiences, there are many links to DSpace from other databases, such as the Higher Education Academy's Evidence Net and the Education Evidence Portal (see: www.tlrp.org/pub/index.html).

Taking stock, TLRP had clear ambitions in relation to user engagement and impact, and the infrastructure of the Programme supported projects in producing a particular set of outputs. However, although it is unlikely that impact can be achieved without the production of outputs, they do not, in themselves, constitute impact. A lot rests on the 'much more collaborative processes' of engagement with users on the specific topics and issues that projects tackled.

Although it is too early to really evaluate what the impact of particular projects has been, we can get a sense of potential if we review some cases of apparent short-term impact.

Illustrations of short-term impact

Nine short narratives offer an impression of the range of impacts by projects and by the Programme itself. These have been drawn across the lifecourse range of the Programme's portfolio.

Consulting pupils on teaching and learning

TLRP's Phase 1 Network, led by Jean Ruddock, engaged hundreds of primary and secondary teachers in classroom enquiry and development work. This led to cultural change in practitioner perception of the significance of 'pupil voice' and to professional confidence in constructive classroom practices that recognize it. The work was influential in teacher associations, General Teaching Councils and the National College for School Leadership. Contemporary school inspection frameworks, for instance, from England's Ofsted, now require pupil consultation as part of inspection activity – though we do not have evidence of a causal link.

Teaching and learning policies for schools

TLRP was active throughout the period and across the UK. For example, in England, the Programme contributed to public discussion of the 2004 DfES policy on 'Personalised Learning' through '2020 Vision'; promotion of 'Principles into Practice' and moderating the 'magic bullet' of neuroscience in education in 2006/7; constructive critique of the Children's Plan in 2008; and a review of primary education in 2009. TLRP could not claim direct leverage on schools' policy, but it has undoubtedly contributed to the climate in which decisions have been taken. For the improvement of standards, TLRP has consistently pressed for teachers to be given more opportunity to develop and exercise professional judgement. The Programme therefore welcomed the 2009 Labour government announcement of withdrawal from National Strategies in England and the 2010 Coalition government's White Paper on *The Importance of Teaching*. These policy decisions were entirely consistent with TLRP's contributions to public debate over many years. Significant contributions have also been made in support of pedagogic initiatives in Scotland, Wales and Northern Ireland. Publication in August 2009 of a TLRP

Commentary in association with the Assessment Reform Group generated public debate on this vital issue concerning school education. This was followed up in 2010 by the Commentary on *Professionalism and Pedagogy* to urge and underpin greater trust in teacher judgement. The Coalition government has announced that it is to back teacher judgement and has requested Ofsted to revise its inspection framework to foreground teaching and learning quality – policies urged by TLRP for many years.

14–19 education and training policy

Four members of TLRP were involved in the Tomlinson Review of 14–19 education and training, as members of the main committee or its specialist sub-committees, arguing the case for greater coherence of provision. The Tomlinson Review highlighted the need to reform many aspects of education and training for 14–19-year-olds, but government pursued a more cautious approach of attempting to make the current system operate more effectively. However, the Nuffield 14–19 Review, in which nine colleagues associated with TLRP were involved, continued to argue the need to implement a broader and more radical vision for 14–19 education and training. TLRP, together with the Nuffield Review of 14–19 education and training, has continued to articulate the choices on how 14–19 education and training might be developed in the future.

The learning and skills sector

A number of projects made written and oral submissions to the Foster Review on the future role of further education; the Leitch Review of skills; and the House of Lords Education Committee. Sir Andrew Foster also read and commented favourably upon a TLRP project report on the structure and operation of the new learning and skills sector in England. The report explicitly acknowledged the TLRP recommendations of the importance of seeking to build a learning and skills system; the need to move away from a target-driven culture; and the problems associated with over-centralized decisions on curriculum delivery and implementation.

Apprenticeships

The government's Task Force on Modern Apprenticeship commissioned Alison Fuller and Lorna Unwin to explore the applicability of TLRP's expansive-restrictive framework with employers and training providers throughout the UK. Their commentary *Towards Expansive Apprenticeships* was distributed to all apprenticeship providers and they gave both written and oral evidence to The House of Lords Select Committee on Economic Affairs on the 'Employment and Training Opportunities for Low-Skilled Young People.'

Science, technology, engineering and mathematics (STEM)

Julian Williams' maths education project has been critical in demonstrating the importance of appropriate pedagogies to support students who want to continue with maths into university, especially for STEM subjects. The team showed the importance of connectionist or inclusive pedagogies rather than trans-missionist approaches both for achievement in maths in sixth forms and for continuing into higher education (HE). Targets for maths education are better achieved through inclusive than instructionist approaches.

Widening participation in higher education

TLRP was active both across the UK and internationally. For example, in England it contributed to a high-level policy seminar for the Learning and Skills Network at the Work Foundation in 2008 in celebration of the 10th anniversary of the Helena Kennedy Foundation and to the 1994 Group's annual conference on research in 2009. We also contributed to the UNESCO report on 'Trends in Global Higher Education: Tracking an Academic Revolution' prepared for the UNESCO 2009 World Conference on Higher Education, 6–8 July, in Paris. The work is often cited and the Coalition government has reiterated its commitment to providing opportunities in higher education.

Interagency learning

In response to (local authority) Children's Services policy imperative of find-ing effective forms of inter-professional work to support vulnerable children, the two projects on *Learning in and for Interagency Working* operated along-side practitioners as they were developing new inter-professional practices. They identified what practitioners needed to know to work across professional boundaries for children's wellbeing, and how their organizations were adapting. The project team focused on working with local authorities and children's trusts to assist them in recognizing and responding to the systemic transformations necessary for the accommodation and sustaining of new ways of working. This work has been influential in Northern Ireland and promoted by the Local Government Association in England.

Strategies for the development of research in the field of education

Discussions took place with the Secretary of State for Education, the Director and Chairman of the National Educational Research Forum (NERF), the Chief Executive of ESRC, BERA Council members and many others, contrib-uting to a 2004 reconstitution of NERF and a progressive re-orientation of its relationship to the education research community. These included liaison with government representatives in Wales, Scotland and Northern Ireland, contributing to events and deploying TLRP resources in support of the capacity building objectives in each country. Later, TLRP led the establishment of the Strategic Forum for Research in Education.

The illustrations above are relatively specific and many more of this sort could have been provided. TLRP's formula – of combining authentic user engagement with high-quality science and appropriate outputs that are then targeted onto contemporary issues – has appeared to be productive in its own terms.

At least, we are able to note the direction of major trends in the last decade and can then explore the relationship of the Programme's work to them.

So, a case can be made that Government education policy in each UK country has been developing in ways that are broadly, though not consistently, consonant with the findings and key messages of TLRP. For instance, the Children's Plan and Widening Participation agendas of the Labour government required awareness of context and of social and informal learning in ways that TLRP had been promoting. The 2010 Coalition government's policy of freeing schools from centralized imposition is known to be drawing on TLRP analyses of professionalism and pedagogy and the government has recruited TLRP researchers as expert advisers on curriculum reform. This reflects the ways in which TLRP's project and Directors' Teams have maintained a policy of 'constructive engagement' with policy makers of all political parties. We believe that the Programme has exerted some influence at many levels, though offering causal proofs of this is extremely difficult.

We can also relate the Programme to its circumstances. As it developed, TLRP benefited from a decade of prosperity and optimism, from growing commitment to evidence in policy and practice, from the need to establish new foundations for twenty-first-century education and from the pressure of international competition. In 2010, with financial retrenchment deepening, TLRP's evidence was being used to inform very different, and arguably more difficult, sets of decisions.

In relation to educational research and the social sciences generally, there appears to have been a cultural and political shift during the period of TLRP's existence. The 'moral panic' and critique of educational research as it was understood in the 1990s shaped the initial focus on 'teaching and learning' and the terms of reference of the Programme. By 2006, the main funder was specifically commissioning sociologically and contextually informed analysis of widening participation in education. There was, quite simply, a more balanced understanding of complementary forms of research and of significant issues in education. We believe that TLRP demonstrated the responsibility and commitment of educational researchers, and that this was one reason for TLRP's total funding of £43m ending up four times greater than initially planned.

We could also claim that the Programme was influential in the policies of the UK's Economic and Social Research Council. In November 2008, at TLRP's Westminster Conference, Ian Diamond, Chief Executive of ESRC, said:

> You should be very proud of TLRP's pioneering nature to enhance knowledge and have impact. TLRP has been an absolute model of the way in which researchers, working closely in partnership with beneficiaries, can cross the dual hurdle of excellence in academic quality and wider impact. The TLRP is terribly important in demonstrating this. The approach is entirely normal practice for ESRC now, but was quasi-experimentally piloted through TLRP and has then been rolled out further. Additionally, TLRP has been a model of communication to a wider public. TLRP has also been great on capacity building, though we acknowledge that much remains to be done for the next generation of researchers. In summary, TLRP has been a wonderful programme – a flagship.

Such statements are very gratifying and it is indeed the case that, in 2010, ESRC changed both its funding application and evaluation systems to explicitly require information on impact. TLRP certainly piloted and illustrated some aspects of this, but ESRC was also exploring these issues in other ways and the real drive has, of course, come externally from pressure to demonstrate the value of social and economic research to UK and national treasuries.

So, TLRP researchers can identify congruent directions of development while also recognizing the complexity of social, political and professional change and the extreme difficulty of documenting causal relationships in rapidly changing situations. There is also the major problem of the misalignment of public aspirations for applied, relevant research and the incentivization of academics to produce work that is perceived to fuel research assessment and career progression (Pollard and Oancea 2010). This is being tackled in new processes for funding and research assessment, but was a major challenge to TLRP. Indeed, it is in fundamental tension with the Programme's aspiration for impact to become seen: 'not as a simple linear flow but as a much more collaborative process: *interactive, iterative, constructive, distributed and transformative*'. At a project level, it was rare for the funding and expectations of both researchers and users to be sufficiently aligned and stable to enable such collaboration. The most favourable conditions existed when leading researchers worked on topics in which they had significant expertise and with users with whom they had pre-existing relationships. At scale, the collaborative goal will only really stand a chance of realization if there are structural changes in the funding and organization of research and in the use of evidence. Rhetoric remains strong (and remains welcome), but there is a long way to go in terms of practical implementation. The case for long-term institutional and personal investment in relation to research and engagement on specific, enduring issues is very strong in my opinion.

Regarding TLRP as a whole, we continue to hope that long-term impact in relation to enduring educational issues will be achieved. The real test, perhaps in 2020 or so, will be whether default assumptions in UK cultures that guide policy and practice on teaching and learning have continued to develop in ways that are broadly consistent with the Programme's 'ten principles for effective teaching and learning'. Recent developments in each of the four UK countries are encouraging – but there is a long way to go and there will be many other factors in play.

Conclusion

At the start of this chapter, I likened TLRP's impact efforts with surfing. In using this metaphor, I wanted to convey a sense of the vast range of the contexts to which research relates and of the vulnerability of the social practice of enquiry. As with the sea, we have to recognize that contemporary events and demands unfold with enormous power and can easily 'wipe out' or even drown a mere researcher. And yet, TLRP experience suggests that ways can be developed for standing up in such situations, of asserting the place of evidence, and of riding the waves. TLRP approached this as a research programme, but a similar stance could be taken by other organizations where there is a commitment to strategic development.

I certainly do not claim that TLRP 'solved how to do it', but the combination of high-quality projects, strategic action and developed infrastructure to support impact activity is certainly worth further consideration by those with an interest in knowledge mobilization. I would claim that the conscious combination of these elements made it easier for the participants in TLRP to take opportunities for impact when they presented themselves. As suitable waves came in, researchers were more prepared to ride them.

To achieve this, the Programme and project teams had to understand and respond to the political context of the UK, to recognize and act within social and cultural understandings of specific stakeholder groups in the sectors to which their projects related and, above all, to take responsibility for the practical mobilization of the knowledge that they had generated.

Our experience suggests that such activity is both interesting and worthwhile. As with tackling storm-driven rollers, there is a risk of being carried somewhere you don't want to go – and you might crash out. But it is also possible that you might really make an impression on those who are watching.

References

Blunkett, D. (2000) *Influence or Irrelevance: can social science improve government?* London: Department for Education and Employment.

Hargreaves, D. (1996) *Teaching as a Research-Based Profession*, London: Teacher Training Agency.

Hillage, J., Pearson, R., Anderson, A. and Tamkin, P. (1998) *Excellence in Research in Schools*, London: Department for Education and Employment.

Pollard, A. (2008) 'Knowledge transformation and impact: aspirations and experiences from TLRP', *Cambridge Journal of Education*, 38 (1): 5–22.

Pollard, A. and Oancea, A. (2010) *Unlocking Learning: towards evidence-informed policy and practice in education*, Final Report of the UK Strategic Forum for Research in Education, London: BERA (British Educational Research Association).

Chapter 3

User engagement and the processes of educational research

Anne Edwards

Educational research and especially pedagogical research in education differs in one important way from research on teaching and learning undertaken in the research practices of psychology or sociology. Pedagogical analyses in educational research necessarily involve close engagement with the complex field of study that is education. Some time ago I argued that educational research is an 'engaged social science' (Edwards 2001, 2002). By that I meant that it engages with the motivations and anticipations of the participants in the research. Recognizing this responsibility as a researcher points to a way of enquiring that is sensitive to the complexities and purposes of educational practices, and that in its most advanced forms involves weaving the knowledge that arises in these practices into the enquiries being pursued. These ideas underpinned a seminar series that was part of the UK Teaching and Learning Research Programme (TLRP). The series examined the impact of engaging users in research on the processes of educational research (Edwards *et al.* 2007; Rickinson *et al.* 2011).

The TLRP concern with user engagement *in* the processes of research reflected a debate that had been underway from the early 1990s (Gibbons *et al.* 1994; Stehr 1994) about whose knowledge was powerful in the new knowledge economy. In those discussions the knowledge produced by researchers outside universities was set alongside the knowledge products of academe in vying for influence on, for example, policies, practices and products.

One response to these challenges to the exclusivity of university-based research expertise was to argue that the boundaries between universities and other sites of knowledge production should be eroded so that *extra-mural* researchers engage in the processes of research, generating research-based knowledge alongside university-based researchers. The arguments put forward by Gibbons *et al.* described 'the new production of knowledge' in such partnerships:

The universities are no longer the remote source and wellspring of invention and creativity but are part of the problem solving, problem identification and strategic brokering that characterise the knowledge industries.

(Gibbons *et al.* 1994: 86)

They suggested that universities should recognize the change underway in how knowledge moves between universities and the fields where it is brought into use. They described the production of what they called Mode 2 knowledge, distinguishing it from Mode 1 knowledge, which was the province of universities and the outcome of the conventions of knowledge production within the academic disciplines. Mode 2 knowledge production, in contrast, is more problem-focused and trans-disciplinary and challenges the more hidebound notions of what 'good science' is (Gibbons *et al.* 1994: 3). Its production, they argued, is based on negotiated relationships across the boundaries of universities and commercial companies, aided by advances in communications technology, as teams from both settings work together to produce knowledge in the site of its application. Mode 2 knowledge therefore depends on good networks to sustain horizontal links between the sites of innovation and university researchers.

These ideas represented the zeitgeist. In 1995 Nonaka and Takeuchi wrote of the knowledge-creating company along similar lines; while Seely Brown and Duguid's 2002 account of the social life of information brought together studies of how knowledge is generated and mobilized in and between organizations from research on information in organizations. But, even in these studies, relatively little attention was paid to the negotiations in the new spaces at the boundaries of different practices where knowledge from each specialist practice came into contact.

The seminar series, which informs this chapter, attempted to address this gap in the context of educational research by examining what happens when the practices of university research come into contact with the practices of those who work in education or use educational services. The horizontal links across practice boundaries between research, pedagogy and management as practitioners work together *in* research is my primary focus. However, I shall point also to the challenges of making vertical or upstream connections so that policy communities might engage *with* research-based knowledge.

The arguments draw on my analyses of inter-professional collaborations, where I have identified the need for a new form of 'relational expertise' (Edwards 2010), which is in addition to one's specialist expertise and enables working across practice boundaries on complex phenomena. I shall suggest that a capacity for recognizing and working with what matters for partners in research projects, while remaining focused on the study, is a crucial attribute when engaging with users in research.

What does user engagement mean for educational research?

Educational research is presented here as a set of practices, inhabited by educational researchers who work alongside practitioners located in other practices as they pursue their research questions. These other practices include teaching children, giving pastoral support or managing organizations. Each practice is imbued with historically accumulated knowledge, driven forward by what matters for participants and freighted with the emotional aspects of work that shape professional identities (Edwards 2010). The rationale for user engagement in research is therefore that educational research is likely to be enriched by the expertise available in these other practices. Studies may be strengthened by insights into problem formulation and data analyses within research projects. User engagement in research is therefore not an easy option, but an added demand that calls for careful planning and sensitive negotiations.

The idea that educational research may be strengthened through user engagement reflects Nowotny's view that specialist knowledge, and the claims for validity that goes with specialist expertise, should be respected (Nowotny 2000); but equally experts need to get closer to the fields in which their expertise is used. She argued as follows:

> Experts must now extend their knowledge, not simply to be an extension of what they know in their specialised field, but to consist of building links and trying to integrate what they know with what others want to, or should, know and do.
>
> (Nowotny 2003: 155)

However, educational research is a broad field encompassing different definitions of acceptable knowledge and different approaches to gathering it and analysing it. For researchers whose epistemological positions take them to objectivist accounts of the relationship between research and the field of study, user engagement is likely to focus on taking findings either to policy-makers who may in turn translate them into guidelines for practice, or to programmes of research dissemination where findings are shared with practitioners with the intention of informing their practices. There are many fine examples of these processes. However, this mode of research is also sometimes characterized as backward-looking, unable to keep pace with the more rapidly moving cycles of policy-making.

Mulgan, writing from his experience in the UK Prime Minister's Office, described 'policy fields in flux', which included education, in the following way:

> The . . . category belongs to areas where most people recognize that things need to change; that policies which worked once are no longer working,

but fewer can agree on either the diagnosis or the solutions. In these areas – a fair amount of education, some environmental policy, crime, the organisation of public services – there is often a great deal of fertility and experimentation. Evidence about what works exists, but it is often patchy. It is more likely to reveal a weakness of policy and find a filter for false claims, than it is to give convincing evidence about what will work in the future.

(Mulgan 2005: 221)

Mulgan argued for a social science version of Mode 2 knowledge:

Today a good deal of conceptual innovation is taking place through practice, with relatively few areas in which academics develop theoretical frameworks which others then apply. More often – in cases as diverse as intelligence-led policing or drugs rehabilitation – the theorists are following behind, trying to make sense of what the practitioners are doing.

(Mulgan 2005: 223)

Mulgan's suggestion that researchers who influence policy should become more forward-looking and develop ideas alongside innovating practitioners resonates with Gibbons' 1999 view that 'experts must now . . . try to integrate what they "know" now with what others want to "do" in the future.' Accordingly, researchers who work on practices need strong links with their fields of study if they are to engage with their practices, anticipations and emergent challenges.

Five broad approaches to user engagement in research

In Rickinson *et al.* (2011) we identified five approaches to managing knowledge flows across practice boundaries:

- creating feedback loops;
- university-led participatory research;
- combining small-scale studies;
- co-research for conceptual development; and
- user-led research.

The first two approaches can be characterized as processes of knowledge exchange across the boundaries of different practices. The remaining three approaches go further than just exchanging knowledge, to include knowledge construction that draws on the expertise of the different practices involved.

Creating feedback loops

This approach does not involve participants in working as researchers, but attempts to keep them engaged with the research over time. It does so by maintaining flows of knowledge between the field and the project, regularly presenting emergent findings to participants and requesting feedback. The boundary between research project and research participants is firmly drawn. Researchers present research-based knowledge at the boundary and participant feedback is elicited to inform the study (Edwards *et al.* 2010).

University-led participatory research

This approach involves potential research users as field-testers or members of expert panels. A boundary is again drawn around a core research team, with the field-testers or panels invited into the team to inform the project. The purpose of the research study and its time-scale are set by the university teams, who also manage the boundaries. Practitioners' expertise contributes to research projects and their feedback is woven into changes in the knowledge products being developed, but practitioners are brought into the service of the study and do not shape its design. They report enjoying the experience, that they are learning and they feel they are making important contributions to areas of professional interest.

Combining small-scale studies

Here practitioners' studies are included within the boundary of the research project. Ideas are tested and developed in schools or classrooms by teachers in cycles of development, which also involve the university-based research teams. However, this approach brings tensions. Although some freedom of move-ment is given to the teachers to develop their own investigations in their schools, the smaller studies are finally embedded in larger-scale projects, which are led by university-based staff towards meeting the research objectives that are the condition of their funding (Sutherland *et al.* 2007). As a result large studies that include action research methods often operate with complex iterative research designs that have a great deal in common with tightly focused design-experiments (Cobb *et al.* 2003).

These tensions can raise the question of who controls the research in large-scale projects, and distinctions of responsibility and expertise between professional researchers and practitioner researchers can become blurred. This blurring can give rise to difficulties for the university-based researchers over being responsive to changes affecting practitioner communities and remaining faithful to the research designs for which they are responsible.

Co-research for conceptual development

This approach aims at developing and refining concepts that explain and take forward understandings of changing practices. It is different from action research because the research teams don't work with practitioners to test developments in practices, but rather to generate fresh ways of explaining what is going on in both existing and emerging practices within relatively long-term research partnerships (Edwards *et al.* 2009; Ellis 2010).

University researchers may use methods from Developmental Work Research (DWR) (Engeström 2007) to reveal the knowledge embedded in practices. They work with groups of practitioners over time, sharing the analytic tools of the study with them to help them to explain their own developing work practices and take forward their own understandings of them. The boundary around the project includes both researchers and participants. However, the researchers are responsible for setting the agenda, organizing meetings and undertaking final analyses.

DWR is a challenging mode of working requiring strong participant commitment to the processes. If participants are not interested in rethinking their practices and exploring developments in their institutional systems they will dislike the process; the powerful analytic tools offered by DWR and the contradictions they unearth will be resisted. Where there is an interest among practitioners, participants become aware of how DWR can disrupt assumptions and lead to profound changes in understandings of practice.

User-led research

Examples of user-led research include work on disabilities led by professional university-based researchers who are also living with disability (Shakespeare 2006). But it also encompasses research relationships like the direct involvement of the Suresearch network of mental health service users as researchers in projects undertaken by the Institute of Applied Social Studies at the University of Birmingham.

The Suresearch example is interesting as the members of Suresearch have developed research skills through sustained involvement in studies with members of the Institute. They work within project boundaries as full members of research teams, both undertaking fieldwork and contributing to analyses alongside university staff. They are also powerful communicators of research outcomes, pointing to the impact of findings. Importantly, user-led research of this kind is quite different from research that aims at giving voice to the less privileged, where these voices are filtered through the analytic lenses of the authors of the texts.

These five approaches are, to different degrees, all underpinned by four assumptions about user engagement in research:

- The relationship between the practice of research and other educational practices is not a simple linear one: it is complex and needs careful management over time.
- Working closely with the field of practice can strengthen educational research as it allows researchers to keep in touch with current intentions in practices.
- Engagement in research alongside university-based researchers can help educational practitioners create a capacity for purposeful questioning of practices and sustaining innovation.
- The word 'relationship' is important: knowledge is mobilized and shared in conversations where each participant recognizes what is important for the others.

Developing relationships for user engagement in research

Some of the challenges arising from designing research studies to achieve user engagement include planning for different time-scales for each group of participants; acknowledging and weaving together the different purposes of research for different participants; and developing new forms of relational expertise that strengthen mutual engagement in and with research (Rickinson *et al.* 2011). These are all aspects of project management. They suggest that project management is not simply a good grasp of the workings of, for example, Prince project management systems. Attention needs to be paid to the relational aspects of knowledge-sharing and generation.

Elsewhere (Edwards 2010) I have described a relational turn in expertise. The argument is that complex problems of professional practice call for both the specific expertise to be found in discrete professional practices and an additional form of 'relational expertise'. The more we recognize that specific expertise is located in practices that are distributed across social systems and that complex problems call for complex interdisciplinary responses, the more we need to develop the expertise that allows us to recognize and work with the expertise of others.

This additional relational expertise is evident when specialists in different practices collaborate to expand understandings of problems of practice and attune their responses to these problems so that the particular expertise that is available in different practices can be brought to bear. The relational turn therefore demands the capacity that Nowotny pointed towards when she suggested that 'experts must now extend their knowledge, not simply to be an extension of what they know in their specialist field, but to consist of building links and trying to integrate what they know with what others want to, or should, know and do' (Nowotny 2003: 155).

Although the arguments for relational expertise were developed while studying inter-professional work, they apply equally to working across the practice boundaries of university-based research and other forms of professional practice. In brief, relational expertise is developed as a two-stage process (Edwards 2009, 2010). First, understanding of 'what matters' in each practice is shared in meetings that occur where the different practices intersect, such as research team meetings. When problems are discussed in these meetings the categories that are employed in each practice to interpret and respond to the topics being investigated reveal what is valued in the purposes of that practice. For example, teachers may discuss pupil outcomes and curriculum, and researchers may discuss methods and validity. These discussions are important and can't be rushed because they build what Carlile (2004) has called common knowledge.

Studying how knowledge is mobilized between sub-units in the semi-conductor industry, Carlile found that knowledge held in common was particularly helpful in linking sub-units within an organization, so that knowledge could be managed across unit boundaries to provoke innovation. He made an important distinction between what he termed transfer, translation and transformation when knowledge enters new practices, and linked this distinction to the ways in which knowledge was mediated across boundaries by drawing on the knowledge that was held in common between units.

His argument was that knowledge mobilization depends on the 'capacity of the common knowledge to represent the differences and dependencies now of consequence and the ability of the actors involved to use it' (Carlile 2004: 557). He suggested that when the difference between what is known and what is new increases, the demands on the knowledge held in common, and therefore the difficulty in working with the new knowledge, also increases.

Accordingly, simple 'transfer' may be possible when new ideas are not too distant from existing specialist knowledge in a practice, such as when a mathematics education researcher talks to a maths teacher about teaching proof, but brief translation may be needed when the researcher offers proof in mathematics as an interesting concept to researchers working on science pedagogy. However, some transformation will be necessary when the researcher explains mathematical proof to her lawyer brother who has his own practice-based understanding of proof. This argument suggests that building common knowledge that enables quick transfer or makes translation easy is an important prerequisite to quick and responsive relational work across practice boundaries.

Common knowledge, it seems, is comprised of knowledge of 'what matters' in each intersecting practice and contains enough background insights to each practice to enable practitioners to recognize the values and standpoints of others when interpreting and responding to a task. In the second stage of the development and use of relational expertise, the knowledge held in common mediates joint work in the field when university-based researchers work with school-based team members in data collection and analysis. They share enough common knowledge to understand each other and have conversations that explore phenomena in creative ways.

Consequently one aspect of project management, when potential users of research are involved in research, is to find ways of easing communication across the boundaries of the different practices, strengthening 'horizontal' links (Edwards *et al.* 2009) between people with different kinds of expertise. It therefore seems that managing team meetings as sites of intersecting practices so that 'what matters' for each set of practitioners is made visible and respected is an important part of preparing people for close collaboration in the field of study.

User engagement and responsible research

This attention to values and purposes when planning for user engagement returns us to the idea of educational research as an 'engaged social science'. I am not alone in emphasizing 'what matters' in the practice of research. Discussing social science research more broadly, Flyvbjerg has suggested that social sciences are strong where the natural sciences are weak. Their strength lies in 'the reflexive analysis and discussion of values and interests, which is the prerequisite for an enlightened political, economic, and cultural development of any society . . .' (Flyvbjerg 2001: 3).

Flyvbjerg is pointing to the demands made on social researchers when they design studies, and analyse and report findings. Social research, from this perspective, is 'responsible' research (Edwards 2002), which, in the case of pedagogic research in education, needs to be close to educational practices to recognize their historical development, embedded purposes and mind-shaping values. All five approaches outlined earlier called for frequent and productive interactions across the boundaries of the practice of research and the various practices that make up education and create opportunities for broadly based 'reflexive analyses and discussion of values and interests'.

However, user engagement can be tokenistic, because of the hierarchies of expertise that persist in research as a result of long-standing relationships between science and society. Arguing that these relationships no longer exist as, for example, university-based researchers find their research programme driven by government priorities, Gibbons has proposed a new social contract between science and society (Gibbons 1999).

Taking as given that knowledge is distributed within and outside universities, Gibbons argues that 'expertise . . . must emerge from bringing together the many different knowledge dimensions involved' (Gibbons 1999: c83). Emphasizing horizontal linkages across fluid knowledge networks, he recognizes that the permeability of boundaries that he is proposing can lead to increased complexity and uncertainty, but argues that these factors only produce more experimentation. At the core of his new social contract is the view that:

the old image of science will no longer suffice. Rather a reciprocity is required in which not only does the public understand how science works, but equally, science understands how its publics work.

(Gibbons 1999: C83–84)

Accordingly, scientists need to consider the 'implications' of their work for society, a much better term than 'impacts'. However, his is not an argument for weakening the expert knowledge base of science by diluting it. Rather, it demands that scientists, like other professionals (Edwards 2010), should constantly negotiate their standing with their publics and develop the relational expertise necessary for reciprocity.

Gibbons' thesis pursues the themes set out in the 1994 book he cowrote with colleagues and focuses on the natural and material sciences, but the arguments are, I suggest, as relevant to the social sciences. Giddens argued that 'the practical impact of social science and sociological theories are enormous' (1990: 16) because of the very reflexivity indicated later by Flyvbjerg. Sociological knowledge, Giddens argued, 'spirals in and out of the universe of social life, reconstructing both itself and that universe as an integral part of that process' (1990: 15–16). I suggest that the responsibilities of researchers are as enormous as the practical implications of their work and demand that they become attuned to the values and purposes of the practices into which they 'spiral'.

The reciprocity that can counteract the overweening impact of social science on the 'universe of social life' can be found in processes of user engagement in research. Where the research team comprises expert members of different practices, as in the last three of the five approaches discussed earlier, there is the potential to share enough common knowledge to work together productively.

Discussing knowledge transfer in knowledge societies, Stehr comments that:

> . . . transfer of knowledge does not necessarily include the cognitive ability to generate such knowledge, for example, the theoretical apparatus or the technological regime which yields such knowledge claims in the first place and on the basis of which it is calibrated and validated.
>
> (Stehr 1994: 98)

User engagement, I suggest, has the potential to bring educational practitioners and researchers into mutually informing conversations where 'the reflexive analysis and discussion of values and interests' of education are core elements and the 'theoretical apparatus and technological regimes' of educational research are as open to scrutiny and development as those of the other practices.

User engagement with research

This chapter has focused on user engagement *in* research; but there are lessons to be learned from these analyses for user engagement *with* research, a topic to be elaborated in other chapters in this collection. I shall only discuss research relationships with policy communities and describe the challenge in terms of vertical knowledge flows, in contrast to the horizontal flows that have characterized the relationships outlined so far.

The themes are familiar: working at boundaries; engagement with knowledge; recognizing motives in practices; building common knowledge; and exercising relational expertise. Here policy-making is seen as a distinct practice that sits in a hierarchical relationship to the practices of research. This relationship is in part because of governments' power over research funding, but also because education as an engaged social science aims at improving the conditions of education, which are ultimately shaped by policies. If policy-making is another practice, the relevance of research goods to 'what matters' in political practices is central to negotiating them across practice boundaries.

However, the difficulty is all too often defined as a communication one, with the fault lying with the academics. The 2003 report on the social sciences in Britain (Commission on the Social Sciences 2003) observed:

> There are significant problems with the exploitation of social science research in government, local government, commerce, the voluntary sector and the media. These come about through 'interface management' and communication problems, though the caution of some academics towards close engagement with practitioners is a source of great disappointment to many users of social science research.
>
> (extracted from the Executive Summary)

However, a former English Minister of Education has suggested that the difficulty lies more in differences in motives in the practices of research and policy. At the 2006 British Educational Research Association Conference, Estelle Morris reminded researchers that policy decisions are usually based on political values and ideology.

In this regard, policy-makers are no different from others who are able to select among different ideas that need their approval for implementation. When discussing the vertical knowledge mobilization in organizations revealed in his study of 570 subsidiaries of US companies in Denmark and of Danish Companies in the US, Schulz (2001, 2003) emphasized the perceived relevance of new knowledge as a crucial component. He observed that the relevance of new knowledge is often recognized 'on less than rational grounds; sentiments and beliefs play an important role' (Schulz 2001: 677). He concluded that relevance is 'a rather curious but under-explored aspect of organizational knowledge that merits much more attention in future' (Schulz 2001: 677).

Schulz's analyses suggest that relevance to 'what matters' in the practices of strategy and policy is important, and that recognition of relevance may need to be negotiated. In the seminar series, the role of knowledge brokers who worked between the practices of research and policy and were familiar with what mattered for each practice emerged as central to mediating research-based knowledge upstream across the hierarchical boundaries between research and policy. As was the case with the horizontal links already discussed, the mediations were complex and rarely involved linear knowledge flows (Nutley *et al.* 2007).

Concluding points

I have taken a practice view of knowledge (Orlikowski 2002, 2006) where it is seen as 'not static or given, but as a capability produced and reproduced in recurrent social practices' and 'always in the making' (Orlikowski 2006: 460). This is not a relativist account that sees all knowledge as equally robust, nor does it propose that knowledge is located only in practices and that practitioners are merely swept along in pre-determined ways of acting. Instead I suggest (a) that professional expertise involves using specialist knowledge to work towards the goals of each professional practice and (b) that working across practice boundaries on goals that are at least partially shared calls for an additional expertise.

This expertise I have characterized as relational, arguing that it is dependent on the building of common knowledge that mediates horizontal, across practices, research collaborations. However, when these concepts are applied to vertical links across the hierarchical boundaries that separate the practices of policy from research to achieve policy engagement *with* research, the challenges are clearly very different. Importantly, although the vertical mobilization of knowledge is helped if 'what matters' in each practice is aligned, the building of common knowledge across hierarchical boundaries may not always be appropriate. This is perhaps particularly so if university research is to sustain the responsible independence that allows it to reach forward to engage with new knowledge in the making.

References

Carlile, P. (2004) 'Transferring, translating and transforming: an integrative framework for managing knowledge across boundaries', *Organization Science*, 15(5): 555–68.

Cobb, P., Confrey, J., diSessa, A., Lehrer, R. and Schauble, L. (2003) 'Design experiments in educational research', *Educational Researcher*, 32(1): 9–13.

Commission on the Social Sciences (2003), Great Expectations: the social sciences in Britain. Online, available: www.acss.org.uk/docs/GtExpectations.pdf.

Edwards, A. (2001) 'Researching pedagogy: a sociocultural agenda', *Pedagogy, Culture and Society*, 9(2): 161–86.

—— (2002) 'Responsible research: ways of being a researcher', *British Educational Research Journal*, 28(2): 157–68.

—— (2009) 'Relational agency in collaborations for the wellbeing of children and young people', *Journal of Children's Services*, 4(1): 33–43.

—— (2010) *Being an Expert Professional Practitioner: the relational turn in expertise*, Dordrecht: Springer.

Edwards, A., Sebba, J. and Rickinson, M. (2007) 'Working with users: some implications for educational research', *British Educational Research Journal*, 33(5): 647–61.

Edwards, A., Lunt, I. and Stamou, E. (2010) 'Inter-professional work and expertise: new roles at the boundaries of schools', *British Educational Research Journal*, 36(1): 27–45.

Edwards, A., Daniels, H., Gallagher, T., Leadbetter, J. and Warmington, P. (2009) *Improving Inter-professional Collaborations: multi-agency working for children's wellbeing*, London: Routledge.

Ellis, V. (2010) 'Studying the process of change: the double stimulation strategy in teacher education research', in V. Ellis, A. Edwards and P. Smagorinsky (eds), *Cultural-Historical Perspectives on Teacher Education and Development*, pp. 95–114, London: Routledge.

Engeström, Y. (2007) 'Putting Vygotsky to work: the change laboratory as an application of double stimulation', in H. Daniels, M. Cole and J.V. Wertsch (eds), *The Cambridge Companion to Vygotsky*, New York: Cambridge University Press, pp. 363–82.

Flyvbjerg, B. (2001) *Making Social Science Matter*, Cambridge: Cambridge University Press.

Gibbons, M. (1999) 'Science's new social contract with society', *Nature*, 402, c81–4: 11–17.

Gibbons, M., Limoges, C., Nowotny, H., Schwartzman, S., Scott, P. and Trow, M. (1994) *The New Production of Knowledge*, London: Sage.

Giddens, A. (1990) *The Consequences of Modernity*, Cambridge: Polity Press.

Mulgan, G. (2005) 'Government, knowledge and the business of policy making; the potential and limits of evidence-based policy', *Evidence and Policy*, 1(2): 215–26.

Nonaka, I. and Takeuchi, H. (1995) *The Knowledge Creating Company: how Japanese companies create the dynamics of innovation*, Oxford: Oxford University Press.

Nowotny, H. (2000) 'Transgressive competence: the narrative of expertise', *European Journal of Social Theory*, 3(1): 5–21.

—— (2003) 'Dilemma of expertise', *Science and Public Policy*, 30(3): 151–56.

Nutley, S., Walter, I. and Davies, H. (2007) *Using Evidence: how research can inform public services*, Bristol: Policy Press.

Orlikowski, W. (2002) 'Knowing in practice: enacting a collective capability in distributed organizing', *Organization Science*, 13(3): 249–73.

—— (2006) 'Material knowing: the scaffolding of human knowledgeability', *European Journal of Information Systems*, 15: 460–66.

Rickinson, M., Sebba, J. and Edwards, A. (2011) *Improving Research through User Engagement*, London: Routledge.

Schulz, M. (2001) 'The uncertain relevance of newness: organizational learning and knowledge flows', *Academy of Management Journal*, 44(4): 661–81.

—— (2003) 'Pathways of relevance: exploring inflows of knowledge into subunits of multinational corporations', *Organization Science*, 14(4): 440–59.

Seely Brown, J. and Duguid, P. (2002) *The Social Life of Information*, Boston, Mass: Harvard Business School Press.

Shakespeare, T. (2006) *Disability Rights and Wrongs*, London: Routledge.

Stehr, N. (1994) *Knowledge Societies*, London: Sage.

Sutherland, R., John, P. and Robertson, S. (2007) *Improving Learning with ICT*, London: Routledge.

Part II

Politics in knowledge flows

Research meets policy

Chapter 4

Affairs of the smart

Will education researchers and decision-makers 'hook up'?

Charles Ungerleider

The 'promise' of evidence-informed public policy

Those advocating evidence-informed decision-making were likely doing their happy dance in March 2009 when US President Barack Obama signed the Stem Cell Executive Order and the Scientific Integrity Presidential Memorandum:

> The public must be able to trust the science and scientific process informing public policy decisions. Political officials should not suppress or alter scientific or technological findings and conclusions. If scientific and technological information is developed and used by the Federal Government, it should ordinarily be made available to the public. To the extent permitted by law, there should be transparency in the preparation, identification, and use of scientific and technological information in policymaking.
>
> (Obama 9 March 2009)

Obama's comments were intended to signal a fundamental change in US government policy regarding stem cell research and in the use of evidence for informing public policy. The change in direction they signalled for the USA was significant. But apart from the implicit swipe at the previous administration's views of science, the announcement regarding scientific integrity was another incremental step by governments under pressure to justify their decisions with reference to the evidence that informs them and to increase the transparency of the decisions they make.

By the time Obama signed the documents in 2009 he had already appointed Arne Duncan as US Secretary of Education. Duncan precipitated the Race to the Top competition in which states compete for US $4 billion by proposing educational reforms. Among the reforms that Duncan is reputed to favour, in contrast to the evidence on their effectiveness, are charter schools and merit pay for teachers (Strauss 2010). Is Obama's commitment to evidence-informed decision-making confined to areas other than education, or is it a political promise he has no intention of keeping?

Appeals for evidence-informed decisions received momentum when, in a *fin de siècle* effort 'to get better government – for a better Britain' (Cabinet Office 1999a: 4), the Blair government embarked upon efforts to modernize government, calling, among other things, for 'better use of evidence and research in policy making and better focus on policies that will deliver long-term goals' (Cabinet Office 1999a: 16). These calls for evidence-informed decisions required a bridging of the chasm.

Blair's desire for the application of evidence to governmental decision-making in Britain was the most recent expression of a question raised by Snow (1960) in *Science and Government* roughly 40 years earlier, namely how can democratic governments make use of science and scientists? In his introductory remarks, Snow makes clear that there are no easy answers to the question:

> No one who has ever thought at all about the relations of science and government, much less anyone who has experienced them directly, is likely to think that positive conclusions are going to be firm or easy to come by. Most of the concepts that administrative theorists use are at best rationalizations, not guides to further thought; as a rule they are unrealistically remote from the workaday experience.
>
> (Snow 1960: 3)

Snow's treatise was a plea for scientists to be active at all levels of government. Snow's belief was that their contribution to government would be to supply what 'our kind of existential society is desperately short of: so short of, that it fails to recognize of what it is starved. That is foresight' (Snow 1960: 81).

In Britain, by 2002, scientist–researchers and policy-makers were living beneath the same roof. The Blair cabinet office had become home to a Strategy Unit, designed to provide strategy and policy advice to the Prime Minister (Cabinet Office 1999b). What kind of a relationship would politicians and researchers have and, most important, could such a relationship last, given the historically dismissive attitude toward research held by policy-makers?

In his seminal and lengthy 1999 volume, *Governing from the Centre: The Concentration of Power in Canadian Politics*, Donald Savoie makes the case that, in the last century, governments in Canada, the United Kingdom, and the United States '. . . would move to strengthen their centre to promote greater policy and programme coordination, to generate policy advice, and to promote better management practices in government operations.' It is revealing that the role of research is of such little consequence in the aforementioned central government processes that it is absent from the book's 27-page index that addresses topics from Aboriginal affairs to youth employment.

Different worlds and different goals

The call for evidence-informed decisions makes strange bedfellows of researchers and politicians. Researchers and political decision-makers live in different worlds, respond to different norms and speak different languages.

Ben Levin, a Canada Research Chair at the University of Toronto who served as a Deputy Minister in both Ontario and Manitoba, tells a story that reveals the distance between the worlds occupied by politicians and researchers. Levin informed a Minister with whom he worked that a course of action under consideration was supported by research, to which the Minister replied, 'You know, Ben, I don't believe that research votes in my constituency' (personal communication).

Levin's anecdote makes clear that the primary audience for the decisions made by politicians is the electorate – or, to be specific, the electorate upon which the politician depends for support. The wider audience for the work of politicians is the various publics (constituents, stakeholders, clients, and/or the media) affected by the decisions that are made. On the other hand, the primary audience for the work of researchers is other researchers in their field of study, and secondarily the agencies that fund their research and the institutions that employ them. The practitioners responsible for education are an audience that receives relatively little attention, though it is largely through their efforts that formal education succeeds or fails.

Sceptics may doubt that it is possible to bridge the chasm that divides decision-makers and researchers. Some may aver that few, if any, of the decisions that most people make are informed by the evidence available. People are often more susceptible to influence by authority and tenacity than by the evidence available. If they seek evidence for the practical decisions they make, it is often after the fact and, if it supports the course of action taken, it is used to affirm prior judgement. If it does not, people discount, dissemble or rationalize.

The worlds in which decision-makers and researchers live are both tightly rational, but, as Levin's anecdote makes clear, the evidence and methods that govern the public policy decision-making process are quite different from those governing research. Although dismissive of research at that moment, the Minister, had he been asked, would have said that he does pay attention to evidence. His reply to Levin points to one source of evidence that politicians consult; the approval of one's constituency is typically the paramount source of evidence, but it is not the sole source. Others include media; lobbyists and advocates; personal, anecdotal experience; ideological and values commitments; and expert advice – what is sometimes referred to as eminence-based advice.

Democracy is government by persuasion. Since those who rule depend upon the compliance of those who are governed, they must secure consent through the selective use of information consonant with the beliefs and dispositions of the governed. The alternative to persuasion is coercion – the use or threat of force to get people to do what they otherwise would not do. Its use signals an ineffective and unstable political system. Thus, in one sense, democracy is a system in which the governed may choose to comply.

Governments use evidence to persuade citizens with varied success. The government for which I worked as Deputy Minister of Education introduced annual assessments of students in grades four, seven and ten. Shortly after their implementation, a right-of-centre think tank used the data to produce school rankings (league tables) published by one of the major daily papers. The government was very disturbed by the think tank's comparison of schools based on raw data indicating more within-school difference than between-school differences and by its use of error-ridden methods.

In an effort to counter the impact that such ranking might have, we developed a strategy to educate reporters about the ranking process. We conducted a technical briefing just prior to the publication of the following year's ranking in the newspaper. The Minister and I would explain the conceptual and technical errors made in the calculation of the rankings by the think tank and illustrate how small changes in school results would produce a large change in a school's position in the rankings. Judging by the questions the reporters asked during the briefing, we thought we had persuaded them to take a more critical stance toward the rankings. When the think tank's results were published, we were disappointed that there was little evidence in other newspapers and electronic media that we had succeeded in engendering a more critical view of the rankings.

Politicians are astutely cognizant that, in democratic societies, ideas are the main instruments for obtaining and maintaining political power and they are keenly aware that persuasion is the main resource at their disposal. As a consequence, propaganda (what we have come to call spin) is a necessary, if insufficient, concomitant of the political process. There is no politics without spin. Politicians will use evidence selectively in securing support for the ideas and ideals they favour. Although writing about the USA, Anderson's comments are applicable to any democratic society:

> The policymaking process in the United States is an adversarial process, characterized by the clash of competing and conflicting viewpoints and interests, rather than an impartial, disinterested, or 'objective' search for 'correct' solutions for policy problems. Public officials – legislators, administrators, and perhaps to a lesser extent, judges – do not stand impartially about the policy struggle. Rather, they have their own values and positions which they seek to advance and hence are often partisans in the policy struggle. Given this, policy analysis done by social scientists, for instance, may have little impact except as they provide support for the positions of particular participants in the policy process.
>
> (Anderson 1984 quoted in Heineman *et al.* 2002: 48)

If they consider evidence, politicians are prone to seek expert opinion. The advice expressed by an expert provides advantages to the politician that a direct reading of the evidence does not. If the expert is charismatic and known to the field, s/he can propel the desired change. If the initiative about which the expert has provided advice fails, the expert provides the politician with a convenient scapegoat.

Expert advice has its drawbacks. Stefan Wolter, Director of the Swiss Coordination Centre for Research in Education, a body co-funded by the federal and cantonal levels of government to ensure the harmonization of education research across Switzerland, makes the distinction between evidence-based and eminence-based decision-making. Evidence-based decision-making relies on systematic research that has been replicated over time and in different settings. Eminence-based decision-making relies on expert advice. The challenge of the latter is that it is impossible for the decision-makers to know what part of an expert's advice, if any, was research-based. According to Wolter, eminence-based 'knowledge' is personal judgment masquerading as evidence (Cappon 2008).

Like Wolter, Phil Davies, who worked in the UK Cabinet Secretariat as Deputy Director of the Government Chief Social Researcher's Office in the Prime Minister's Strategy Unit, contrasts evidence-informed approaches with opinion-based policy. He notes that 'opinion-based policy, which relies heavily on either the selective use of evidence (e.g. on single studies irrespective of quality) or on the untested views of individuals or groups, [is] often inspired by ideological standpoints, prejudices, or speculative conjecture' (Davies 2004: 3).

Both decision-makers and researchers are risk-averse. In fact, managing risk is a key concern among decision-makers because visible decision failures undermine their credibility and legitimacy, threatening the longevity of their authority, especially if they are elected officials. Neither the visibility nor the consequences of risks faced by researchers are as great as those facing decision-makers, especially political decision-makers.

Researchers manage risks – primarily threats to the validity of their research – but they are better able to manage the visibility of such risks since the primary medium for the communication of their research is typically blind, peer-reviewed publications. Consequences are also more manageable for researchers. They are typically offered the opportunity to revise their work before it is disseminated. The primary medium of dissemination is publications of limited circulation. There are professional consequences of poorly conducted investigations for researchers, but they are – given the system of review – less likely to occur and typically less cataclysmic than the public humiliation or loss of position that decision-makers face.

Decision-makers will take risks, but they carefully calculate the likelihood of failure. My own experience provides an illustration of risk management from the point of view of researcher and decision-maker. I was an academic seconded to serve as Deputy Minister who had, among other things, responsibility for the implementation of a major technological change. The project faced challenges. For example, the large corporation with which government had contracted had fallen behind in its commitments and had not tackled the most difficult installations.

One of the Ministers to whom I was responsible thought it desirable that some of the work should be redirected to small, inexperienced local suppliers. That action – something permitted under the terms of the government's contract – would build capacity among local suppliers to do such work in the future, a form of local economic development. The Minister in question called a meeting late one afternoon to discuss his idea and to seek advice. I approached the situation as a researcher, feeling that I had evidence on my side. I recommended against the direction that the Minister favoured, reasoning that, given the delays and the difficulty in completing the work faced by a large, experienced corporation and the disparity between it and the small, inexperienced, local suppliers, it was highly likely that government would not be able to meet its commitment to a timely roll-out within budget. The Minister was not persuaded, and decided in favour of his plan to provide the work to the local suppliers and develop the local economies of the communities in which the suppliers were located. As we left the Minister's office, we were reminded that, despite the change in plans the Minister had made, the timelines and budgetary restrictions were to be met.

As it turned out, the Minister's reasoning was correct. The local suppliers used the government contract to borrow money to buy the material they needed and acquired the expertise to do the work. Because they were more familiar with the local settings in which the work was performed, they were able to complete the work faster than the larger corporation. The project was completed on time and under budget, and the government garnered considerable support, although not enough to secure re-election!

This experience and others like it point to another of the many differences between research and policy-oriented decision-making. After considering the evidence of importance to him, the Minister arrived at a conclusion that he hoped could be achieved easily and would produce wide benefit to the community. Researchers are attentive to nuance and circumstance, and, thus, want to qualify their conclusions.

The Minister was typical of decision-makers; they seek resolution of conflict and elimination of problems as rapidly as can be achieved. Researchers usually do not. The pace of research is designed to engender thoughtful and careful reflection, while the pace of decision-making is more pressing and resolution-oriented. Decision-makers also seek results, but they are less concerned with specific mechanisms so long as the anticipated outcomes can be achieved; they seek answers and impact. Though they, too, may want their immediate investigation to provide a solution to the problem that animated it, in the long run researchers want their work to beget more – if not more problems, certainly more research.

Can research improve decision-making?

It is not inevitable that research will improve decision-making about policy. Research evidence will not inform decisions if the need for a decision is urgent or if the decision-maker has an established position on the matter. If the matter is one that has attracted significant visibility and is highly divisive, the decision-maker might call for research evidence as a way of deferring decision-making – but the strategy is unlikely to work if the process of gathering such evidence will itself keep the issue's visibility high.

The pay-offs for decision-makers are the benefits or improvements brought about by the decisions made. These include reducing (if not eliminating) problems, or managing the conflicts (or the visibility of the conflicts) that the allocation of scarce values produces. The payoffs for researchers include the recognition that their work receives from their peers and the translation of peer approval into support for further research, tenure and promotion.

Politicians walk a fine line between seeking recognition for good work and avoiding visibility for making decisions that will be contentious. Researchers, on the other hand, seek visibility for themselves and for their research – albeit among audiences where their visibility is more easily controlled. Notwithstanding the substantive contribution that research makes to the creation of new knowledge, research, like politics, is also a form of self-promotion.

Despite visible instances such as the ones by Blair and Obama, calls for increased use of evidence by politicians in education decision-making are infrequent, if not completely absent. Calls are more typically made by researchers and advocates. Such calls are often an implicit indictment of a particular educational decision and/or post-positivistic expressions of belief that the conduct and outcomes of education would be improved if only decision-makers made more and better use of research.

Evidence-informed decision-making in education and health

A frequent, and I think misplaced, comparator for the use of research in education is the field of health. There are a number of key differences between health and education that deserve mention with respect to the part that evidence should play. The flow from evidence to policy and practice appears to be more direct and more rapid in health than in education – though there are no established benchmarks. This is probably true because the incentives for profit from undertaking and encouraging the use of research in health are greater than they are in education – especially where, as a consequence of careful study, pharmaceutical companies are able to garner significant economic rewards. Being first matters in medical research since those who are first can patent their discoveries. Leading investigators can reap further rewards in attracting resources to support further research. Although not without opportunities for economic reward, educational research rarely leads to a patentable discovery or huge economic returns.

A second difference between health and education is the notion of protecting the public from harm. We are not accustomed to considering the harm to the public that may result from poor educational practice, at least not in the way that we do in the health field. Health-related malpractice is typically more visible, both in its impact on the individual and in the attention that it receives in the media, in part due to the visibility of litigation, large awards and those rare, but significant, instances where a practitioner's licence is revoked. The notion of professional regulation in the public interest is of longer standing in health than education. The criteria for performance of health professionals – especially physicians – are seemingly more clear-cut and evidence-informed than for educators.

We do not have established or even useful benchmarks for such matters in education. Nonetheless, implied and explicit comparisons are often made between the fields of education and health – typically to the detriment of the former. It might be more appropriate to compare evidence production and use in education with social work, social welfare or criminal justice.

Politics and policy exist because of conflict between parties who seek authorization of a decision that will see one party's value preferences prevail. The process is one in which values are paramount and all other considerations – including decisions about evidence – are subordinate.

Politicians and senior decision-makers are responsible for setting the broad directions for education – an exercise that is primarily values-driven, not evidence-driven. Improved student achievement, development of artistic abilities and standards, civic engagement and similar goals are value stances. They express what is desirable and desired. Research evidence cannot inform which among them should be emphasized or diminished.

Advice to educational researchers

Many researchers think that dissemination of their peer-reviewed results in refereed publications will contribute to the improvement of policy and practice. It may, but there are heavy odds against its happening quickly or directly. Public policy and, by extension, educational policy is a values-driven activity. The policies adopted by any particular regime will depend upon a fit between the policy objectives and the values that the regime holds. Regimes that favour diminishing the part that government plays in the lives of citizens are unlikely to approve a policy of state-supported early childhood care or education. If they do provide support for early childhood care or education, it will more likely be in the form of tax credits or income tax deductions for families who purchase care or education for children during the early years, rather than funding for public institutions. The opposite is true of regimes that see the state as a mechanism of ensuring equity of access to such programmes. Thus, the first lesson for researchers is to recognize that the opportunity to influence policy will depend on the prevailing political ideology.

People matter significantly in politics. Politicians are acutely attuned to what constituents want. In fact, if sufficient in number and intensity, constituent preferences can often reshape a politician's ideology or cause a politician to ignore ideology. Educational researchers are unlikely to be able to mobilize constituent preferences. If they can communicate the policy implications of their research in media to which the public pays attention, they have a chance to influence public policy. Timing plays a crucial part in the process. The opportunity for influencing public policy on an issue depends upon whether the issue that the policy addresses is seen by the public to be important. If failure to address the issue threatens the legitimacy of the regime in power, the likelihood that the regime will act is significantly increased.

Lovaas' research devoted to therapy for autistic children received considerable prominence when families argued that the failure to fund Lovaas' approach was a violation of the equality provision of section 15 of the Charter of Rights and Freedoms. The petitioners' argument failed, but, in its ruling, the court commented:

> ... Applied Behavioural Analysis, ('ABA') or Intensive Behavioural Intervention ('IBI') therapy is not uncontroversial. Objections range from its reliance in its early years on crude and arguably painful stimuli, to its goal of changing the child's mind and personality.
>
> (Auton 2004: 10)

It is arguable whether researchers would welcome such attention to their work.

Researchers interested in influencing public policy are better off developing relationships with those who advise decision-makers than trying to directly influence politicians. In the Westminster system of government, ministers change portfolios, often frequently. During my three-year tenure as Deputy Minister, I worked with four Ministers. Civil servants with domain expertise do not change positions as frequently as Ministers or Deputy Ministers. Thus, developing relationships with the civil servants who prepare the briefing notes and cabinet submissions on behalf of their ministries will increase the likelihood that one's views will be sought on matters that fall within what is perceived to be the researcher's ambit.

Whether in the face-to-face relationship with civil servants or in the material that is prepared for their consideration, it is imperative that ideas are expressed clearly; that the limitations of the evidence are made clear; that, most important-antly, the direct and indirect costs of implementing a policy based on the evidence provided are disclosed; and that the factors affecting what it will take to bring the effort to scale are evident. Civil servants are typically well-educated professionals. However, they often do not know the arcane terminology used in the field and, like most people, are unsympathetic with jargon. Brevity and clarity are essential.

A number of politicians have been credited with the demand that a policy brief be written on a single sheet of paper. The demand for brevity is understandable given that politicians are busy people. In addition, the one-page requirement signals the necessity of being able to communicate the analysis of a problem and a recommended solution clearly, conveying its essential elements succinctly. If the material cannot be communicated in a single page, it is unlikely to be clarified in a longer document.

Candid appraisals of the evidence are welcome. It is imperative to explain when the evidence is not sufficiently developed to support policy or practice. If the policy or practice has sufficient evidence to warrant support, researchers must be able to explain the steps necessary to implement the policy and the attendant direct and indirect costs. If there are alternative and less costly policies or practices that will address the issue, the researcher ought to be able to explain them.

Evidence-informed teaching practice

Interest in the use of the research to inform the education decisions of politicians and senior policy-makers may be misplaced. Perhaps efforts to increase the use of research to inform decisions in education should be focused upon educational practitioners. Educational practitioners are responsible for decisions about how the value preferences (expressed as goals) might best be achieved. Indeed, we express our confidence in educational practitioners by according them autonomy about how the goals expressed by politicians might best be achieved.

We do not know what it would look like if research played a greater and more regular part in the decisions about education. We assume that the increased application of research would improve education and can even point to instances where it has. Today, for example, most elementary schools employ a balanced approach to literacy in recognition that phonological awareness and comprehension are important components of reading.

There have been negative instances as well. James Coleman *et al.*'s (1966) study of educational opportunity in the USA had at least one unintended negative impact. Coleman's work showed that, taken together, out-of-school factors explained more of the variance in student achievement than school factors. Though true, recognition of the impact of out-of-school factors – especially poverty, and low parental education and expectations – on student achievement appears to have had a deleterious impact on teacher efficacy and their expectations for the performance of some students, limiting opportunities and the outcomes achieved.

Conclusion

While a marriage of research and decision-making is unlikely, long-term liaisons are becoming more frequent than one-night stands, at least rhetorically. Decision-makers, especially those occupying public office, are increasingly paying lip service to what the research has to say, averring to use research evidence along with a variety of other forms of evidence to inform the decisions they make. Unless we are prepared to substitute a technocracy for a democracy (and coercion for compliance), we should not expect more or demand that public policy decisions be determined by research evidence alone.

Less emphasis on the use of evidence by politicians and senior decision-makers in education may be warranted by recognition that their decisions are primarily expressive of the community's aspirations rather than of the means for achieving those aspirations. However, when it comes to the means, evidence about the efficacy and cost of various approaches becomes more salient. If we seek more than episodic relations between evidence and decisions in education, we should focus on practitioners and on the conditions favouring a marriage of research and practices, rather than on brief affairs between researchers and politicians.

References

Auton (Guardian ad litem of) v. British Columbia (Attorney General), 2004 SCC 78, [2004] 3 S.C.R. 657. Online, available: www.canlii.org/en/ca/scc/doc/2004/2004scc78/2004scc78.html (accessed 31 August 2010).

Cabinet Office (1999a) *Modernising Government*, White Paper, London: Cabinet Office. Online, available: http://archive.cabinetoffice.gov.uk/moderngov/download/modgov.pdf (accessed 3 October 2010).

Cabinet Office (1999b) *Professional Policy Making for the Twenty-First Century, Cabinet Office Strategic Policy Making Team*, London: Cabinet Office. Online, available: www.nationalschool.gov.uk/policyhub/docs/profpolicymaking.pdf (accessed 3 October 2010).

Cappon, P. (21 May 2008) Interview with Stefan Wolter. Online, available: www.ccl-cca.ca/ccl/AboutCCL/PresidentCEO/20080624StefanWolter.html (accessed 17 August 2010).

Coleman, J.S., Campbell, E.Q., Hobson, C.J., McPartland, J., Mood, A.M., Weinfeld, F.D. and R.L. York (1966) *Equality of Educational Opportunity*, Washington, DC: US Department of Health, Education and Welfare, Office of Education.

Davies, P. (2004) 'Is evidence-based government possible?', Jerry Lee Lecture 2004, presented at the 4th Annual Campbell Collaboration Colloquium, Washington, DC, 19 February 2004.

Heineman, R.A., Bluhm, W.T., Peterson, S.A. and E. N. Kearney (2002) *The World of the Policy Analyst: rationality, values and politics*, London: Chatham House Publishers, Third Edition.

Obama, B. (9 March 2009a) *Scientific Integrity. Memorandum for the Heads of Executive Departments and Agencies*, The White House: Office of the Press Secretary.

Obama, B. (9 March 2009b) *Signing of Stem Cell Executive Order and Scientific Integrity Presidential Memorandum: Remarks of President Barack Obama – As Prepared for Delivery*, Washington, DC: The White House, Office of the Press Secretary.

Savoie, D.J. (1999) *Governing from the Centre: the concentration of power in Canadian politics*, Toronto: University of Toronto Press.

Snow, C.P. (1960) *Science and Government*, Cambridge, MA: Harvard University Press.

Strauss, V. (22 April 2010) 'Bill Gates' college tour – The Answer Sheet: a school survival guide for parents (and everyone else)', *The Washington Post*. Online, available: http://voices.washingtonpost.com/answer-sheet/l-gates-on-a-his-college-tour. html (accessed 23 June 2010).

Chapter 5

Knowledge stocks and flows

Data and education governance

Jenny Ozga

Introduction

This chapter discusses knowledge and its relationship to governing. It considers the representation of knowledge as data and the use of data in governing education in the UK and in Europe in recent years.[1] Governing knowledge developed in relationship with performance management regimes, alongside decentralization and deregulation: data enabled goal-governed steering of outputs and outcomes, accompanied by the monitoring of targets. In brief, the so called 'governance turn' is a shift that is highly dependent on the appearance of deregulation, but that is equally marked by strong central steering through various policy technologies, especially data collection, analysis and use. Knowledge and information play a pivotal role both in the pervasiveness of governance and in allowing the development of its dispersed, distributed and disaggregated form. Data support and create new kinds of policy instrument that organize political relations through communication/information and hence legitimize that organization (Lascoumes and Le Galès 2007). Data derived from indicators and in such policy technologies as the apparatus of quality assurance and evaluation (QAE) have the purpose, in the words of Lascoumes and Le Galès (2007: 6):

> of orienting relations between political society (via the administrative executive) and civil society (via its administered subjects) through inter-mediaries in the form of devices that mix technical components (measuring, calculating the rule of law, procedure) and social components (representation, symbol).

From this perspective, evaluation is a policy instrument; the new governance forms of decentralization and deregulation create a need for steering through evaluation; evaluation and performance data fill the space between the state and the new consumer-citizen (Fägerlind and Strömqvist 2004; Clarke 2008). New governance forms promote ways of controlling and shaping behaviour that mix material and discursive strategies: the discursive mobilization of new norms and values is combined with external regulatory mechanisms (such as competitive indicators of performance) that together seek to transform the conduct of organizations and individuals in their capacity as 'self-actualizing' agents, so as to achieve political objectives through 'action at a distance' (Miller and Rose 2008). In the discussion that follows I review some recent history and current developments in data use, including examples of the forms of 'translation' necessary to make data-based knowledge intelligible and actionable, which reveal the gap between the fluid dream of data-based governance and the sticky reality. I then consider the recent shift towards installing data monitoring at the level of individual learners, through processes of self-evaluation, which requires individuals to take much more responsibility for learning from information and for translating knowledge into action. This shift seeks to produce learning organizations – and learning governments – whose knowledge is accumulated and translated into use through the action of knowledge on itself.

Governing data

Developments in the mode of governance and its relation to data can be tracked in a shift in Europe from government as an enabler of provision, then as a market regulator, and more recently as the driver of 'integration' of action and delivery with a range of partners in the provision of services. Data are now conceptualized as aids to self-evaluation, and self-evaluation is spreading as the new governing mode. One feature that is constant is the rapid growth of information produced by the new agencies and actors involved in public service provision, and the growth of demand for more information, and for more to be done with the information available. This creates new central demands for data about operations and resources. In other words, data production and management were and are essential to the new governance turn; constant comparison is its symbolic feature, as well as a distinctive mode of operation (Grek 2009; Grek and Ozga 2010). Similarly, at the international level, the ranking and rating of educational achievement by international organizations like the OECD or the European Commission has become one of the prime tools for education systems to evaluate their competitive status against that of other countries in the global economy (Grek 2009). Such developments indicate a radical change in the relationship between knowledge and policy. Knowledge, in parallel with governance, appears as far more distributed and apparently democratic, in comparison with the operation of traditional bureaucracies and forms of knowledge production. If bureaucracy was based on local, elite, simplified, static and centrally controlled knowledge stored in large files, the knowledge of post-bureaucracy is decentralized, future-oriented, networked, processual, autonomous and fluid (Isaakyan et al. 2008). Its networked nature (in the sense that it is co-produced by different networks of policy-makers, experts and practitioners) promotes its easy exchange and hence its operation as one of the prime engines for its marketization within neo-liberal economies (Thrift 2005).

The shift from government to governance – and now to self-governance – thus relates to changes in data capacity and use. The recent emphasis on self-evaluation may reflect a crisis in information management: data about performance are unmanageable, information grows without limits, policy ambitions are pre-occupied with generating more and better data, and data use is an unexamined principle, its existence assumed to be evidence of evidence-based practice and policy-making. The huge costs of data systems are no longer affordable. The speed with which data move and the technical capacity of new systems means that data analysts at all levels – schools, central and government agencies and the European Commission are pre-occupied with updating information – are constantly maintaining data rather than making sense of the information, as this extract from an interview with a senior EU analyst suggests:

> Yes, we are overwhelmed with data and then we don't use them enough. We go to the next survey and then we have new data and so on. Well. I think there is a great difference between the data that countries need for monitoring the quality of their systems, [and systems] like the English system which is monstrous. I always ask what is the cost–benefit? Have you ever made a cost–benefit analysis of what you are doing?
>
> Interviewer: What is the answer?
>
> They smile.
>
> (EU3)[2]

Data about performance are in constant movement, building new relations between key actors, creating new knowledges and helping both to shape and justify policy. Performance across provision of education/learning is made visible and transparent in the form of indicators and targets that can be constantly scrutinized. Data enable comparison, and comparison is a new mode of transnational governance that creates an international 'spectacle' (Nóvoa and Yariv-Mashal 2003; Grek 2009). Data also create the space in which comparison can be carried out. In Europe this space is constructed through data, benchmarks and indicators that carry governing principles and establish rules and meanings (Grek *et al.* 2009: 8–9) and that create relations among actors at a distance from each other in schools, local authorities, agencies and government offices. These local, national and European networks of actors are integrated by technologies – including data – as much as by explicit policy; their networks carry and shape new models of European governance (Kohler-Koch and Eising 1999). Some further reflections from the European Commission analyst quoted above illustrate the data–governance relationship:

> It is exploding. Extraordinary. And the reason is the role of indicators and statistics in the open method of coordination. . . . Inside the Commission we had a clear understanding that we had to develop that area because it is the strongest element in the open method of coordination. This is how the Commission can say that you can engage with certain objectives, you are not following them . . . [we can identify] who is following, who succeeds, where the performance lies . . .
>
> (EU3)

This informant goes on to say that the Commission's analysts know more about national systems than do the members of any national system. From Brussels, the Commission can 'see' a system more clearly:

> because when you sit up to your neck in the . . . Scottish system, everything is Scottish. Everything is Scottish. This is our system, we defend it as a fortress and all these influences from outside, they should be kept away. By sitting here and making comparative analysis, you identify what is specifically Scottish to the Scottish system. What is it that you should actually defend to keep these roots in national culture and national institutions that are set up. We know it, or we could know it, we have the information, we have this distance that is necessary to do it. And we can compare and find out what is it that shines in the Scottish system.

National systems are thus brought into view, constituted and reconstituted, by Europe, and simultaneously develop their own data-driven initiatives, in part in response to transnational pressures. In this development England claims the status of world leader.

Data and governance in England

Modernization of education policy, accelerated under New Labour in England from 1997 to 2010, tied education very firmly to the economy (DfEE 1997) and involved a shift towards 'implied consent' by the public to the problem-solving initiatives of government. These also required the widespread collection and use of data in order to enable the public to be informed, and the displacement of expert or professional judgement. Managerialism reinforced a technical and pragmatic approach to policy-making, driven by a calculus of economy and efficiency (Clarke, Gewirtz and McLaughlin 2000). In education policy-making in England these developments promoted integration ('joined-up policy-making') and involved new partners, particularly private partners (Ball 2008).

Data grew in England from the 1980s onwards because of the policy pre-occupation with measuring attainment levels (of pupils, schools and the system). Regulation of the system through inspections that followed highly prescribed forms also ensured the growth of data collection and analysis and supported a narrative of sustained improvement in education linked to the creation of objective 'depersonalized' judgement and increasingly driven by apparently objective data. At the same time, these developments also created an impression of knowledgeable governance. The analysis of key policy texts since the 1990s (Ozga, Grek and Lawn 2009) identifies education/learning as both an economic and a *governing* resource. Governing education is done in these texts through a combination of shared 'interests' in attracting mobile capital, while regulatory instruments at all levels measure and compare performance, create governing knowledge and also, importantly, construct an image of governing *through* knowledge. The government discursively constructed a narrative of problems to be overcome by 'evidence-based' or 'evidence-informed' policy, derived from trustworthy, data-rich sources. That narrative largely excluded knowledge production that remained locked into traditional research-based practices of self-doubt and reflexive questioning (Nassehi *et al.* 2008). Instead, government presents re-formed, data-driven knowledge production as informing, justifying and legitimating policy and also clears the ground for the construction and circulation of an overarching narrative of knowledge–policy relations, redefined in relation to governance.

In this development, data use is greatly expanded and this creates and sustains an imaginary of governance informed by data, constantly moving to respond to change, and focused on the future. In the central government department for England, for example, a senior official conveys the live nature and visibility of education stocks and flows:

> It's interesting to reflect on how the work of a central government policy department has evolved. . . . In fact actually we've been developing a concept here in the Department which we've called 'the bridge' where we corral all of this data and information and at a glance now across all local authorities in England you can go downstairs and look at a big screen and you can look across all the key performance areas and that's actually across all the social care areas as well as education. So at that level we're doing quite active performance management of the system and that's quite a powerful tool.
>
> (CP7 E)

This process of system surveillance takes place in 'real time': data are constantly required about the rate of progress towards a given target. Powerful data systems, at all stages, from procedure, to input, distribution, analysis and access, create the vision from the performance. School and system actors are focused on the data and come to see it as specifying the future: the policy trajectory of improvement is built into the data production process. The range of data collection widens constantly (and the speed of collection and analysis also increases constantly), including school and pupil performance; contextual school data; statutory target-setting; school censuses; and establishing centralized databases for children. This is a highly centralized system, but local authorities still attempt to maintain a role in research and evaluation, obtaining feedback from parents and pupils, providing guidance and training for staff on the interpretation and use of performance data for setting targets, tracking pupil progress and evaluating outcomes.

These flows of data are not weightless: they demand heavy, complex work from data workers who maintain the flow and bring it into a relationship with existing data – this is not a simple or automatic task. Data software becomes 'a practice of government' (Thrift 2005: 172), but it is a practice that needs interpretive work. People are required to operate codes that may be at odds with the knowledge they have of the situation on the ground. In England, there are two connected developments that increase the problems of 'trans-lation' of data: the removal of the local education authority from its traditional brokering role between the centre and the schools, and the handing over of large parts of the responsibility for data collection to commercial organizations, often with difficult consequences.

> And then they really messed it up, they had a company in doing the collection which might have been different to the other companies doing the collection . . . So again you've got all these big companies blaming each other – one's responsible for one thing, one for another . . . if something does go wrong, even though we are not supposed to be involved, we get the phone call and we don't say its not our problem, we sort it out.
>
> (LP6E)

Here local knowledge is disregarded until it is needed to restart the flow:

> We weren't part of what they were planning, we couldn't tell them they weren't doing it properly . . . we were not involved, they were doing their own thing again, you see it always seems as though they are introducing new things and when it goes wrong, we were picking up the pieces, finding out the problem and then telling them about it [laughs] and how to do it.
>
> (LP4E)

Ironically, these interventions to smooth the flow of data contribute to the idea of data as independent, objective and intelligent information that guides and shapes action, often invisibly. Working with software demands observation of codes that may shape understanding: the need for speed and movement standardizes distinctive practices and experiences. The capacity to know seems infinitely expandable: the data-driven systems of 'the database state' (Andersen *et al.* 2009) promise a new form of intelligence, a system that has the capacity to think for itself. Yet, as we have seen, the scale of the activity means that the data dream of infinite interoperability is more accurately conveyed as 'layered, tangled, textured: they interact to form an ecology as well as a flat set of compatibilities . . . lodged in different communities of practice' (Bowker and Starr 1999: 31, quoted in Thrift 2005: 173).

Those communities of practice are being reshaped, through the creation of a framework of data about integrated children's services, including education, social work, health and the police, which is creating a shared language of provision to ensure translations across these services and their work cultures. There are considerable difficulties in achieving 'interoperability' conceived in technical terms that do not reflect the cultures and practices of different professional communities, who understand knowledge in conflicting ways and who also see the translation of knowledge into action as shaped by different priorities. This extract from an interview with a local authority data manager illustrates some of the issues in achieving understanding across different communities of practice:

> I think it would be really good if we would understand ourselves, first of all, how we work in terms of our own field, understand how our colleagues work and try to find a way of coming together, getting some energy there and creating our processes, reviewing our processes, looking at technology, looking at the structure of the data, how do we do that to best meet the needs and try to do any potential changes. Get a model that is capable of dealing with the integration or some new configuration . . . I don't know if this is kind of one of those data dreams, I don't know if it can be delivered but we kind of think, you know, it must be possible to do something to improve.
>
> (LP10S)

Attempts to produce flatter 'compatibilities' are contained in the development of shared sets of references in joint inspection frameworks, and the learners, teachers and citizens engaged through these frameworks are increasingly drawn into activity through self-evaluation processes that also seek to promote compatibilities at the level of the individual learner. I turn now to Scotland to explore the development of self-evaluation and its relationship to governing knowledge.

Self-evaluation

Self-evaluation is becoming the favoured form in the improvement of performance: it is both a continuation and a shift in data use, as it moves from the regulation of performance associated with external mechanisms that monitor and test teachers and learners to a focus on the school as a learning organization, and on engendering in the school a commitment to the constant production and review of knowledge about performance that defines a learning organization (Senge 1999). School self-evaluation (SSE) reflects the knowledge economy paradigm in its most developed form: that is, transforming organizations (whether schools or businesses) into learning institutions that, through their constant production of knowledge about what and how they know, become sites of competitive advantage and also of 'governing knowledge' (Ozga 2009; Ball 2010). The reflexive nature of self-evaluation is key here: thought and action are demanded on the basis of knowledge about knowledge – from the individual learner, from the school/organization and from government and its agencies. The turn towards self-evaluation also locates processes of knowledge sharing, generation and retention in organizational processes and thus offers a more attractive, engaging and creative version of knowledge use than performance management: it is a technique of soft government, following the ground-clearing and standardization work done by regulation.

Self-evaluation, and its use of data, connects to greater urgency in economizing schooling/learning and draws on contemporary developments in the 'economics of knowledge' (Foray 2004) that stress the heightened significance of knowledge management and the redesign of organizations in 'post-bureaucratic' forms. Members of learning organizations contribute added value through their continuous learning, which generates new, productive knowledge, not for the individual learner, but for the organization (OECD 2000). This approach, it is argued, also reduces costs, because it is less reliant on external mechanisms to monitor performance, while engendering relations of trust, transparency and openness within the organization that are conducive to 'real' learning. The regulatory regimes associated with new public management policies had, of course, been criticized in terms of their costs and their installation of performative cultures of distrust within organizations, so self-evaluation may be understood as a response to those problems and also as a logical development from them.

Learning government in Scotland

SSE in Scotland is connected to change in political control in May 2007, when the Scottish National Party (SNP) formed a minority government. Political control in Scotland had previously been exercised by a Labour–Liberal coalition government that closely followed UK Labour government policies, including practices of strict target-setting and performance monitoring across the public sector, leading to more than 400 separate agreements/targets that required monitoring. Critics argued that preoccupation with meeting targets stifled innovation and led to 'delivery anxiety' (Keating 2005). With the election of an SNP government there was a shift to an outcomes focus, along with referencing of evidence: the SNP government claims to promote evidence-based policy.

The Scottish government has developed an approach to policy-making based on wider consultations with stakeholders (Arnott and Ozga 2010). The SNP simplified the policy agenda to focus on an overarching purpose of government: 'To focus government and public services on creating a more successful country, with opportunities for all of Scotland to flourish, through increasing sustainable economic growth' (TSG 2007: 1).

This overarching purpose is delivered through 15 national outcomes and 43 national indicators. The purpose of government: 'to make Scotland wealthier and fairer, healthier, safer and stronger and greener' is thus reflected in the adoption of a relatively small number of key outcomes and indicators, giving the impression of a realizable ambition (Arnott and Ozga 2010: 338):

> All performance management systems will therefore be aligned to a single, clear and consistent set of priorities. The transition to an outcomes-based approach with delivery partners, including local government, will leave the detailed management of services to those who can best understand and tailor their resources and activities in line with local priorities. The Scottish Government will concentrate on providing leadership and direction, and focus on strategic priorities.
>
> (TSG 2007: 1–2)

There was a wide-ranging review of policy-making in 2008 that advocated a further move towards more collaborative approaches, especially in a new relationship (described as a Concordat) with local government in the co-production of policy. There is considerable emphasis, in the documentation produced for this review, on the need to free up knowledge through more experimentation and on ensuring more system learning at all levels. In this the role of evidence, alongside and in relationship with evaluation, is seen as a critical driver of learning. The capacity of government to integrate and evaluate data has been increased, while responsibility is shifted downwards to an increased range of partners, whose capacity for self-monitoring is required to increase. These developments demand the very considerable expansion of the use of self-assessment, so that it becomes the core tool of accountability across all public sector services:

> Over time Ministers and the Parliament should rely more on self-assessment by providers, enabling a reduction in the volume of external scrutiny. In future Ministers and Parliament should consider the extent to which the assurance they require can be provided by providers, before commissioning external audit, inspection or regulation.
>
> (Crerar 2008: 5)

SSE thus represents an element of a larger policy paradigm shift. SSE is about creating a school evaluation framework that claims to bring about constant comparison and improvement, broadly focusing on answering two key questions about educational practice: 'How good are we now?' and 'How good can we be?' As a key policy text makes clear, the shift in responsibility produces a holistic approach to evidence and learning: 'schools are not islands. They work with other schools, colleges, employers and a number of other services' (HMIE 2007: 55). SSE is used as a means of encoding school knowledge, creating 'compatibilities' and promoting self-managed and self-sufficient individuals (teachers and pupils) in a decentralized, inclusive system. In other words, schools and their teachers and pupils become members of learning organizations, embedded within the larger learning organization of the local authority and of government itself. The coding of knowledge through self-evaluation enables flows of knowledge within and across new networks of knowledge production. Furthermore, as schools and learners do more, they produce more and more new knowledge about themselves, which becomes productive for the constant improvement not only of the individual school, but for the governing of the system as a whole.

The knowledge produced through self-evaluation is integrated knowledge in which the learner is recognized as an agent in knowledge production and use: 'there is a developing view of the child as an *active agent* in their world

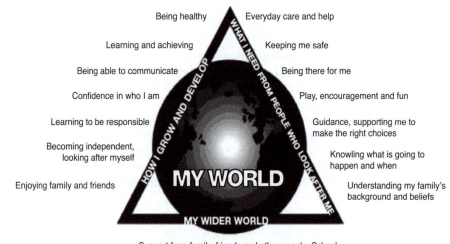

Figure 5.1 The whole child: physical, social, educational, emotional, spiritual and psychological development (Scottish Executive 2005)

and a commitment to *empowerment* as a key in any change or recovery process' (Scottish Executive 2001: 15).

'Personal learning plans' (PLPs) encapsulate the shift in emphasis to the individual child: 'The objective of PLPs is to encourage self-evaluation by pupils *of their own needs* and participation in negotiating personal learning targets to empower the learner and help encourage independent learning habits' (Scottish Executive 2001: 15). This is achieved through a template 'to structure thinking and information gathering' for all children and young people. Figure 5.1 sets out the key dimensions through which active learners (children and their teachers, as well as their managers and governors) are enabled to accumulate and evaluate knowledge, and plan accordingly.

Conclusion

The shift from centralized and vertical hierarchical forms of regulation to decentralized, horizontal, networked forms, noted in the literature on governance, also applies to knowledge. Yet, rather than representing the potential for democratization of either knowledge or governance, these forms closely resemble the networking practices, open communications and systems of global business, along with its increasing tendency to blur public and private distinctions. New data technologies reflect the processes and instruments of knowledgeable/ knowing capitalism and their 'economic imaginaries' establish new organizational forms that have 'a performative, constitutive force' (Jessop 2008: 18).

Data reconstitute knowledge in governing form, but the 'data dream' of infinite interoperability is disrupted by incompatibilities, by the inert mass of accumulated information and by the continued need for processes of brokering and translation of knowledge into action. The development of self-evaluation is an attempt to enrol communities of practice in processes of constructing compatibilities through an emphasis on learning and self-evaluation, and children are also asked to develop and monitor their situations, to evaluate these and act appropriately. The discourse surrounding this new knowledge is one of agency, malleability, flexibility, multi-purpose resources, volatility and heterogeneity (Stehr 2004). Inter-agency professionals, children and government itself are seen as having the capacity and the responsibility to learn through constant self-scrutiny: 'to move new scientific and technical knowledge, and thereby the future, into the centre of the cultural, economic and political matrix of society' (Stehr 2004: ix).

Notes

1   The argument in this chapter is based on research in a number of European research projects, namely Fabricating Quality in European Education/Governing by Numbers (ESRC: RES 00-23-1385) and Knowledge and Policy (EU FP6 IP 028848–2). This chapter is particularly indebted to the work of Sotiria Grek and Martin Lawn on these projects.

2   The acronyms used in this chapter relate to policy actors interviewed in the course of the 'Fabricating Quality' project; EU denotes a European commission policy actor, CPE a central government policy actor in England, CPS a Scottish central policy actor, and LP a local policy actor. The numbers are codes that protect the identity of our interviewees.

References

Andersen, R., Brown, I., Dowty, T., Inglesant, P., Heath, W. and Sasse, A. (2009) *Database State*, York: The Joseph Rowntree Reform Trust.

Arnott, M. and Ozga, J. (2010) 'Education and nationalism: the discourse of education policy in Scotland', *Discourse: Studies in the Cultural Politics of Education*, 31(3): 335–50.

Ball, S.J. (2008) 'New philanthropy, new networks and new governance in education', *Political Studies* 56: 747–65.

—— (2010) 'New voices, new knowledges and the new politics of education research: the gathering of a perfect storm?' *European Educational Research Journal*, 9(2): 124–37.

Bowker, G.C. and Starr, S.L. (1999) *Sorting Things Out: classification and its consequences*, Cambridge, MA: MIT Press.

Clarke, J. (2008) 'Performance paradoxes: the politics of evaluation in public services', in H. Davis and S. Martin (eds), *Public Services Inspection in the UK. Research Highlights in Social Work* (50), London: Jessica Kingsley Publishers, 120–34.

Clarke, J., Gewirtz, S. and McLaughlin, E. (eds) (2000) *New Managerialism, New Welfare?*, London: Sage.

Crerar, L. (2008) *The Crerar Review: The Report of the Independent Review of Regulation, Audit, Inspection and Complaints Handling of Public Services in Scotland*, Edinburgh: The Scottish Government.

Department for Education and Employment (DfEE) (1997) *Excellence in Schools*, London: Stationery Office Cm 3681 (July).

Fägerlind, I. and Strömqvist, G. (eds) (2004) *Reforming Higher Education in the Nordic Countries: studies of changes in Denmark, Finland, Iceland, Norway and Sweden*, Paris: International Institute for Educational Planning.

Foray, D. (2004) *The Economics of Knowledge*, Cambridge, MA: MIT Press.

Grek, S. (2009) 'Governing by numbers: the PISA "effect" in Europe', *Journal of Education Policy*, 24(1): 23–37.

Grek, S. and Ozga, J. (2010) 'Re-inventing public education: the new role of knowledge in education policy-making', *Public Policy and Administration* 25(3): 271–88.

Grek, S., Lawn, M., Lingard, B., Ozga, J., Rinne, R., Segerholm, C. and Simola, H. (2009) 'National policy brokering and the construction of the European Education Space in England, Sweden, Finland and Scotland', *Comparative Education*, 45(1): 5–21.

HMIE (Her Majesty's Inspectorate of Education) (2007) *How Good is Our School? The journey to excellence, Part 3*, www.hmie.gov.uk/documents/publication/hgiosjte.3html (accessed 10 May 2010).

Isaakyan, I., Lawn, M., Ozga, J. and Shaik, F. (2008) *Scotland: Education Knowledge and Policy Report on Orientation I*. Online, available: www.knowandpol.eu (accessed 31 January 2011).

Jessop, B. (2008) 'A cultural political economy of competitiveness and its implications for higher education', in B. Jessop, N. Fairclough and R. Wodak (eds) *Education and the Knowledge-Based Economy in Europe*, Rotterdam: Sense Publishers.

Keating, M. (2005) *The Government of Scotland* (first edition), Edinburgh: Edinburgh University Press.

Kohler-Koch, B. and Eising, R. (1999) *The Transformation of Governance in the European Union*, London: Routledge/Falmer.

Lascoumes, P. and Le Galès, P. (2007) 'Understanding public policy through its instruments – from the nature of instruments to the sociology of public policy instrumentation', *Governance*, 20(1): 1–21.

Miller, P. and Rose, N. (2008) *Governing the Present: administering economic, social and personal Life*, Polity Press.

Nassehi, A., von der Hagen-Demszky, A. and Mayr, K. (2008) 'The structures of knowledge and of knowledge production literature review', *KNOW&POL*, 8. Online, available: www.knowandpol.eu (accessed 20 June 2010).

Nóvoa, A. and Yariv-Mashal, T. (2003) 'Comparative research in education: a mode of governance or a historical journey?' *Comparative Education*, 39(4): 423–39.

OECD (Organisation for Economic Cooperation and Development) (2000) *Knowledge Management in the Learning Society*, Paris: OECD.

Ozga, J. (2009) 'Governing education through data in England: from regulation to self-evaluation', *Special Issue of Journal of Education Policy*, 24(2): 149–63.

Ozga, J. Grek, S. and Lawn, M. (2009) 'The new production of governing knowledge: education research in England', *Soziale Welt*, 4: 353–71.

Scottish Executive (2001) *For Scotland's Children – better integrated children's services*, Edinburgh: Scottish Executive.

Scottish Government (TSG) (2007) *Scotland Performs: the national performance framework*. Online, available: www.scotland.gov.uk/Publications/2007/11/1309 2240/9 (accessed April 2009).

Senge, P. (1999) *Challenges of Sustaining Momentum in Learning Organizations*, New York: Doubleday.

Stehr, N. (2004), 'Introduction: a world made of knowledge', in N. Stehr (ed.), *The Governance of Knowledge*, Edison, NJ: Transaction Publishers.

Thrift, N. (2005) *Knowing Capitalism*, London: Sage.

Chapter 6

Art, community and knowledge flows

Margaret Somerville

Introduction

In this chapter I explore knowledge mobilization and educational research in the policy context of water conservation. The chapter is based on Indigenous[1] partnership research about water in the drylands of the Murray–Darling Basin in south-eastern Australia. The research was collaboratively designed with U'Alayi researcher Chrissiejoy Marshall as an emergent, arts-based project. It began as a study of the Narran Lake in north-western New South Wales (NSW), a Ramsar-listed wetlands, and an iconic site in the connection between the northern and southern Basin. Through a series of emergent circumstances, the project moved and changed with the flow of the waters, ending at the Murray River in Victoria. The emergent nature of the methodology that enabled the flow of knowledge between Indigenous and non-Indigenous researchers was the basis for the learning and knowledge exchange that happened between the project and the wider communities with which it engaged.

One of the main features of the project, which emerged in its making, was a series of art exhibitions in regional galleries. It is the role of these art exhibitions in the mobilization of knowledge that I focus on in this chapter. I use the metaphor of water to track the ways that different knowledge systems block or facilitate flows of knowledge in parallel to the ways different story-lines and cultural practices block or facilitate the flows of water.

Global water issues and water knowledges

The work of water has traditionally been the work of community. The knowledges associated with caring for water and water places in sustainable ways have been passed down in families and communities as processes of knowledge transmission. Indigenous communities all over the world have harvested and managed water in sustainable ways throughout history (Shiva 2002). The knowledge and practices to manage water sustainably for the production of food and maintenance of all life forms was learned in families and communities. During the first major wave of global colonization, new tech-nologies of water in the form of large dams and irrigation schemes were intro-duced for the benefit of the imperial colonizers (Shiva 2002; Pearce 2006; Schama 1996), enabled by 'a profound belief in the possibility of restructuring nature and re-ordering it to serve human needs and desires' (Adams and Mulligan 2003: 23). Under the so-called 'green revolution' in the latter part of the twentieth century, large-scale farming further required massive dams and irrigation schemes to harvest water on most of the major rivers of the world. Most of those river systems are now in crisis (Pearce 2006) and the water crisis is described as 'the most pervasive, the most severe, and most invisible dimension of the ecological devastation of the earth' (Shiva 2002: 1).

Australian issues of water: the Murray–Darling Basin

Australia is a particular example of the politics of water. Living on the driest inhabited continent on earth, the Australian population consumes more water per capita than any other country in the world. The most prominent example of the current water crisis is the case of the Murray–Darling Basin (MDB), which includes parts of the Australian Capital Territory (ACT), Queensland, NSW, Victoria and South Australia. It can be located and described as a physical entity, but even this description is already determined by particular discourses and modes of governance that impact on the flows of water. The following, for example, is a standard description of the MDB: 'The MDB covers 1061469 square kilometres, about 14% of Australia. The Basin . . . accounts for 41% of the nation's gross value of agricultural production, and for 70% of all water used for irrigation in Australia. It is described as "the nation's food basket"' (Nicholls 2004: 323). There is much that is not said here about the fact that there is no longer enough water and why, but even prior to this there was another way of thinking about the MDB as a geographical entity. The map of the region overlaps almost perfectly with the map of the Riverine language group of 46 Aboriginal languages that share a common stem, lang-uages of that country. What does it mean to think about the MDB as a region composed of a series of intersecting catchments with related cultural stories? What stories enabled people to know water in this country and how were those stories shared across tribal boundaries so that the flows and connections were not blocked?

   The MDB is made up of a system of rivers and networks of tributaries and floodplains that begin in the headwaters of the Balonne and Condamine Rivers in Queensland, flow down through the Narran, Culgoa and Bokhara Rivers to the Darling, eventually join the Murray River and flow into the sea at the Coorong in South Australia. Each of the six states and territories imposes different regulatory and allocation practices over the waters within these artificial boundaries, constructing blockages to its flows. It is now well recognized that 'the way water is managed in Qld [Queensland] controls how much water eventually flows into NSW with obvious ecological and financial implications (ABC Radio 2003)'. The situation worsens the further down the system one travels. The first MDB agreement was set up in 1987, but it was not until 1998 that the Commonwealth and all state governments signed the agreement. In 2008 the Federal Government enhanced the powers of the Commonwealth over the states and the agreement is currently under review. Meanwhile the system continues to decline. In November 2009 the regular Drought Update by the MDB Commission declared that the Darling River had ceased to flow, the Lower Lakes were at record low levels for that time of year, and the situation remained very serious for the environment (MDBA 2009b: 6).

In the same year a single page of a 150-page report on the 'Socio-economic context for the Murray–Darling Basin' (MDBA 2009a: 122) was devoted to the situation of Indigenous people in relation to the waterways under the heading, 'Water for culture and recreation'. The report notes that, 'for Indigenous Australians, their personal, cultural and spiritual identity, their sense of belonging and sense of security are inextricably linked to water and country'. In the report it is suggested that it is not within the brief to represent the views of Indigenous groups, but it does draw on the published management plan of the Ngarrindjeri people of the Coorong to make some brief points about the current situation of Indigenous peoples in relation to the waterways. The Coorong is the system of shallow lakes, lagoons and wetlands at the Murray mouth, the very end point of the system of water. The Ngarrindjeri people state that they 'wish to hand on to their younger generations the knowledge of local animals and plants, and the language, stories and sacred knowledge that is tied to this environment. If the environment is not healthy, then the culture tied to it cannot be so easily passed on and kept alive' (Birckhead et al. 2008). The report goes on to quote, however, a starkly ironic description by the Government of South Australia of the reality of the situation for the Coorong as 'unprecedented', with 'water levels dropping, salinity levels increasing and soils on the drying lakebeds and wetlands acidifying' (MDBA 2009a: 122).

In 1990 the MDB Commission had launched a strategy of 'integrated catchment management' that emphasized 'the importance of people in the process of developing a shared vision and acting together to manage the natural resources of their catchment' (Murray–Darling Basin Ministerial Council 2001: 1). A study of Aboriginal involvement in MDB Commission initiatives, however, found a 'chasm between the perception of the available opportunities for involvement and the reality experienced by Aboriginal people' (Ward et al. 2003: 8). The most significant barrier to Aboriginal involvement was identified as a 'lack of respect and understanding of Aboriginal culture and its relevance to natural resource management' (Ward et al. 2003: 8). Discourses of 'management' have blocked the exchange of knowledge between Aboriginal and non-Aboriginal Australians in relation to the environment generally, and the MDB in particular. Significant inclusion of Aboriginal peoples in issues of land takes the language to a completely different plane. One study found, for example, that 'the presence of Indigenous others in NRM [Natural Resource Management] debates shifts the terms of the debate to include issues of justice, history, identity and recognition' and concluded that 'literacy in cultural landscapes is fundamental to reframing these relationships' (Suchet-Pearson and Howitt 2006: 118). Literacy, understood here as possessing the fundamental representational tools necessary for the survival of human and non-human others, is about the necessity for learning by non-Indigenous Australians before any change can take place. How this might happen, and what might be the process, has not yet been articulated.

Emergent arts-based methodology

The study *Bubbles on the surface: A place pedagogy of the Narran Lakes* was designed to address these questions. An emergent arts-based methodology sits within a conceptual framework of Place and an Enabling place pedagogies approach that I have outlined elsewhere (Somerville 2010). The methodology was developed by combining U'Alayi researcher Chrissiejoy Marshall's 'thinking through country' (Marshall 2007) and the author's 'postmodern emergence' (Somerville 2007). Marshall's methodology, based on her relationship to her birth country of the Narran Lakes, involved producing a painting and an accompanying oral story to structure and inform each cluster of meanings. By moving between the paintings, oral storytelling and academic writing, she expressed new meanings that were not possible in academic prose alone. Postmodern emergence argues for an ontology and epistemology developed from the space in between binary constructions of thought, and moving beyond deconstruction to creative possibilities. The essence of this methodological position is to set up the conditions within the research to work from the space between Indigenous and non-Indigenous paradigms and knowledges in order to explore how knowledge can flow between them. As the project evolved, the emergent nature of the methodology proved to be critical to the development of languages, forms, processes and pedagogies for this flow of knowledge.

In the first instance Chrissiejoy Marshall became too chronically ill to be actively involved in the research. At a serendipitous meeting with the author in their shared local community, Daphne Wallace, a Gomaroi artist and cultural knowledge holder from Lightning Ridge, became the second partner researcher. Daphne had an exhibition space booked at the New England Regional Art Museum for later that year and invited Badger Bates, a Paakantji artist from the Darling River, to join the exhibition and the project. The author moved to Victoria and became involved with the fourth partner, Yorta Yorta artist and researcher Treahna Hamm from the Murray River. A very close working team developed between the Indigenous artists, the author as project leader, Sarah

Figure 6.1 Badger Bates, 2007, *Iron Pole Bend, Darling River, Wilcannia*, linocut print
30 × 43 cm

Martin, an archaeologist and ethnohistorian, and Phoenix de Carteret, Research
Fellow, as the project moved literally and conceptually through the MDB
following the flow of the rivers.

Each year we developed artworks and stories that were presented in a series
of exhibitions. The artworks and stories provided both the form and content
for the exchange of knowledge. A reading of one of the works, a lino print of
Iron Pole Bend, Wilcannia by Badger Bates (Figure 6.1), illustrates this process.

The artwork is already a contemporary translation of Indigenous knowledge
of country that gives us access to its meanings in a familiar form. Badger says
that he learned to carve emu eggs from his grandmother and that the designs
carved on his lino prints are an extension of her mark making. We know from
the English title that the place in this image is known by a sign of the
colonization of the River, the iron pole, but the iron pole itself does not appear
in the work. The image is structured around the Ngatyi, or rainbow serpents,
who play a central part in the creation storylines, particularly in relation to
water. In this print the Ngatyi are deeply immersed in the radiating lines of
force that represent the energy of the waters. From their mouths the flow of
waters bursts forth; their bodies create the shape of the rivers and travel with
the waterways. The waters of the river are alive with the river's creatures – cod,
catfish, shrimp, yabby and mussels. It is a story of the everyday – of the place
where Badger's granny caught their daily food, near where Badger grew up in
a tin hut on the banks of the Darling River.

Around the edges of the water we can see the mythical creatures whose
movement and storylines link to other places: the Kangaroo with the hump of

Koonenberry Mountain, the Goanna from its story place, and the Brolga, flying in from elsewhere. At the top of the print, in a hybrid combination of a bird's eye view and a more typical Western landscape, we can see the moon and the emu in the Milky Way. The shape of the emu within the stars of the Milky Way tells people the time for collecting emu eggs for feasting and for ceremony. Earth country, water country and sky country are interconnected in this print that opens the intimate attachments of the everyday and home to the rhythms of water, earth, moon and stars.

Space, and the way the artwork delineates the spaces and places of these stories, is conceived differently than the way space and place is understood and represented in Western knowledge frameworks. The frame of the print does not foreclose meanings within its square boundaries, because the meanings are both allusive and elusive. It points always to connections elsewhere in the flow of the waters and the storylines. The waters flow in from somewhere else and travel to elsewhere. The mythical creatures travel into the frame of the print but are not bounded by it. The meanings of the storylines are *elusive* too, in the sense that we cannot know all the layers and complexity of these stories. They can be read, but they refuse the closure of the already-known; we are positioned as Other, as the unknowing learner.

Each year for the three years of the project we presented the artworks and stories around the themes that we had developed as a collective during that year. Like the waters in Badger's lino print, the project had developed a life force of its own. After a series of three exhibitions and the formal end of the project there were requests from regional and metropolitan galleries to stage an exhibition. *Water in a dry land* was developed to exhibit the best of the works produced during the three years of the project and provided us with an opportunity to focus on the question of art exhibitions as a public pedagogy of place. Previous poststructural and postcolonial theorizing of place learning that led to the development of an enabling pedagogy of place had focused on a general application of the teaching and learning of place. In this instance we wanted to explore how the artworks and stories functioned as a pedagogy of place in relation to an unknown public audience with no formal teaching learning curriculum. During the staging of the first of these exhibitions at the Albury City Gallery from May to July 2010, we asked: What constituted the elements of the exhibition of *Water in a dry land* as a public pedagogy? Was there a process of knowledge mobilization from the research activities and representations to the viewing public? Did the knowledge generated in this research have an impact, and through what processes did that occur?

Narrative analysis of events

We conducted a micro-ethnographic analysis of the three main elements that contributed to our study of art as a public pedagogy of place in relation to the

Water in a dry land exhibition at Albury on the Murray River. The first was the 'Welcome to Country' performed at the beginning of the opening of the exhibition. The second was the talk given at the opening by the author and project leader, and the third was the artists' talk session organized for the following day. Each of these elements had its own contribution to make towards analysing the overall nature of the pedagogical experience.

Welcome to Country

There were about 80 people present at the launch, which began with a 'Welcome to Country' from Wiradjuri Elder, Aunty Nancy. Wiradjuri is one of the languages that make up the Riverine language group. The Welcome to Country ceremony is based on the traditional protocol of welcoming out-siders across the boundaries of the 500 Aboriginal tribal areas that existed in Australia. Today it is a common protocol associated with ceremony through which visitors are invited into country. Aunty Nancy was dressed in a ceremonial possum skin cloak made as part of a Victoria-wide community arts project of revitalization of the possum skin cloak tradition. Possum skin cloaks featured strongly in both everyday life and ceremony for Aboriginal people in south-eastern Australia. Their practical functions in providing warmth and protection were essential; babies were wrapped in them at birth and people were buried in their cloaks. On one side the cloaks revealed a patchwork of furry pelts and the other was incised with designs that showed people's connections to country. The designs 'symbolized country, geographical features and the wearer's clan and tribal affiliations' (Reynolds *et al.* 2005: 13). In ceremony the cloaks were used to display the wearer's identity in country. Aunty Nancy spoke about the possum skin cloak and her connection to the country of the Murray River.

Project leader address

The public address at the launch was an opportunity to frame the intellectual content of the exhibition in relation to issues of water in the MDB. There were three main ideas offered to frame the project and the exhibition, and the main mode of communicating them was storytelling. The collaboration between the U'alayi cultural knowledge holder and the project leader was described as the basis of the project. The emergent and dynamic nature of this collaboration was told through story. The aim of the project was identified as being to explore how we can think about water differently in this country. The nature of thinking differently was articulated as being expressed by the Indigenous artists in the artworks and stories presented in the current exhibi-tion, which 'We hope will change worlds' (quoted extract from unpublished opening talk).

The two stories invited the audience into a deeper engagement with these ideas. The first story was about Chrissiejoy's intense attachment to the Narran Lake and her fear on our return with the project, that it would be like 'viewing a body after an autopsy'. The second story was about a baby possum skin cloak that appeared in the catalogue but was not on display. It was held up during the telling of this story, my story.

> Treahna and I [Margaret Somerville] talked about whether we should exhibit the baby cloak because she made it for my granddaughter when she was in trouble just after her birth. She was born very small and would not feed. The hospital sent her home with no support and my daughter called me when Eva was just a few days old to tell me that she could not wake the baby and she was cold. I was sure she was going to die. I was living far away in Gippsland and she was in Sydney. Treahna made the baby possum skin cloak to protect my baby girl. Eva is now 22 months old and her little sister has just been born. The baby cloak is part of the exhibition but Treahna says my daughter and her babies need the cloak for protection so I will take it back to them.

Treahna's words were then read to make the connection from the baby cloak back to the river:

> Imagine the river without a map
> having it in your head
> that's how people found their way
> if they got lost.
> The little ones would start with a small cloak,
> as they got older they would come along with it on
> just throw it down, talk with the mob
> 'This is my country, where I come from'
> you could use it as a cloak and a map together.

The cloak is held out so that the story of identity in country is visible. The audience is then invited to touch the cloak, which is laid on the plinth in the middle of the room, symbolically occupying centre place. When the many people feel the cloak with their hands it looks as if they are participating in a ritual of place, touching identity, and touching country. Through the cloak as a sensory object they are offered a bridge into a different way of knowing.

The event of the launch is a critical part of enacting the concept of art as public pedagogy in relation to the research about water in a dry land. The ritual of 'Welcome to Country' foregrounds Indigenous knowledges and practices of place, especially in relation to the nearby Murray River. The ritual is inclusive and permission-giving, invitational and open-ended. Although it has no political power in itself in relation to land, it opens up the possibility of a different storytelling space, one in which the Aboriginal stories and histories can be listened to and heard. In this space the cloak functions as a metaphor or bridge between past stories and practices of country and the present. The possum skin cloak as object is a continuing presence in the pedagogical possibilities of the art exhibition that arose serendipitously from the performance of the occasion.

The address by the project leader is an opportunity for an academic researcher to present to the audience the underpinning ideas that shaped the project and the exhibition. These are communicated through the stories and artworks as an invitation to participate in singing the waterways back to life, an invitation that is expressed in the catalogue as an enduring feature of the exhibition. The artworks are used as a way to illustrate the stories and to make connections between the intellectual project, the artists, the audience and the places of the project. They act as transitional objects in the same way as the possum skin cloak. The story of the possum skin cloak is a deeply personal story of connection between the project leader and one of the artists, but also a connection to continuing themes of renewal and creation – of babies, of the next generation, of the creation of the cloak as an artwork, of the creation story of the river inscribed on the cloak and the re-creation of the waterways.

Artists' talk

Yorta Yorta artist Treahna Hamm and Paakantji artist Badger Bates organized the space and structured the process of the artists' talk session on the Saturday morning after the exhibition opening. There was a large crowd, with a noticeable presence of Aboriginal participants in the audience. The artists arranged the chairs in concentric circles around the perimeter of the gallery, reshaping the square space into a circle. In the centre of the circle a white painted plinth displayed Treahna's woven turtles. Her Murray cod made from chicken wire and woven thread, filled with items of rubbish commonly found in the fish, was suspended above the plinth. The artists sat in the circle on a colonial antique chaise longue, and the artworks on the square white walls were a still backdrop to the dynamic space of people and conversation. The artists introduced themselves and their work, communicating their openness and inclusion, doing the translation and emotional work of the contact zone.

Early in the conversation the artists opened the floor to questions and comments. An older white woman spoke about her attachment to the land as a long-time landowner in the area who is passionate about the land and its creatures. She said she tells stories to the grandkids about the land over and over so that they don't forget. She argued against the weirs that stop the flow of the waters at a recent meeting but when she did the meeting stopped. Later in the discussion she said that she would take up Treahna's metaphor of the River as a body, with the kidneys being the system of flows that clean out the water and the weirs the blood clots that stop this flow, to explain more forcefully her feelings about the River and its needs to a public audience.

This is just one example of audience engagement and learning offered in this session. The artists reinforced all the audience stories, questions and responses and the conversation flowed from the space of the exhibition with its artworks and stories, to larger questions of caring for the environment, to climate change, to the fate of the earth and to the relationship of all this to global indigenous knowledges of place. The final conversation was about the importance of cultural flows. An Indigenous woman talked about the relationship between flows of water and flows of Indigenous cultural knowledge. Badger placed this idea back into the audience circle of the contact zone and said that everyone has a cultural connection to the rivers: cultural flows are everyone's responsibility. The space inside the circle enabled ideas, feelings, thoughts, the inchoate, and the not-yet-thought, to reside there where they were mediated by the safety of mutual concerns about place and waterways.

Story, body, contact zone as analytical categories

The performance elements described and analysed above offered a sequence of teaching and learning activities from ritual engagement and public address, to open participatory conversations. Each of these contributed in different ways to the sequence of thought and to the pedagogical processes that constituted the whole. In the absence of the Welcome to Country and the public address for visitors who would participate in the ongoing exhibition, the catalogue remained as a permanent feature to perform similar functions, although the immediacy of performance was absent. The nature of the contributions of each of the parts of these events, and thence the nature of how they functioned as technologies of knowledge mobilization, is further illuminated in the following meta-analysis. The meta-analysis draws on the principles of a poststructural and postcolonial 'enabling place pedagogy' (Somerville 2010) of *story, body, contact zone* which underpinned the project.

Story: our relationship to place is constituted in stories and other representations

In the analysis of these events it is evident that storytelling is the line along which knowledge flows. It is both content and process. Australian Indigenous storylines, in common with many indigenous narrative forms, connect the events in the creation stories of the ancestral beings to particular material formations of the landscape. The project brings this characteristic of Indigenous storylines into the contemporary relationships between peoples and between peoples and places. The storylines are about collaboration in the contact zone, about attachment to local places, illness and wellbeing of bodies and places, the caring and protection of bodies and places, and the making of artworks as participating in the renewal of waterways. The stories invite the audience to engage in a physical, emotional and spiritual sense as well as an intellectual sense. They are the main means of exchange between the Indigenous artists and the mainly non-Indigenous audience. The artists tell stories about their place making through art; the audience-participants tell stories about their attachment to local water places, their concerns about the waterways and the environment, and their desire to hand on stories and places to the next generation. The stories/storylines flow from one topic into another, developing collective as well as individual meanings in the flows of stories and knowledge making.

Body: place learning is necessarily embodied and local

The body is the vehicle, the means of carrying the flows of knowledge. The actual physical materiality of our human bodies, linked to the body of places and their wellbeing, is an essential continuing thread in the presentation of the exhibition and the associated performances. The body is most aptly symbolized by the possum skin cloaks, worn in the Welcome to Country ceremony, presented to the audience to touch as the baby cloak artwork, and told as a map of the river to be worn. It is the physical and embodied act of making the artworks that connects the artists to country. The traces of that *making* reside in the works and it is these material traces that, in turn, connect the people who are viewing the artworks to the country of their making. The artworks, as body, are material objects with a life of their own. They are a permanent feature of the exhibition; they are exhibited in other places and contexts; they are purchased and circulated to different people and places; they are given as gifts both within and outside the project; and they have their own particular material qualities according to the media of their production. They have travelled to new homes in Russia, the UK and Canada. The artworks as material objects mediate the crossing of the binaries/boundaries between bodies and places that helps the knowledge to flow.

Contact zone: deep place learning occurs in a cultural contact zone of multiple contested stories

The contact zone is the space where different storylines and knowledges come together to clash, separate, merge, or grow into new knowledges, in recognition of sameness and difference. The audiences at the exhibitions are invited into the circle of the contact zone, opening up a space where previously silenced and invisible Aboriginal stories and histories can be told and heard. It is an invitation to enter a different country, a space of difference. The space inside the circle of chairs created by the artists is a powerful demonstration of the contact zone where participants hesitantly put their words and wonderings into that space. It is a space of uncertainty, of openness, where people can put half-formed ideas, questions and thoughts, and they can make new stories. The contact zone is a site of productive tension where new knowledge can be generated. The artworks function as transitional objects in the contact zone to create a bridge for different understandings to emerge from the space between cultures, peoples, and people and country: 'We use transitional objects to imaginatively put our selves in a transformative relation with the outside' (Ellsworth 2005: 6).

Conclusion

It is evident that there are parallel processes of the blocking of flows of water through the introduction of dams and irrigation schemes in the processes of global colonization, and the blocking of the transmission of Indigenous cultural stories related to a sustainable relationship with water. What is not so evident are the processes whereby this erasure and loss of cultural stories can be reversed and stories and places can be revitalized through processes of knowledge mobilization. In the case of the Murray–Darling Basin in Australia, Aboriginal people continue to inhabit all of the waterways, but the stories and practices through which they have survived as the longest continuing culture inhabiting the world's driest continent have not entered the public arena. This is related to the vast difference in paradigms between Aboriginal stories and Western scientific knowledge. The question that this chapter addresses is: How do these Australian Indigenous stories and knowledge systems work, and how can we create a knowledge flow between Indigenous and non-Indigenous under-standings and practices of water?

Art making and oral storytelling were an integral feature of the project that addressed these questions in recognition of the fact that Indigenous water knowledge is expressed in song, music, dance, body painting and perform-ance, in place. The events that took place in association with the opening of an exhibition of the artworks and stories were analysed in fine-grained ethnographic detail to explore local processes of knowledge exchange. A central feature of Aboriginal stories of place was identified as the mapping of *connections*. Their greatest potential for change lies in their capacity to create flows of knowledge between places, between peoples, and between people and places. The concepts of story, body and contact zone illuminated the nature of the flows of knowledge that occurred, and will enable a continuing investi-gation of the ways that the outcomes of educational research can impact on community learning and public practice through the knowledge mobilization processes enacted in this research.

98   Margaret Somerville

Note

1   The terms Indigenous and Aboriginal (capitalized to represent the specificities of
     Australian Indigenous peoples) are used interchangeably in this chapter depending
     on the 'feel' of the word in its particular context. Our partner researchers identified
     not as either Aboriginal or Indigenous but by the particular language groups into
     which they were born. Chrissiejoy Marshall, the co-designer of the project, preferred
     'Aboriginal' and had a strong objection to the use of 'Indigenous', but other partners
     did not share this preference. For the author, Indigenous is a more objective and
     objectifying term and Aboriginal a term of fondness of address. The use of indigenous
     with a small 'i' is used to refer to indigenous peoples all over the world who share
     some common connections to their lands.

References

ABC Radio Country Hour (2003) 'Water wars flare between Queensland and NSW
    Farmers', ABC Radio. Online, available: www.abc.net.au/rural/nsw/stories/s1011
    922.htm (accessed 10 February 2004).
Adams, W. and Mulligan, M. (eds) (2003) *Decolonizing Nature: strategies for conservation
    in a post-colonial era*, London: Earthscan Publications Ltd.
Birckhead, J., D. Greiner, S. Hemming, M., Rigney, G., Trevorrow, T. and Rigney, D.
    (2008) *Economic and Cultural Values of Water to the Ngarrindjeri People of the Lower
    Lakes, Coorong and Murray Mouth*, CSIRO Water-For-A-Healthy-Country, Flagship
    Report, Canberra: CSIRO.
Ellsworth, E. (2005) *Places of Learning: Media, Architecture, Pedagogy*, New York:
    Routledge/Falmer.
Marshall, C.J. (2007) *Thinking through Country (Immiboagurramilbun)*, [DVD]
    revised edition, Armidale, NSW: University of New England.
Murray–Darling Basin Authority (MDBA) (2009a) Murray–Darling Indigenous
    Forum. Online, available: www.mdba.gov.au/services/publications/more-information?
    publicationid=37 (accessed 18 April 2011).
—— (2009b) *River Murray Drought Update*, Issue 1, Canberra: Murray–Darling Basin
    Authority.
Murray–Darling Basin Ministerial Council (2001) *Integrated Catchment Management
    in the Murray–Darling Basin 2001–2010: delivering a sustainable future*, Canberra:
    Murray–Darling Basin Commission.
Nicholls, N. (2004) 'The changing nature of Australian droughts', *Climatic Change*
    63(3): 323–56.
Pearce, F. (2006) *When the Rivers Run Dry: Water, the defining crisis of the twenty-first
    century*, Boston: Beacon Press.
Reynolds, A., Couzens, D., Couzens, V., Darroch, L. and Hamm, T. (2005) *Wrapped
    in a Possum Skin Cloak: The Tooloyn Koortakay Collection in the National Museum of
    Australia*, Canberra: National Museum of Australia Press.
Schama, S. (1996) *Landscape and Memory*, London: HarperCollins.
Shiva, V. (2002) *Water Wars: pollution, profits and privatization*, London: Pluto Press.
Somerville, M. (2007) 'Postmodern emergence', *International Journal of Qualitative
    Studies in Education* 20(2): 225–43.
—— (2010) A place pedagogy for 'Global Contemporaneity', *Educational Philosophy
    and Theory* 42(3): 326–43.

Suchet-Pearson, S. and Howitt, R. (2006) 'On teaching and learning resource and environmental management: reframing capacity building in multicultural settings', *Australian Geographer* 37(1), March, 117–28.

Ward, N., Reys, S., Davies, J. and Roots, J. (2003) *Scoping Study on Aboriginal Involvement in Natural Resource Management Decision Making and the Integration of Aboriginal Cultural Heritage Considerations into Relevant Murray–Darling Commission Programs*, Canberra: Murray–Darling Basin Commission.

Chapter 7

Fighting for the role of the nation state in knowledge mobilization and educational research

An autoethnography of a mobile Vietnamese scholar

Phan Le Ha

Introduction

In this chapter I argue for the role of the nation state and locality in knowledge mobilization and educational research in relation to mobility and transnationality. I will engage critically with the literature that over-emphasizes the 'global' dimension of research and knowledge and simultaneously overlooks the role that the nation state and the sense of national identity play in mobile global sites of knowledge construction and reconstruction. While acknowledging the limitations associated with narrow and rigid perspectives shaped by the nation state and locality discourses, I will demonstrate that, together with the need to understand these two notions more creatively and openly, it is also necessary to be critical of the over-enthusiasm about globalization and its power over the nation state, particularly in terms of what knowledge, responsibilities and contributions may mean to different mobile researchers. Drawing on my own autoethnography, I will discuss how my sense of being a mobile Vietnamese working in Australia and operating internationally has shaped my research interests as well as my approach to research and knowledge. I will address two areas in which mobility and transnationality have been playing an important role: mobility and the sense of being Vietnamese/sense of belonging/sense of a particular locality; and mobility and my endeavours to introduce more 'Eastern' knowledge and philosophies to the 'West'. I will also discuss what I mean by 'making contributions' at the national, international and global levels and suggest 'brain gain' rather than 'brain drain' and in what ways mobility is not a given, a face value notion, but a site of struggle and negotiation in itself when it comes to knowledge construction and identity making.

Throughout the chapter, I treat the concept of the nation state in close relation to cultural national identity and the sense of belonging to a place, which also includes diversity of local regional identities within a nation. While acknowledging the political as an irreducible defining feature of the nation state, I also argue that this very feature makes 'the nation state' both contested and desirable.

Identity in relation to the nation state and mobility

Identity should be seen as both 'being' and 'becoming'. Together with viewing identity as being dynamic, hybrid, fragmented, multiple and constructed and reconstructed, which often suggests identity more as becoming (Hall 1997; Farrell 2000), it is also important to understand identity with regard to fluidity, continuity, having a 'core' and connectedness (Phan Le Ha 2008, Phan Ngoc 1998, Tran Ngoc Them 2001, Tran Quoc Vuong 2000). Importantly, my argument of identity pays great attention to identity as cultural national identity that often relates to the sense of belonging, the sense of a coherent growth and wholeness and the important role of locality and culture in identity formation, which also suggest identity as being. I argue that the understanding of identity as both 'being' and 'becoming' helps fill the gaps in the literature that are often created by the tendency to take either view of identity. For example, my earlier work on identity studies demonstrates that the understanding of identity as always changing, fragmented, transformed and retransformed fails to explain why the identity formation of mobile Vietnamese teachers of English studying TESOL (teaching of English to speakers of other languages) in Australia largely reflects the sense of belonging, connectedness and fluid continuity in relation to their Vietnamese cultural and national identity (Phan Le Ha 2008). By the same token, my previous work indicates that the understanding of identity as solely national identity and as being makes it impossible to gain insights into how these Vietnamese teachers of English negotiate their contradictory roles and selves (for example, the teacher learner in Australia and/or the teacher in Vietnam, the professional and/or the personal, and the facilitator and/or the moral guide). Either way of understanding identity alone is insufficient to understand thoughtfully complicated processes of identity formation, in which the 'being' and the 'becoming' often play significantly equal roles; this is particularly so in the context of globalization; together with the desire to be global, individuals also wish to declare their affiliations with specific nationals. This argument is further supported by Yang and Welch (2010), in which they discuss the experiences of Chinese diaspora scholars, who despite their working and living in English-speaking countries consistently express a strong attachment to China as their origin, a place they always identify themselves with and a locality that gives them a sense of who they are, regardless of their mobility.

The subsequent sections of this chapter justify my argument of identity by examining it in relation to mobility, transnationality and diaspora. My reading of these interdependent notions and my previous work demonstrate that discussion of identity makes little sense without the sense of belonging. Thus, my proposal to view identity as both being and becoming and in relation to the sense of belonging is the key argument in this chapter.

Mobility, transnationality and diaspora

These concepts – mobility, transnationailty and diaspora – are discussed in relation to one another. I have often been seen as belonging to the 'Vietnamese diaspora community' just because I live and work in Australia, although I would consider diaspora in a very different sense. While the 'Vietnamese diaspora community' tends to be associated with the Vietnam War (or the Anti-American War, as we call it in Vietnam), talked about and researched as 'refugees', 'political asylum seekers', 'Viet Kieu' (Overseas Vietnamese) or 'boat-people' (Nguyen 2009), I see myself as none of these. Mobility, a contested concept and a value-laden and prejudice-embedded notion as I would argue, has created a unique transnational space for me to operate in as an academic who feels 'global', yet strongly a Vietnamese who belongs to Vietnam as a nation. I will elaborate this argument as the chapter develops.

Mobility often refers to human/population movements/flows at different levels worldwide. Movements can be at local, regional, national, trans-national or global levels (Appadurai 1996; Lin 2002; Paasi 2002; Crang et al. 2003). These movements necessitate identity formation to take place in multidimensional directions, resulting in different kinds of negotiations of identities. As demonstrated in my earlier work (Phan Le Ha 2008), while the concept of mobility on the one hand problematizes the existing narratives of fixed regional identities and the closed local/national cultures (Paasi 2002), on the other hand it confirms the importance of locality or place-based identity in identity formation (Lin 2002). Paasi (2002: 146) argues that the links between space, boundaries and identity have new meanings in this mobile world. Thus, she suggests that 'we have to analyse critically any discourse of "regional identity" or "our identity" that is based on roots or common heritage, since these often hide the influence of mobility'. This argument corresponds to Tsagarousianou (2004: 52), who urges us to see 'the complex nexus of linkages' between mobility, transnationality and connectivity when studying diasporic communities. Taking Anderson's (1983) concept of nations as 'imagined', Tsagarousianou (2004: 60) proposes to approach diaspora as 'imagined communities', moving the understanding away from the physical boundaries, physical place or a place-based 'home' side of the concept, and instead focusing on the processes of its members interacting at all levels, in both local and transnational contexts. Paasi (2002) and Tsagarousianou (2004) would fall into the category of work that Crang et al. (2003) criticize for their enthusiasm toward 'rosy' globalization and 'the world without border' mentality, when they discuss transnationalism and mobility.

In the context of transnationality, the relationship of identity, mobility and locality is of vital significance, as I will argue later in what ways mobility is not a given, a face value notion, but a site of struggle and negotiation in itself when it comes to knowledge construction and identity making in transnational space. Yeoh *et al.* (2003) recognize the role of transnationality in strengthening the significance of the 'national'. Transnationality, instead of treating the world in the dichotomy of the global and the local, acts as 'a bifocal one which views the nation-state and transnational practices as "mutually constitutive"' (p. 208). In this view, 'transnationalism studies open up the possibilities and politics of simultaneity where transnational subjects, from a range of social groups, can now "think and act simultaneously at multiple scales" and fashion transnational social practices by being both "here" and "there"' (Smith 2001: 164, cited in Yeoh *et al.* 2003: 208). This argument is closely associated with the question of identity formation and identity politics in transnational social spaces, which my autoethnography as a mobile Vietnamese scholar is situated in.

Specifically, Crang *et al.* (2003: 441) review a variety of work on transnationalism and comment that several authors criticize the term for being used 'too sweepingly, with too little attention to place-specific variations in the form of cross-border activities and sensibilities'. Transnationalism and the notion of 'a world without boundaries' are so powerful and romanticizing that various discourses have enthusiastically adopted them, and this adoption seems to neglect that 'a world without boundaries' is not for everyone yet (Kaplan 1995: 45, cited in Crang *et al.* 2003: 442). Among these discourses are those that over-emphasize the 'global' dimension of research and knowledge and thus simultaneously overlook the role that the nation state and the sense of national identity play in mobile global sites of knowledge construction and reconstruction. Examples of these include Appadurai (1996) and Fahey and Kenway (2008). Together with the romanticization of globalization, some work in transnationalism implies that the nation state no longer plays a significant role in social analysis (Crang *et al.* 2003). However, as these authors argue, in spite of preferences of transnationalism, 'the nation state continues to play a key role in defining the terms in which transnational processes are played out' (p. 442). Transnationalism should not neglect this role and instead it needs to take into account the specificity and particularity of histories, times and places, since every identity formation process in the mobile world makes little meaning if it is separated from its origins of locality.

Transnational identities are not only fluid, flexible, dynamic, but also attach to specificity and particularity of places and times. While transnational identities go against essentialist and fixed notions of identity, they put emphasis on 'interconnectedness across borders' (Yeoh *et al.* 2003: 213). This way of understanding transnational identities suggests that identities are constantly constructed and reconstructed along the lines of 'simultaneous embeddedness in more than one society' (p. 213). This nature of being 'here' and 'there' and simultaneity enables the understanding of transnational identities in ways in which 'the "individual", "group", "national" and "transnational" relate to one another – whether in collusion or collision, or both – in shaping a world with increasingly, but also complexly, fluid borders' (p. 215).

In the context of mobility and transnationality, diaspora and hybridity have become some of the most important notions relating to identity formation of different groups of people, communities, places and nations. These notions, however, do not enjoy a unitary definition. Tsagarousianou (2004) asserts that much understanding of mobility in diaspora studies tends to suggest displacement, and therefore fails to capture the complexities and multilayeredness of the phenomenon and various forms of mobility, which are far from displacement and disorientation. Tsagarousianou, hence, argues for the need to shift from 'mobility' to 'connectivity' when talking about diaspora. I am in line with this viewpoint. However, I do not share her stand regarding the concept of 'home', which she considers 'becomes somewhat irrelevant' (p. 56) within contemporary diasporas, as 'diasporas themselves are deeply affected by their position at the centre of contemporary globalization flows' (pp. 56–57). In her view, there seems to be a tension between global aspects of mobility and a locality, a 'home' and a sense of belonging. This is also evident in work centred around hybridity in which there is a lack of engagement with specificity and particularity of the location and the moment, as in light of Hallward's (2001) critiques of Bhabha (1990, 1994). According to Hallward (2001: 35), Bhabha's work is challenged for 'totalis[ing] a hegemonic global ideology, neither much tainted by its conditions of production nor transformed by the pragmatics of colonial encounters and struggles'.

As argued in my earlier work (Phan Le Ha 2008), identities are subject to dynamic change, construction, reconstruction, negotiation, hybridization and reproduction, but hold on to continuity as well as connectedness. As such, these questions of home, locality and sense of belonging remind researchers that, together with celebrating hybridity and global mobility, we need to work on notions of hybridity and diaspora that are critical and useful for recognition and appreciation of difference and cultural creativity. Engagement with these notions should not result in denying the right to be different and disregarding the emotional aspect of mobile individuals. Hybridity must respect and retain 'a local sensibility in a globalizing world' (Werbner 2001: 149), so as to lead to 'a double consciousness, a global cultural ecumene', not to 'a polarization of discourses'.

This understanding of diaspora and hybridity helps address the flaws of the global/national binary and at the same time reinforces the sense of belonging that many mobile or diasporic scholars would be identified with. Equally important is how identity as both 'becoming' and 'being' makes sense of the mobility experience of these scholars. The following section specifically focuses on academic mobility and the diaspora intellectual community. I acknowledge the complexities, variations and exceptions underlying these concepts.

Academic mobility and the knowledge diaspora

Over the past few years, in talking about academic mobility, knowledge diaspora has emerged as a key theme in the work of several scholars, such as Singh (2009), and Welch and Zhang (2008). Knowledge diaspora 'as trans-national human capital' (Yang and Welch 2010) is seen as being created, generated and produced by diaspora intellectuals, including academics, scholars, researchers and research students, who often move from the 'global South' to developed countries, largely the English-speaking West. Dominant ways of looking at this phenomenon often suggest a brain-drain problem faced by developing countries, where brain is seen as belonging to and thus a property of a nation (Fahey and Kenway 2008). As such, Fahey and Kenway (2008) criticize discourses associated with the nation state for limiting our under-standing of academic mobility and the concept of 'brain'. Thus, in their report on Australian mobile scholars, Fahey and Kenway (2008: 6) propose 'a mind-shift away from simple equations of loss and gain and territory and identity – notions still perpetuated in policy conceptions of "brain drain-gain/mobility" and "diaspora"', and suggest 'national reputation and relationships' as the alternative that mobile researchers take to create the 'global public good'. In the same vein, knowledge mobility should be viewed in more creative and open ways, in which knowledge should not be seen as 'embodied and territorial' and belonging to 'a particular territory' (p. 9). While, on the one hand, all these arguments speak to my positioning as a mobile Vietnamese scholar/academic working in Australia, on the other they still fail to capture the emotional side of the multiple positionings I hold and why and how I identify myself as a Vietnamese in all my work and in all contexts. This is partly addressed in Welch and Zhang (2008) and Yang and Welch (forthcoming) in their studies about the Chinese knowledge diaspora with Chinese mobile intellectuals residing in Australia. They consistently prove how influential the Chinese culture, identity and China as a people are on the ways these intellectuals talk about themselves as the mobile diaspora community and individuals, in relation to other Chinese and non-Chinese. A strong sense of belonging to China and attachment to its culture and history is evident throughout and with every mobile Chinese participating in these studies, who see themselves as Chinese and consider that their work always serves China either directly or indirectly, in the immediate or long term. In addition to this, these diaspora scholars tend to talk about Australia as a country and place where they work, rather than a place where they belong and that they are attached to. While 'global' is not yet for all and what it means to be 'global' still remains 'vague', the nation state, a particular locality and a place-based home continue to play a significant role in the identity formation and positioning of many mobile individuals, be they sojourn academics, diaspora intellectuals or transnational scholars. All this confirms my argument that identity formation and knowledge mobilization make little sense when individuals are separated from locality/localities, be it/they 'imagined' or 'out there'. What is greater is the emotional feeling each individual has towards that locality, which ties mobility and transnationality to a place rather than detaches them from it.

Autoethnography of a mobile Vietnamese scholar working in Australia

This section is autoethnographical and contains a selected narrative of my positioning as a mobile Vietnamese academic/scholar working in Australia. Drawing on my own autoethnography, I will discuss how my sense of being a mobile Vietnamese working in Australia and operating internationally has shaped my research interests as well as my approach to research and knowledge. I will address two areas in which mobility and transnationality have been playing an important role: mobility and the sense of being Vietnamese/sense of belonging/sense of a particular locality; and mobility and my endeavours to introduce more 'Eastern' knowledge and philosophies to the 'West'. I will also discuss what I mean by 'making contributions' at the national, international and global levels and suggest 'brain gain' rather than 'brain drain'.

Mobility and the sense of being Vietnamese/sense of belonging/ sense of a particular locality

Perhaps the most precious things I had in my luggage on my first trip to Australia were my parents' and friends' words that, whatever happens, I must always remember one thing, that *I am Vietnamese*.

'*I am Vietnamese*' matters to me more as a mobile individual whose work is centred on questions of language, identity, culture, difference and the politics of knowledge. Instances in my everyday interactions with Vietnam, whether directly, indirectly, from within or from afar, first-hand or second-hand, always remind me that 'I am Vietnamese' and that 'I belong there'. The recollection presented below of my first days in Melbourne speaks for this positioning ever since. It is not something I have recently 'made up' and 'dramatized' to reclaim this identity, as one may say that I am influenced by my work and the readings I do in my field.

As an international student in Australia in the late 1990s, when most Vietnamese people there at that time were refugees, I was at times sarcastically referred to as belonging to the privileged 'plane people' group, not the 'boat people', by several Vietnamese refugees in Melbourne while shopping for

Vietnamese food in the community. I have the Hanoi accent, and Hanoi where I come from is considered the cradle of the communist, so all of these disqualified me as 'belonging' to the local Vietnamese community in Melbourne. I acknowledge that the community itself is diverse, not unitary, complicated and mixed in terms of ideologies as well. Many questions I received from people around me (most of whom were not Vietnamese) were about whether Vietnam was still partitioned into two parts, or was it already united as one. Much suspicion and curiosity about the so-called 'communist' regime was poured out onto me when I travelled, shopped and talked to others. This was so much so that the legacies of the 'Vietnam War' positioned me in a certain way in Australia, a place so far away from my homeland. This very foreign land did shape Vietnam in a particular way that was so alienating to me and what I had known as Vietnam. I realized Vietnam meant different things to different people, including Vietnamese themselves, and still does. However, what I had known about Vietnam did not seem to be accessible and appreciated by the new social and academic context, where memories, accounts, representation and tales of Vietnam were dominantly related to the war, poverty and communist ideals. A strong passion in me to communicate the Vietnam I had been familiar with emerged and has been growing since then.

Mobility has offered me the opportunity to see Vietnam from different angles, yet consolidated my attachment to this place in such a way that holds me firm as a Vietnamese first and foremost in how my positioning as a mobile Vietnamese has influenced my work and research in education. I do not suggest that this being Vietnamese only holds one meaning, rather, it enjoys multiple meanings depending on where and when I talk it and feel it. In each context and setting, on talking about me as being Vietnamese, multiple positionings are often operating simultaneously. These include being a Vietnamese, being a Vietnamese scholar, being a scholar in Vietnam, being a Vietnamese working in the West, being a Vietnamese in Australia, and being a young female academic with a PhD 'talking' about Vietnam with scholars in Vietnam and scholars who work on Vietnam. These are not unproblematic positionings. They can be disturbing at times, particularly when how I see myself as a Vietnamese is not 'approved' by some audiences who place me as an 'overseas Vietnamese', implying that I am not Vietnamese and that the 'overseas' part associated with 'wealth', 'pro-West' and 'individualism' is more dominant than the 'Vietnamese' side. These audiences conflate being physically in Vietnam with being Vietnamese. At this very point, I am disturbed by this rigid understanding of belonging as physical and of identity as only being fixed to a bounded territory. Nevertheless, at the same time I feel more strongly about this particular place that has nurtured my being and becoming; while the feeling of being a 'global' citizen frees me from any national affiliations, it makes me float. And as I am floating I see myself closer to Vietnam, at least to a sense of this place with a language, history and culture to which I feel I belong.

Being Vietnamese and enjoying a sense of national identity involves making contributions to Vietnam, the country and its people. This very positioning has allowed me to be more creative with what meaning I give to the common discourses of 'contributions' that are often based on the brain gain-drain dichotomy. Most importantly, I argue for the sense of always being 'Vietnamese' in the simultaneity of my 'here' and 'there', past, present and future, 'real' and 'imagined', 'emotional' and 'physical', 'academic' and 'personal' in the inter-section of my 'global', 'local' and 'transnational' sites of knowledge mobilization and educational research. The section below exemplifies how mobility has shaped my research interest and in what ways my work makes contributions to Vietnam, while operating transnationally.

Mobility and my endeavours to introduce more 'Eastern/ Vietnamese' knowledge and philosophies to the 'West'

I first came to Australia as an international student from Vietnam for my Masters degree in 1998. I started my study in Australia with confidence and eager-ness, assuming that what I had learnt before would be valued and desired. But then, I found out that much of what I had known and learnt in Vietnam was irrelevant in the new context, both socially and academically; that being an international student from Vietnam (Asia) was not something 'fancy' as I thought it would be in Australia; and what Vietnam meant for me could be something very different for other people around me. All this questioned my own thinking and knowing.

Then, I learnt that very little written by Vietnamese scholars in the field of education, social sciences and humanities had been acknowledged and engaged with. I learnt that even the way we wrote in English and in Vietnamese was seen as lacking critical analytical engagement in the new context. And then, questions were jumping up and down in my head. My very first research project on Vietnam was to revisit '*my route*' and '*root*' as a Vietnamese writer in English. I started to engage with both Western and Vietnamese scholars' work on writing issues and cross-cultural writing adjustments.

My second trip to Australia was to do my PhD in mid-2000. My research examined the identity formation of Western-trained Vietnamese teachers of English, which was later turned into my first authored book (Phan Le Ha 2008). I was one of these teachers, so the project in a sense was helpful for me to understand my identity formation as a mobile transnational Vietnamese. Since the start of my doctoral study, I have been more and more engaged in the literature on language, culture and identity and able to create a cross-cultural dialogue between Vietnamese and Western scholars in this field of studies. Although the arguments about language, culture and identity developed and pursued by many Western and Vietnamese scholars are from two almost com-pletely different traditions, bringing them together is helpful in understanding the identity formation of Vietnamese teachers of English who were trained in the West. On the one hand, when Western theorists fail to decode why a strong sense of belonging was shared among these teachers, Vietnamese authors are able to do the job persuasively with their theory of the '*being*' and '*becoming*' of identity. On the other, while Vietnamese authors seem to ignore the notion of individual identity and thus fail to acknowledge its existence, Western theorists help by introducing their constructivist approach to identity formation. According to them, identity is constructed minute by minute, and is multiple, dynamic and hybrid. They pay attention to fragmented identities rather than one overall identity, as suggested by Vietnamese authors. Moreover, the very idea expressed by a number of Western theorists of identity presents a paradox. They argue the central formative and responsive role of culture and cultural values in identity formation, yet at the same time do not seem to consider and acknowledge the validity of views shaped by other cultures which may emphasize quite different aspects of identity. For example, Vietnamese thinkers emphasize the importance of a national identity based on the study of culturally shaped values. As a result, the introduction of Vietnamese scholars' views of identity is helpful in harmonizing or resolving this paradox. Thanks to both traditions, Western and Vietnamese, the multiple identities of these teachers are acknowledged, and the issue as to why they perceived a consistent sense of being Vietnamese within these multiple identities is answered with reference to the ways in which culture can shape our sense of self. Through the lenses of both traditions, the complexity and sophistication of the identity formation of these Western-trained Vietnamese teachers of English are best revealed, understood, and argued. The notion of the influence of culture is the thread that brings these two very different sets of views together, despite their apparent contradictions.

My endeavours to introduce more 'Eastern/Vietnamese' knowledge and philosophies to the 'West' partly stems from debates around the hegemonic nature of the West and Western knowledge (Lal 2002, Chakrabarty 2000). My mobility and transnational space as a scholar working with different theories in different languages grants me the 'power' to speak from within the 'Centre', and thus be able to get 'what I know' heard. The West and/or Western knowledge has been questioned, criticized and challenged from multiple angles by postcolonial theorists, among whose ideas the hegemonic and imperialist nature of Western knowledge is most often contested. Postcolonial theorists contest the assumption that Western thought is superior and the only truth worldwide. Its assumed superiority has been constructed, sustained and presented to the world in every way.

Chakrabarty (2000: 7) criticizes the European ideology of the 'first in Europe, then elsewhere' structure of global historical time, which, for instance, implies that modernity or capitalism originated in Europe first, then spread outside it. Thus, Chakrabarty urges the need to see in what way 'historicism . . . posited historical time as a measure of the cultural distance . . . assumed to exist between the West and the non-West' (p. 7). As stated on the back cover of Chakrabarty's

(2000) book, his work indicates that 'the mythical figure of Europe that is often taken to be the original site of the modern in many histories of capitalist transition in non-Western countries [and] this imaginary Europe . . . is built right into the social sciences.' However, taking India as an example, Charkrabarty shows that European thought can neither understand adequately nor explain meaningfully the political and the historical in a country like India. Provincializing Europe also teases out how powerful and taken-for-granted European thought is in social sciences. Its power and the way it is presented in scholarly works have treated non-European thinking as 'truly dead' (p. 6) and at the same time made non-Western scholars accept the European way as the only 'alive' tradition (p. 5) based on which they can develop their knowledge. That is why 'South Asian(ist) social scientists would argue passionately with a Marx or a Weber without feeling any need to historicize them or to place them in their European intellectual contexts' (p. 6), whereas few of them if any would argue seriously with their own philosophers and theorists. His argument points out that the idea of the non-West has been interpreted in binary terms in ways that have masked its colonial constructions and continuing hegemonic role. In talking about 'Eastern/Vietnamese' knowledge, I acknowledge the likelihood of the hegemonic role of the West in the complex development of Eastern/Vietnamese scholars' views on identity and knowledge formation. Nevertheless, I am relying on the argument that many other social and historical layers of meaning inhabit these Vietnamese scholars' views in addition to Western ideas. Because of this complexity of layeredness of the Vietnamese scholars' views, I feel it necessary to represent them alongside current Western thought on identity and knowledge (Phan Le Ha 2008).

The need to bring more 'Southern theory' (Connell 2007) to scholarly discussions in Western academia is further advocated by Singh (2009). With specific reference to Vietnam as a country, a nation, a people, there is so much about Vietnam that needs to be communicated to the world and that the world needs to know and learn about, rather than just the 'Vietnam War' and 'food' – the spring rolls and 'pho' (beef noodle soup). What Vietnam has produced in terms of knowledge and scholarship deserves more serious attention and engagement from academia; and I see myself as contributing to making this happen, particularly in the field of social sciences and humanities. At this level, I do not limit my contributions to Vietnam only, but more importantly to knowledge in general as a Vietnamese. I see myself as 'making contributions' at the national, international and global levels and that I (and my brain) are not 'leaving' Vietnam in any way; rather I am always there holding firm to that place, despite my other multiple positionings enabled by my mobility and transnational experiences. Contributions in this context are not confined within any physical border of any bounded territory, but are more meaningful to a mobile transnational scholar like me when they adhere to a specific place that initially gave birth to my being and becoming, Vietnamese.

This corresponds to Fahey and Kenway's (2008) notion of 'national reputation', and once more confirms the significant role of a sense of belonging and locality (either 'real' or 'imagined') evident in the work of many authors I have engaged with above.

Some afterthoughts

Bringing together all that I have discussed and argued so far about knowledge, the West, Vietnam/Vietnamese, mobility, identity, transnationality, diaspora, and hybridity, I do not want to suggest myself that I am not speaking from the position of the 'privileged', and that being a 'global' citizen is meaningless to me. I am well aware of the danger of representing myself as being 'ungrateful' to and 'unappreciative' of Australia, while being associated with Australia has indeed made me more attached to Vietnam. Perhaps the emotional side of being attached to a place must be taken into consideration in the ways we do research, talk about knowledge and engage with ideas. As I am closing this chapter, I could see mobility is not a given, particularly when it places me in positions that signify my 'Otherness' as discussed in my autoethnography. Likewise, mobility is not a face value notion, but a site of struggle and negotiation in itself when it comes to knowledge construction and identity making.

References

Anderson, B. (1983) *Imagined Communities: reflections on the origin and spread of nationalism*, London: Verso.

Appadurai, A. (1996) *Modernity at Large: cultural dimensions of globalization*, Minnesota: University of Minnesota Press.

Bhabha, H. (1990) *Nation and Narration*, London: Routledge.

—— (1994) *The Location of Culture*, London: Routledge.

Chakrabarty, D. (2000) *Provincialing Europe: postcolonial thoughts and historical difference*, Princeton, NJ: Princeton University Press.

Connell, R. (2007) *Southern Theory: the global dynamics of knowledge in social science*, Australia: Allen & Unwin.

Crang, P., Dwyer, C. and Jackson, P. (2003) 'Transnationalism and the spaces of commodity culture', *Progress in Human Geography*, 27(4): 438–56.

Fahey, J. and Kenway, J. (2008) *Brain Drain or Mind-Shift: reconsidering policies on researcher mobility*, Melbourne: Monash Institute for the Study of Global Movements.

Farrell, L. (2000) 'Ways of doing, ways of being: language education and "working" identities', *Language and Education*, 14(1): 18–36.

Hall, S. (ed.) (1997) *Representation: cultural representations and signifying practices*, London: Sage in association with The Open University.

Hallward, P. (2001) *Absolutely Postcolonial: writing between the singular and the specific*, Manchester: Manchester University Press.

Lal, V. (2002) *Empire of Knowledge: culture and plurality in the global economy*, London, Sterling, VA: Pluto Press.

Lin, G. C. S. (2002) 'Hong Kong and the globalisation of the Chinese diaspora: a geographical perspective', *Asia Pacific Viewpoint*, 43(1): 63–91.

Nguyen, N.H.C. (2009) *Memory Is Another Country: women of the Vietnamese diaspora*, Santa Barbara, CA: Praeger.

Paasi, A. (2002) 'Bounded spaces in the mobile world: deconstructing "regional identity"', *Royal Dutch Geographical Society KNAG*, 93(2): 137–48.

Phan Le Ha (2008) *Teaching English as an International Language: identity, resistance and negotiation*, Clevedon, UK: Multilingual Matters.

Phan Ngoc (1998) *Ban Sac Van Hoa Viet Nam*, Hanoi: NXB Van Hoa Thong Tin.

Singh, M. (2009) 'Using Chinese knowledge in internationalising research education: Jacques Rancière, an ignorant supervisor and doctoral students from China', *Globalization Societies and Education*, 7(2): 185–201.

Tran Ngoc Them (2001) *Tim Ve ban Sac Van Hoa Vietnam* (third edn), Ho Chi Minh City: Nha xuat ban TP Ho Chi Minh.

Tran Quoc Vuong (2000) *Van Hoa Viet Nam: Tim Toi Va Suy Ngam*, Hanoi: Nha xuat ban van hoa dan toc and Tap chi van hoa nghe thuat.

Tsagarousianou, R. (2004) 'Rethinking the concept of diaspora: mobility, connectivity and communication in a globalized world', *Westminster Papers in Communication and Culture*, 1(1), 52–65.

Welch, A., and Zhang, Z. (2008) 'Higher education and global talent flows: brain drain, overseas Chinese intellectuals, and diasporic knowledge networks', *Higher Education Policy*, 21(4): 519–37.

Werbner, P. (2001) 'The limits of cultural hybridity: on ritual monsters, poetic licence and contested postcolonial purifications', *Journal of the Royal Anthropological Institute*, 7(1): 133–52.

Yang, R., and Welch, A. (2010) 'Globalisation, transnational academic mobility and the Chinese knowledge diaspora: an Australian case study', *Discourse: Studies in the Cultural Politics of Education*.

Yeoh, B. S. A., Willis, K. D. and Abdul Khader Fakhri, S. M. (2003) 'Introduction: transnationalism and its edges', *Ethnic and Racial Studies*, 26(2): 207–17.

Part III

Languages and enactments of knowledge mobilization

Chapter 8

Finding common perspectives

Knowledge mobilization in a transnational museum project

Ian Dyck

Introduction

Museums are important sites for the assembly, generation, structuring and mobilization of knowledge, tasks that are usually undertaken in reference to an established network of interests and agencies (Lord and Lord 2009: 63–72). In recent years, like many organizations, museums have been pushed to extend their reach into wider-ranging interdisciplinary and multi-partner collaborations (Hill and Nicks 1992; Tien 2006; Waibel and Erway 2009). The effects of this trend have been subject to critical analysis for some organizational sectors (e.g. Hall 1999), but rarely for museums. This chapter traces the complexity of one international museum collaboration, the Ancient Nomads project, which was aimed at mobilizing archaeological knowledge across two very different cultures.

We began the project in September 1999 as a partnership between the Canadian Museum of Civilization (CMC), Gatineau, Canada and the Alabin Museum of Historical and Regional Studies (AMHRS), Samara, Russia. The purposes were (1) to undertake a scholarly comparison of the ancient cultures of the Russian Steppes and Canadian Prairies and (2) to disseminate the results to a broad cross-section of Canadian and Russian publics through an exhibition, book, and website. The website was launched in November 2006. The exhibition opened in Gatineau in December 2006, then moved to Samara in June 2008, where it closed in February 2009. The book was released in both Samara and Gatineau in 2009. In this chapter I will analyse the context for this collaboration in knowledge mobilization, the process it followed and the results it produced, and will conclude with some observations on the efficacy of the endeavour.

Museum context

A museum is a non-profit, permanent institution in the service of society and its development, open to the public, which acquires, conserves, researches, communicates and exhibits the tangible and intangible heritage of humanity and its environment for the purposes of education, study and enjoyment.

(International Council of Museums 2010)

This definition certainly applies to the two museums under consideration. The CMC is a large, 150-year-old, federal institution with a human history mandate that is focused on Canada within a world context. The CMC attracts about 1.2 million visitors annually. In addition, its website receives about 2.8 million visits plus another 17.3 million page views per year. The AMHRS is a medium-sized, 125-year-old, oblastic institution[1] with both human and natural history mandates. This museum receives about 200,000 visitors annually and its website an additional 100,000.

People come to museums for a variety of reasons – social experience, entertainment, learning, discovery, and opportunities for introspection and self-restoration (Graham 2006). Visitor profiles indicate that the CMC audience mirrors the Canadian public in respect to age and gender. Surveys also show that 45% of the CMC audience have a university education, which seems to reflect an inherent interest in learning among a substantial portion of visitors (CMCC 1999). One of the characteristics of museums is that they are centres for free-choice or self-directed learning. They are places that children and adults can trust as they browse for objects, information and ideas; they are places where people can find both meaning and connection (Falk and Dierking 2000: 2). Collectively, museums appeal to a very wide range of interests. However, individual museums, driven by their mandates and by economic considerations, generally yearn to expand and refresh their content in order to appeal to ever broader audiences. Collaboration is part of the answer to this desire.

Collaborative context

Origins

The Ancient Nomads project had serendipitous origins in a 1990s meeting between an émigré Russian soil scientist, Elena Ponomarenko, and me, a Prairies archaeologist. Elena had considerable experience in the Russian Steppes. Her approach to soil science is well suited to collaborative work with archaeologists and, at the time I met her, she wanted to gain experience in the Canadian Prairies by working with Prairies archaeologists. I arranged for that to happen. Subsequently, she offered me the opportunity to gain exposure to Russian Steppes archaeology. I took advantage during the fall of 1999 by attending a regional meeting in Samara, where I presented an overview of Canadian Prairies archaeology and participated in several field trips and museum visits.

It was soon clear that the Steppes had some amazing similarities to the Canadian Prairies. For example, the natural landscapes seemed almost identical.

Moreover, herd-based nomads had dominated both regions until recent centuries. Ancient conical and linear burial mounds are present in both regions, although they are vastly more numerous in the Steppes. And some ceramic vessels and stone artefacts look strangely familiar. But there are also some striking differences. For example, the Steppes have had a much longer period of human occupation – 120,000 years as opposed to 12,000 years for the Prairies. Furthermore, Steppe nomads' subsistence depended on domestic animals, while Prairie nomads' subsistence was based on wild animals.

During the visit, Elena and I and several Russian archaeologists formed a working group and roughed out a collaborative plan to compare the archaeological record of the Steppes with that of the Prairies. That plan eventually became an institutional collaboration between the CMC and the AMHRS – we will come to the details shortly. First, however, some information about the considerations and expectations that underlay the collaboration.

Considerations

Collaborations are generally aimed at (1) building on the strengths and/or ameliorating the weaknesses of the institutions involved, and (2) taking advantage of opportunities and/or overcoming constraints in the environments facing those institutions (University of Western Australia 1999). The CMC looked on AMHRS strengths as including: excellent Steppes archaeological collections; unrestricted access to those collections; a small but expert archaeological staff with intimate involvement in a strong research tradition in the Steppes region; valuable connections with regional and national archaeological associations; strong public knowledge of and support for Steppes archaeology; a certain institutional distance from the everyday constraints of big bureaucracy; and a strong interest in the intellectual potential and challenge of an international collaboration. At the same time, AMHRS weaknesses included: a decaying physical infrastructure (except for their information technology and capacity for scientific publication); weak ethnographic collections;[2] low and unreliable operating resources (except for special travel, publication and project grants); and susceptibility to obstruction by some federal and oblast agencies (e.g. Customs).

On the other side of the world, CMC strengths included a grand new facility; a large museum staff with many technical specialists; a more advanced exhibitions programme; a larger and more reliable operating budget; excellent Prairies ethnographic collections; a small core of expertise in Prairies archaeology with good connections to related regional and national organizations; a modicum of experience with previous Russian collaborations; and a desire to take part in an innovative collaborative project that would add novelty to its research and exhibition line-ups. As to CMC weaknesses: its Prairies archaeological collections are small in comparison to its holdings from other parts of the country; access to some of its collections is restricted out of respect for Aboriginal sensitivities; the CMC is somewhat more prone to the burden of bureaucratic process; and although its public is generally sympathetic to ancient Canadian history and archaeology, only a tiny fraction of that audience has any substantial knowledge of either the Canadian or Russian grasslands or their ancient cultures (CMC 2004; Pokotylo 2002).

Expectations

Past international collaborations in archaeology have often produced imbalanced relationships in which Westerners entered with superior funding and training and left with results that were strongly oriented to their own needs. Today, due in large measure to the spread of protective heritage legislation around the world, collaborative relationships are generally more equal (Lanata and Duff 2008). From the Western perspective, this usually means paying closer attention to matters such as financial assistance and training, mutual respect, trust, reciprocity, joint publications, patience, good communications, team decision making, and shared celebration of success (Boivin et al. 2008).

The Russian–Canadian collaboration that I experienced was definitely not a case of Western archaeologists making a one-way incursion into a foreign place. From the beginning, it was intended that this would be a two-way collaboration involving an equal exchange of information. Members started on a fairly equal footing, all drawing on substantial museum and university experience. Each side had to contribute data, artefacts and interpretation from its own region, and the two sides had to work together to find workable units of comparison and means for presenting the results. This meant that any intellectual or professional imbalance was expected to be small. Because of the CMC's greater experience in national and international projects, it was agreed that our staff would lead the project. But major decisions were to be consensual, with input from both sides. As it turned out, although we did experience intellectual differences, these were not due to an imbalance in professionalism. I'll come back to some of these differences later.

On the financial side, because some resources – specifically funding for construction and for adjunct professional and technical services – were much harder to find in Russia than in Canada, the Canadian Museum of Civilization agreed to carry most of the technical planning and fabrication costs. The CMC also agreed to bear the salary of a team liaison person, Elena Ponomarenko, to overcome the Russian–English language barrier, to contribute her own scientific expertise and to smooth cultural differences. Alternatively, because grants for book printing and team travel were generally easier to obtain in Russia, the Samara Museum agreed to assume a large share of those costs. They also agreed to take lead responsibility for overcoming the obstacles presented by Russian Customs.

With these general provisions agreed to, in 2001 the CMC and the AMHRS approved funding for the collaboration. The time frame allowed for preparations was five years.

Collaborative approach

The approach we adopted required the creation of five teams:

(1) First was a research team that included Steppes archaeologists Anna Kochkina, Dmitry Stashenkov and Liudmila Kuznetsova from the AMHRS, Prairies archaeologists Richard Morlan and Ian Dyck from the CMC, plus Elena Ponomarenko, who was hired part-time as liaison and researcher for the duration of the project. The tasks of the research team were to generate the scholarly comparison for the exhibition and to find the objects and illustrations to support it; at the same time to contribute to and coordinate the assembly of text and illustrations for a book and website. The work of the research team was carried beyond the exploratory stage before the other teams were created.
(2) After the research team had generated a detailed approach paper, an exhibition team was struck. It was comprised of the research team plus a group of exhibition specialists from the CMC: specifically, a project manager, a designer and an interpretive officer. The job of the exhibition team was to create an approximately 475 m² multilingual exhibition that would be of high quality and broad public interest.
(3) Next, we created a book team consisting initially of the research team, from which specific writers were designated and to which publishing coordinators from both museums were added. The team's task changed through time. In the end, we researched, wrote and published a book describing the results of the comparison in separate English, French and Russian editions.
(4) As the exhibition was approaching its final form, the CMC created a Web team consisting of a communications officer, website manager and representatives of the research team. The website was designed to summarize the exhibition in words and photographs. The Samara museum was expected to use the CMC website material for its own website.
(5) Finally, after the exhibition had been taken down at the CMC, a travelling exhibition team was established to coordinate the packaging, transportation, set-up and publicity of the exhibition in Samara, then the dismantling, repackaging and return of artefacts to their repositories. This team consisted of a travelling exhibition manager, loan officer, preparator and two researchers from the CMC, plus two researchers, a preparator, exhibition officer and other staff from the AMHRH.

Each team drew on additional assistance as required. There were also some changes in membership of the core teams. Morlan had to withdraw from the research team for health reasons and we could not find a replacement. Over the life of the project, at least nine different persons held the exhibition manager position; two the interpretive officer position; and two the book manager position. Aside from the loss of Morlan, which was a serious blow, the project ran well in spite of the changes, showing the strength of the talent pool we drew upon.

Research – what to compare and how to make the comparison

In doing research for the exhibition, our initial idea was to compare the whole human history of the Russian Steppes with that of the Northern Great Plains, but with emphasis on the nomadic era, extending from about AD 5000 to about 200 years ago in both regions. We also planned to give some attention to the overlapping period of indigenous agriculture and the subsequent era of European colonization. The first problem we faced was how to present such a complex comparison. We debated whether to develop one exhibition in which Steppes and Prairies materials were fully integrated, or two semi-integrated exhibitions with juxtaposed parts. In the end, we merged these ideas into one fully integrated exhibition with juxtaposed parts.

A question that I raised early, based on previous experience at the CMC, was what sort of content should be included or excluded. Our Russian colleagues didn't understand the question at first and thought it was ridiculous to limit ourselves in any way. After all, they commented, shortages of materials for some subject areas would be limitation enough. However, I explained that North American museums have conceded that ancient Aboriginal burial materials and sacred objects are generally too sensitive for public exposure. Our Russian colleagues were astounded by this revelation, since ancient burials are a major part of their work and are routinely shown in exhibitions. When I asked how their visitors reacted, they replied that visitors really appreciated such exhibits. The compromise we reached was that the CMC would use no burial or sacred materials in the exhibition, except a few replicas, and that we would not engage in a comparison of burials. However, the Russians would use real grave goods throughout the exhibition.

The question of ancient burials and their avoidance in North America led us to another realization. During at least the last half century, Steppes archaeology has been primarily mortuary archaeology while Prairies archaeology has concentrated mainly on campsites and bison kill sites. How do artefacts recovered from camp and kill sites compare with those from burial sites? It is easily imagined that burial goods are often exceptionally fine, whole and rare examples of their kind, whereas camp and kill site materials are generally worn out, broken, everyday discards – treasures versus trash. Those on the Canadian side did not want to pursue such a mismatched comparison, fearing it would cast an unfairly negative reflection on the lives and material culture of ancient Prairies inhabitants. The Russians agreed, but with a little different twist. For them, with Canadian burial and sacred materials removed, the remaining archaeological collections held little prospect for an interesting comparison.

At this point, we decided to plumb the nature of Steppes archaeology a little more deeply. I asked what our Russian colleagues knew about Steppe nomads' campsites and they replied, almost nothing from archaeology, but a fair bit from the historical literature extending back more than a thousand years. When I asked about animal kill or management sites, the answer was similar. To date, very few nomadic camp or butchering sites have been found or examined. Thus, it was apparent that the archaeological gap between the Russian Steppes and Canadian Prairies was broader than I had expected.

We decided that one means to bridge this gap would be to supplement the archaeological base with ethnographic collections. Our Russian colleagues seemed keen for us to do this as an improvement to what they saw as the impoverished quality of our archaeological collections. Since the Plains ethnographic collections available to us in the CMC are strong and beautiful, we were certainly willing to comply. In addition, we thought that an infusion of Russian ethnographic information and collections might fill some of the obvious blanks in the archaeological picture available for the Steppe nomads. Our Russian colleagues cautiously agreed.

Another measure we decided upon was a shift from traditional preoccupation with time and culture change toward a comparison of subjects such as resource use, travel, dwellings and so forth. In fact, this was not an easy discussion. On the Canadian side we pushed for this approach in the expectation that it would be of greater interest for Canadian audiences. Our Russian colleagues did not agree, arguing that the Russian public was generally familiar with Russian chronology and culture history, archaeology being a mandatory subject in primary, secondary and normal school curricula. Eventually we compromised on a plan that emphasized a thematic approach but was prefaced with a historical framework for both regions.

Converting research results into an exhibition

After seeing the CMC exhibition halls, our Russian partners agreed to adopt the CMC method of exhibition preparation. They may have had only the vaguest idea about the implications of this decision, yet they embraced it as a learning experience that might benefit their own work. Since moving to its new building in 1989, the CMC has tried to appeal to larger audiences by better understanding the nature and interests of potential visitors and by constructing exhibitions that better answer those interests (MacDonald and Alsford 1989: 72). The process that the Museum has developed to achieve this goal is complicated, and I'll not go into it here except to say that each new exhibition project begins with an exhibition team consisting of a researcher (or researchers), a project manager, an interpretive officer and a designer who collectively navigate a series of guidelines, milestones and approval points (see Moser 2010 for an overview of this kind of planning environment).

The addition to our team of these highly skilled non-archaeologists brought new perspectives to the planning. For one thing, they demanded to know the main messages we expected to relay to visitors. Searching for significant messages at the right level of generalization can only be described as a ponderous task. The honing of messages went on and on and on. In addition, our exhibition specialists told us that the scheme we had developed was far too complex. According to them, we needed to both simplify and reduce the scope of the comparison. While we researchers agreed to many of their suggestions, we found it difficult to accept proposals that skewed evidence-based inter-pretations, undermined the comparative intent or strayed into subjects where the evidence was weak. Collectively, we finally decided to focus on the nomads of each region and to forego comparisons of the pre-nomadic societies, the Indigenous agriculturists and post-nomadic colonial societies. We also agreed to disregard culture change within the nomadic societies in order to deal with major social themes. Yet, when it came to the suggestion to discard the general archaeological/historical outlines for each region, we refused – our Russian colleagues quite fervently. It would have meant the loss of an important contextual reference for each area and we were not prepared to do that. In addition, when the non-archaeological specialists argued that we should drop the section summarizing the comparison, because it was likely to be overburdened with text, we again refused.

The negotiation of what was to be included in the exhibition took a long time, extending over several years. Although the resulting modifications made use of much of what we had already done, they also called for additional material research. In the end, we developed a plan having 14 modules: (1) Introduction, (2) Culture Histories, (3) Environments, (4) Crucial Features of Subsistence, (5) Transportation, (6) Citing Camps, (7) Dwellings from the Outside, (8) Activities inside Dwellings, (9) Children, (10) Gatherings, (11) Warfare, (12) Trade, (13) Comparative Summary and (14) Nomads' Descendants Today.

The book – enlarging the exhibition comparisons

In regard to the book, our initial idea was to do a catalogue of the exhibition artefacts enlarged with a couple of essays describing and comparing the archaeologies of the two regions. Our advice from the publications division of the CMC was that this sort of book was almost always a financial failure and they would not support it.

The next possibility we considered was a large scholarly tome comparing the two regions, with essays from a number of expert contributors describing the environments, the histories of archaeology, the culture/histories and the colonial histories and wrapping up with comparisons. This kind of volume would have been a complement to the exhibition, dealing with the temporal dimension that we had set aside. We actually got started on this book, but with the departure of Morlan, who was expected to be a contributor and co-editor, and in the rush to complete the exhibition, work on this book fell behind. Eventually, it became evident that a major scholarly book could not be completed before the exhibition opened or even soon after.

This was difficult news for our Russian colleagues since their publishing grant came with a deadline that was already overextended. It was also worrisome to CMC management, who countered with a suggestion that we write a short popular book, using the materials already under development for the exhibition. I will not detail here the negotiations and compromises we worked out with our Russian colleagues. Suffice it to say that we aborted the scholarly tome and instead wrote a popular book that elaborates the main themes of the exhibition (Ponomarenko *et al.* 2007).

The website(s)

The website was developed primarily as a publicity and communication device – as a teaser for the exhibition using materials already in hand. It was launched on the CMC website just before the CMC opening of the exhibition and is still available there (CMC 2006). Subsequently, the Samara Museum used some of the CMC website material in describing the project on its website (AMHRS 2008).

Retrospection on the results

The exhibition opened in Canada on schedule amid considerable publicity – television and print – and with a grand public reception attended by more than 500 people. After the public reception, the CMC honoured the exhibition team with a private dinner attended by the Mongolian Ambassador, delegates from the Russian Embassy and Canadian Foreign Affairs, representatives of the CMC and AMHRS management, and other cultural luminaries. Over the course of its showing, the exhibition drew more than 103,000 visitors – a record for the particular hall in which it was situated. Alas, we have only a general idea about the knowledge that visitors took away.

Academic studies indicate that museum visitors do learn from exhibitions, but in very complex, personal fashions. It appears that traditional models of learning, such as the transmission–absorption model, are not applicable in museums. Instead, a contextual model of learning has been developed to understand the organic, integrated learning experience that actually happens (Falk and Dierking 2000: 10–14; Lord 2007: 13–19). Studies relevant to this model show that exhibition visits do facilitate learning in virtually all museum visitors, although not necessarily the exact learning that the exhibit developers would expect (Falk and Dierking 2000: 173).

We did not attempt a formal evaluation for this exhibition. However, the visitor reaction that I observed was generally interested, contemplative and positive, albeit muted, as it drew less than the usual written reaction at the visitor comment station in the rotunda of the museum. Incidentally, it seemed to me that Canadian visitors gave approximately equal attention to Canadian and Russian sides of the exhibition. Newspaper reviews indicated that the exhibition was attractive, that the main messages of comparison were understood and that some of the specific artefacts were remembered. But reporters also tried to situate the exhibition in other terms, for example in terms of supposed museum aspirations, the place of various objects in respect to grand artistic traditions, the comparative coverage of the Russian and Canadian subject matter (Canadian coverage was found wanting, particularly in ceremonial objects) and the cultural opportunities provided by the fall of Russia's Iron Curtain. The variety of comment in the media is consistent with the contextual model of learning.

The showing of the exhibition in Russia was delayed first by political events (a federal election and change of power in the oblast) and then, in spite of the greatest diligence on the part of Canadian and Russian collaborators, delays and huge unexpected expenses in Customs (there are Customs controls at both federal and oblast levels in Russia). In fact, the grand opening was changed from a public event to a much smaller private affair for dignitaries and the media, because the exhibitry[3] was not released from oblast Customs in time for a full set-up. The set-up had to be finished during the following week. However, the media coverage of the exhibition was extensive, both nationally and locally, as well as being interested and supportive. In the coverage I saw, reporters tended to focus more on the collaboration than the exhibition, finding it to be a worthy exercise in which the Canadian part of the team was meticulous in all stages of the planning while 'our fellow [Russian] countrymen showed skill to operate quickly and thus in absolutely true direction'. Russian reporters touched on the themes of the exhibition, but quickly turned to the richness of results that had come out of the Russian archaeology. The only direct observation I made on the reaction of Russian visitors is that, unlike the Canadian visitors, they tended to pass from module to module looking only at the Russian part of the material. Starting from what one knows is also consistent with the contextual model of learning. Some 60,000 visitors saw the exhibition while it was in Samara, which was judged to be satisfactory by our Russian colleagues and their museum management.

In regard to the book, after the already mentioned planning and writing delays, we delivered printer-ready files for English and French versions[4] to our Russian colleagues for printing in late 2007. We also helped with the preparation of the Russian version. However, the delays had resulted in loss of our position in the printing line-up and the books, although dated 2007, were not ready for distribution until the exhibition was being taken down in Samara in 2009. Books related to exhibitions generally sell slowly in museum boutiques after the media coverage of an exhibition has ended. And since neither museum has effective means for distributing popular books outside their boutiques, the roughly 2,000 copies that were printed have not been widely circulated in either country. The few comments that we have received, mostly academic, give the book genteel praise. Although it enlarges and preserves the comparison we made, it is sad to admit that the book has had little impact on the public readership for which it was intended.

In closing, I can say that the project achieved its goals, producing an innovative comparative exhibition, book and website by means of an intricate international collaboration. The comparison threw light on historical subjects that are only partially known in Russia and almost unknown in Canada. The exhibition was widely publicized and more than 160,000 people in the two countries made their way to the sponsoring museums to see it. As a participating researcher, I found the project to be demanding and deeply engaging. The comparative thematic approach we adopted forced us onto a steep learning curve and this was not simply a matter of assimilating already existing knowledge. In a few cases, we actually generated new knowledge. Little of this would likely be appreciated by visitors, who might simply accept what was presented as given.

It is difficult to know what impact this project may have in the long run. I suspect that, in mixing a comparative, thematic approach into a balanced, collaborative, international project, we may have stretched the limits of practicality one step too far. Both museums appreciated what we were trying to do, but both also chafed at the delays, insecurities, working difficulties and added costs we had to contend with. These problems seem to be inherent in such projects. Beyond that, comparative studies, even though they are the heart of most learning, are rarely attempted in museum exhibitions. Thus, there is little experience to draw upon in developing such exhibitions – at least this is so for culture-historical topics. I would like to think that our Ancient Nomads project made a contribution to knowledge transmission in this area, creating a model that seems to have worked. Yet, I suspect that most museums that examine our experience closely will balk at the time, effort and money that is required for such a complex endeavour. Museums and museum scholars will likely continue to engage in collaborative, balanced, international, multilingual, thematic and probably even comparative knowledge projects in the future, but probably not all at once.

Acknowledgements

I am grateful to Elena Ponomarenko for catalyzing the Ancient Nomads project; the CMC and AMHRS for funding and other support; the team members and many others who assisted us; Karen Graham for information about visitors and exhibition evaluations; Sandra Hamel and Dmitry Stashenkov for information concerning the CMC and AMHRS websites; and Victor Rabinovitch and Tara Fenwick for encouraging the development of this chapter.

Notes

1   A Russian oblast is an administrative and territorial unit that is roughly equivalent to a Canadian province.
2   An ethnographic collection is an assemblage of objects made, modified or used by people of a particular ethnic group during historic or contemporary times, that has been collected and documented for the interpretation and descriptive study of human culture (based on a definition in the Agreement between the Inuit of the Nunavut Settlement Area and Her Majesty the Queen in Right of Canada).
3   Non-artefactual components of the exhibition; in this situation, the glass cases, bases, mounts, labels, text panels and backgrounds among which the artefacts were displayed.
4   A requirement for Canadian federal government projects.

References

Alabin Museum of Historical and Regional Studies (AMHRS) (2008) Российско-канадская выставка 'Хозяева степей: древние кочевники России и Канады'. Available: www.alabin.ru/alabina/exposure/exhibitions/canadasteppes/ (accessed 20 October 2010).

Boivin, N., Korisettar, R. and Petraglia, M. (2008) 'Successfully negotiating international collaboration: an east–west example', *The SAA Archaeological Record*, 8(2): 8–11.

Canadian Museum of Civilization (CMC) (2004) *A Front-End Evaluation for an Exhibition on Ancient Grasslands at the Canadian Museum of Civilization Corporation*, unpublished report prepared for the Ancient Grasslands Exhibition Team by the Office of Audit and Evaluation, Canadian Museum of Civilization, Gatineau.

—— (2006) 'Masters of the plains: ancient nomads of Russia and Canada'. Available: www.civilization.ca/cmc/exhibitions/cmc/maitres/masterse.shtml (accessed 20 October 2010).

Canadian Museum of Civilization Corporation (CMCC) (1999) 'Attracting a diverse audience', in *Canadian Museum of Civilization Corporation, Summary of the Corporate Plan (1999–2000 to 2003–2004)*, p. 12. Available: www.civilization.ca/app/DocRepository/1/About_The_Corporation/Corporate_Reports/Corporate_Plans/corp99e.pdf (accessed 20 October 2010).

Falk, J. H. and Dierking, L.D. (2000) *Learning from Museums: visitor experience and the making of Meaning*, Walnut Creek: Altamira Press.

Graham, K. (2006) *Satisfying Visitor Experiences at the Canadian Museum of Civilization and the Canadian War Museum*, unpublished technical report on file at the Canadian Museum of Civilization, Gatineau.

Hall, C. M. (1999) 'Rethinking collaboration and partnership: a public policy perspective', *Journal of Sustainable Tourism*, 7(3&4): 274–89.

Hill, T. and Nicks, T. (1992) *Turning the Page: forging new partnerships between museums and first peoples*, a joint report sponsored by the Assembly of First Nations and the Canadian Museums Association, Ottawa.

International Council of Museums (2010) *ICOM Statutes*, Article 3, Section 1. Available: http://icom.museum/statutes.html#3 (accessed 6 May 2010).

Lanata, J. L. and Duff, A.I. (2008) 'International cooperative research – an introduction', *The SAA Archaeological Record*, 8(2): 7.

Lord, B. (2007) *The Manual of Museum Learning*, Toronto: Altamira Press.

Lord, G.D. and Lord, B. (2009) *The Manual of Museum Management*, Toronto: Altamira Press.

MacDonald, G. F. and Alsford, S. (1989) *A Museum for the Global Village: The Canadian Museum of Civilization*, Hull: Canadian Museum of Civilization.

Moser, S. (2010) 'The devil is in the detail: museum displays and the creation of knowledge', *Museum Anthropology*, 33(1): 22–32.

Pokotylo, D. (2002) 'Public opinion and Canadian archaeological heritage: a national perspective', *Canadian Journal of Archaeology*, 26(2): 88–129.

Ponomarenko, E. and Dyck, I., with contributions by A. Kochkina, L. Kuznetsova, D. Stashenkov, M. Turetzky and E. Dubman (2007) *Ancient Nomads of the Eurasian and North American Grasslands*, Gatineau and Samara: Canadian Museum of Civilization Corporation and Alabin Museum of Historical and Regional Studies.

Tien, Chieh-Ching (2006) 'Collaboration in museums: the evolution of cross-sector collaboration', in Lai Ying-Ying (ed.) *New Roles and Missions of Museums: Intercom 2006 Symposium*, pp. 351–61, Taiwan: ICOM–INTERCOM, Council for Cultural Affairs.

University of Western Australia (1999) 'Collaboration policy statement'. Available: www.registrar.uwa.edu.au/–data/page/65555/CollabPolicy.pdf (accessed 25 May 2010).

Waibel, G. and Erway, R. (2009) 'Think globally, act locally: library, archive, and museum collaboration', *Museum Management and Curatorship*, 24(4): 323–35.

Chapter 9

Bridging journalistic–academic divides to promote democratic dialogue and debate

Deirdre M. Kelly and Michelle Stack

Introduction

A common concern among journalists is that academics are remote or abstract in their concerns and speak in a language difficult to convert into news for a popular audience (Stack 2007). A common concern among academic researchers is that their valuable research and ideas rarely make it into the popular discussion managed by journalists and that, when they do, journalists tend to get their findings wrong or present them superficially (Kelly and Stack 2011). It is even more complicated when we look at academics' ideas that do not coincide with dominant or status quo thinking about issues of public concern (Kelly 2006). Our aim in this chapter is to think through whether it is possible to bridge what we see as a *double divide* in knowledge exchange and, if so, how. The *first divide* refers to the gap between academe and journalism in terms of how knowledge is represented and for whom (e.g. specialized, professional versus large and diverse publics). The *second divide* refers to the exclusion or marginalization of some areas of knowledge production and dissemination *vis-à-vis* mainstream media and university life (e.g. sexuality, disability, Indigenous and feminist studies).

In this chapter we analyze divides between researchers and journalists that have sometimes led to misunderstandings and dismissal, particularly around issues of systemic injustice. Central to our interest is thinking about practices that make and maintain spaces for counter-narratives. Counter-narratives are interpretations that call dominant or status quo narratives 'into question by foregrounding an alternative set of arguments, images, key words and facts salient for people who share particular life experiences and the constraints and possibilities associated with belonging to a subordinated social group' (Kelly 2010: 292).

In the first section, we discuss the importance for a more inclusive democracy of changing communications between academics and journalists. We argue that it is not a matter of academic researchers enlightening journalists but, rather, of understanding the different rules of the game (Bourdieu 1990) under which academic researchers and journalists operate. In the second section, we explore what it means to be a public intellectual for journalists and academic researchers through comparing and contrasting dimensions of their respective fields (Bourdieu 1990, 2005), including understanding of reward systems, time, definition of research, audience and ideology. In the third section, we draw on the first two sections to suggest strategies for institutions and researchers who want to bridge the double divide.

Before developing our main argument, a caveat is in order. When we write of bridging the double divide, we do not mean to imply that a technocratic solution is at hand that would ease travel between two worlds. The metaphor of a physical bridge might suggest that the significant differences between academe and journalism could or should be eliminated. The nuance of our argument – that knowledge exchange between these two fields could be better understood and perhaps improved – is better captured by the metaphor of a musical bridge. Bridging in music consists of a contrasting section within a song that provides a transition from one major section to another; a bridge is a distinct entity. In classical music, for example, a bridge can help to smooth what might otherwise be an abrupt move from one key to another key; journalism and academe might be thought of as two different keys. In some cases, the bridge or shift between the two keys may be relatively subtle. Analogously, academics within the mainstream of, say, economics, are more likely to find that their views resonate within mainstream news media; conversely, radical economists, who start from premises that may be counter-intuitive to mainstream journalists' 'common sense', are likely to strike a discordant note, despite attempts at bridging (Schor 2004).

Brand enforcer or democratic facilitator?

There are tensions inherent in the calls for academics to be more engaged with diverse and larger publics. The call for public intellectuals to speak truth to power contrasts with 'knowledge transfer' as a branding activity that universities engage in to maximize their research dollars and attract students. We distance ourselves from knowledge mobilization driven solely by commercial interests, because we see it as eroding public education and civic values and spaces. We recognize the tendencies of today's universities toward the market model – 'from spin-off companies and patenting claims, to internal charging regimes, logo-branding, and the commercialisation of instruction' (McLennan, Osborne and Vaux 2005: 243). And yet we place ourselves among those seeking 'to raise broader questions about the social, economic, and political forces shaping the very terrain of higher education – particularly unbridled market forces, or racist and sexist forces that *unequally* value diverse groups of students [and, we would add, fields of study and forms of knowledge] within relations of academic power' (Giroux 2004: 501). We support the idea of *knowledge exchange* as the responsibility of academics to communicate beyond the peer-reviewed journal to diverse publics. Knowledge exchange should be an active process of interpretation; it provides space to challenge long-standing ways of looking at the world based in status quo sociopolitical and economic structures. We see this responsibility for knowledge exchange as central to the mission of any public university charged with, among other things, helping to form and educate citizens capable of contributing to and sustaining an inclusive democratic society.

There are multiple ways in which academics share their scholarly work with broader and multiple publics: teaching, consulting, textbook and trade book writing, collaborating with communities, and so on. We focus here on media engagement, because media constitute a key arena where groups engage in political discussion (while acknowledging that mainstream media in our actually existing democracy can operate more as a 'forum for communication among elites' [Schudson 2002: 263]). In our media-saturated world, popular media (albeit corporate-dominated) are the town square where ideas circulate, understandings of social inequalities can form and be challenged, and issues can be framed for public debate, dialogue and action.

In our review of the literature on knowledge exchange, we found relatively little attention paid (in the context of higher education) to media engagement compared with other modes of knowledge exchange. Critical literature on academic–media engagement has highlighted pressure on academics not to harm the university brand. Brass and Rowe (2009) examined media policies at Australian universities and found that they implicitly categorized academics as 'assets' or 'liabilities' based on whether they were likely to generate positive publicity and thus attract students without offending potential funders.

In this promotional culture, we understand the pressure on university administrators to maintain funding for their institutions through marketing and public relations. We need to insist, however, that these efforts be kept from encroaching on the role of academics to facilitate and contribute to debates that might be controversial and discordant. An important dimension of academic–media engagement is the potential circulation of counter-narratives that move beyond individualistic understandings of various inequities and provide support for policy alternatives.

Within each field – journalism and academia – there exist traditional and often hegemonic approaches to knowledge production and distribution that act, more often than we would care to admit, to obstruct the development of more democratic social relations. We acknowledge the huge structural differences between these two fields as well as the hierarchies within both. In the next section we will explore these differences and hierarchies using some concepts from Bourdieu.

Competition and collaboration: journalists and academics as knowledge workers

Rowe (2005) notes that both academics and journalists are 'knowledge workers' but that they play this role in different ways. Academics 'are seen to exercise command over specialised knowledge,' whereas journalists ' "translate", re-fashion and relay that knowledge on behalf of wider publics in the partial (in both senses) constitution of the contemporary public sphere' (p. 271). The fields of academia and journalism are changing, of course, in the face of financial constraints and other forces. Just as a new 'structure of diverse academic roles and career paths' is emerging in the academic profession in countries around the world (El-Khawas 2008: 34), so, too, the field of journalism and the very definition of *journalist* are being transformed by, for example, the rise of blogging and citizen journalism (e.g. Project for Excellence in Journalism 2010).

In the following comparison, we focus largely on professors and educational researchers at internationally ranked, Tier-I research universities; we assume that they work within similar parameters for what constitutes an academic in good standing. For journalists, we focus on news journalism in papers of record and national broadcasts, and although there are some differences in journalistic practices across Western countries, there is enough similarity in terms of what is considered good journalism to warrant the broad comparisons between journalism and academe that we make in this section (see e.g. Dimitrova and Strömbäck 2009; Kunelius 2006; Schudson 2002).

How academics think about research and how journalists think about translation of research is shaped by their professional education. Both sets of knowledge producers belong to what Bourdieu conceptualized as *fields* and *subfields*. A field such as social science or journalism, according to Bourdieu,

> is the site of actions and reactions performed by social agents endowed with permanent dispositions, partly acquired in their experience of these social fields. The agents react to these relations of forces, to the structures; they construct them, perceive them, form an idea of them, represent them to themselves, and so on.
>
> (Bourdieu 2005: 30)

By looking at fields, we are examining how the parameters of what is seen as 'good academic research' or 'good journalism' are embodied in professionals through membership in their respective field(s). To be accepted within a field requires acceptance of deep or implicit rules of the game; fields, however, do change. Individuals come with different backgrounds and ideological framings of scholarship and journalism and operate 'with a margin of freedom' (Bourdieu 2005: 30). They also come with different and fluid levels of power and influence within their field. For example, high-profile research academics engage in 'frequent media commentary, serving on national commissions, or writing as a public intellectual on issues of the day' (El-Khawas 2008: 37), whereas other academics may be too busy meeting institutional demands to communicate with broader public audiences. Within journalism, some beats (such as 'hard' news areas like politics and business) are more prestigious than other areas of news (such as education).

Reward systems

In academe, the reward structure is evident in the criteria for hiring, tenure, promotion and the awarding of grants and prizes. There are new pressures for academics to engage with media. This call for engagement, however, still takes place within an environment where traditional, discipline-based scholarship is highly prized by peers and the 'publish or perish' mantra continues its hold. Despite inducements by research-granting councils, recent evidence shows that Canadian universities have not moved significantly beyond traditional models of reward (Phaneuf et al. 2007). There are signs, though, that this may be changing or that new demands are being added to traditional ones (McLennan et al. 2005; Rowe and Brass 2008). In considering whether to engage with media, academics must balance the need to demonstrate specialized knowledge as well as a comprehensive understanding of their area against demands by funding and other agencies to show the 'impact' of their research outside of scholarly communities. Refusal to engage with media can result in a low profile and failure to obtain grants, but being seen as a 'media tart' (Rowe 2005: 284) can lead to a loss of credibility among one's academic peers.

Journalists compete for the attention of readers and advertisers, and journalism's reward structure centres around the field's definition of newsworthiness. Journalists frequently express frustration with arcane language used by academics (Stack 2010) and with ideas for stories that do not meet criteria needed to gain recognition within the field of journalism, such as novelty, impact, providing a fresh look at an old issue, usefulness to readers and timeliness.

There are similarities between journalistic and academic reward structures. Journalists and news organizations gain prestige when influential individuals within their field cite their stories; similarly, academics measure their success through various mechanisms of peer recognition. Furthermore, journalists are prized for obtaining 'scoops', but also for following the pack (Bennett et al. 2007: 180). Academics face the similar tension between pressure to say something new and different but that also resonates with intellectual fashions. There are also potential rewards for bridging the academic–journalistic divide: talking to academic sources is an excellent way for journalists to get a fresh perspective on a news issue; journalists, in turn, can help academics translate their ideas to reach wider audiences.

Time

Academic time has traditionally been measured in years, not hours. The time from conceiving a study, researching it and sending a manuscript out for review to time of publication easily amounts to years. Such a concept of time in journalism would lead to the collapse of an industry based on newness and advertising revenue. With the advent of the 24/7 news cycle, the Internet and cable channels, the temporal rhythms of journalism have become even faster. Warner (2002: 68) captures this 'more punctual and abbreviated' circulation of journalistic discourse with the metaphor of the *headline*, which he contrasts with the temporality of the *archive* that characterizes academe.

Journalism's shortened news cycle, combined with the hollowing out of newsrooms in many Western countries, means reporters have little time to find reliable sources and thus rely on formulas for quick news. The need for sources provides academics with an opportunity to engage with journalists and possibly influence how an issue is framed. Journalists' need for quick turnaround and efficient sound bites, however, goes against academics' scholarly practices that emphasize comprehensive development over timeliness. Most educational researchers do not have much practice in reducing their response to 30 seconds or a few well-chosen words.

Definitions of research

Bound up in these different temporal conditions are differences between the fields in terms of how journalists and academics define research. Academic enquiry is often systematic, in-depth, detail-oriented and rooted in the rigour of various disciplinary traditions. By contrast, journalists might begin their research with Google and a scan of LexisNexis citations to see what other journalists have had to say on a particular subject, followed by seeking out sources to speak to the issue.

These differences noted, there are affinities between what counts as evidence in news journalism and the sort of research that has the power to persuade within and beyond the academy. Empirical research, claiming to be objective (in the sense of detached and value-neutral), generalizable and statistically significant can be attractive to policy makers looking for clear answers to 'What works?'. In contests playing out in the media – or in decision-making bodies or courtrooms that are then reported in the media – partisans like to appeal to 'objective' research to support their preferred policy solutions. In countries throughout the world, there has been a resurgence of demand for 'rigorous' empirical studies to inform education policy, preferably with quantitatively measured outcomes (such as standardized test scores to measure student learning) and specifying interventions that can be used by policy-makers to improve those outcomes.

It should come as no surprise, then, that academics who are experts in this type of research and can speak authoritatively within the parameters set by the public debate among policy makers and other elite actors are often seen as the most credible sources for news stories. 'The positivism of journalism's inquiry and the concomitant attention to notions of facts, truth, and reality' (Zelizer 2004: 111) may lead mainstream journalists to see the work of academics adhering to other epistemological approaches as lacking rigour, objectivity or common sense. An Indigenous scholar, for example, who points to storytelling-based research or anti-colonial studies (rather than, say, survey research) as evidence of the need for change in the educational system may be discounted by mainstream editors. As one critical feminist scholar discovered in her encounters with mainstream media: 'Unreflexive, plainspoken positivist discourse is the prerequisite lingua franca for entry into a realm that misreads signs of subjectivity, let alone advocacy, as evidence of unprofessional, ideological "bias"' (Stacey 2004: 143).

Primary audiences

Journalists see that they are experts in their audience; they know what their audience will understand and care about. Of course, there are incentives within corporate media to imagine the audience as more customer than citizen, because the business model requires renting as many eyeballs as possible to demonstrate worth to advertisers. Still, the imagined primary audience for journalism is more general than that for academics, who tend to communicate primarily to specialized audiences that are often peers within their discipline or scholarly area. The differences in the imagined primary audience are reflected in the nature of the two fields' respective discourses. Journalists are experts in storytelling, and their communication style is more colloquial as compared with the expository, formal style of much academic communication.

Ideology

By virtue of the differences in how journalists and academics see their primary audience and define research, it becomes easier to understand why members within one field develop beliefs about the other as fundamentally different. In short, while journalists may mutter among themselves that academics are obtuse eggheads who can't speak in plain English, academics may be prone to imagining journalists as simplistic dilettantes who mangle their ideas. At issue in such clichéd images of each other are core beliefs: for academics, a belief in the importance of detail, precision, context sensitivity, depth and nuance; for journalists, a belief in getting to the bottom line and communicating that to a wide audience.

Guiding ideologies shape professional ethics and the direction of accountability for both journalists and academics. For journalists, the audience's right to know, as well as having sources speak openly 'on the record', are important; for academics, the protection of research participants, often through the anonymizing of sources, is paramount.

Despite these differences, many journalists and academics perceive public service, broadly defined, as central to their professional purpose. Members of both fields, for example, speak about contributing to, or helping to sustain, forums for public debate (Gardner, Csikszentmihalyi and Damon 2001). Both see themselves, in their loftier moments, as informing citizens and supporting democracy. Other values linked to promoting a more vibrant democracy include questioning orthodoxy ('speaking truth to power') and serving as watchdogs against abuses of power. Such civic ideals have motivated academics and journalists alike to enter their respective fields. Allied to these ideals are fundamental beliefs in academic freedom and freedom of the press, watchwords for maintaining professional autonomy and fending off attempts by government, corporations or other powerful agencies to censor and exercise undue influence.

A shared sense of democratic purpose, we believe, sometimes motivates knowledge workers to cross the first divide, but ideological differences within and across both fields make bridging the second divide much harder. Academics and journalists who are relatively comfortable with the status quo may have more difficulty seeing their own ideologies as anything other than common-sense assumptions circulating within popular culture. Long-Scott, an African-American reporter whose career dates from the civil rights era in the USA, for example, noted the capacity of middle-class journalists to filter out the importance of persistent class inequality:

> We journalists talked about urban violence as if race was by far the most important issue, and poverty, if it played a role at all, was a distant second. We talked about it this way because the popular culture talked about it this way, regardless of mountains of evidence to the contrary.
>
> Long-Scott (2004: 13)

Among critical journalists and scholars, there is awareness of structural biases in news and knowledge production more generally; yet it remains difficult to communicate critical work to broad audiences through the general press, particularly when the topics and perspectives stray too far from dominant culture experiences and understandings. It is ironic that complex argumentation aimed at democratizing knowledge can come across as inaccessible. 'Despite the more democratic aspirations of critical ideologies, the often counterintuitive social structural analyses that undergird them demand from audiences comparatively sophisticated, "elitist" intellectual skills' (Stacey 2004: 141; cf. Bourdieu's defense against charges of elitism, 1996b: 64–67).

For these reasons, it is difficult for academics to cross the second divide. As we discuss in the next section, however, new opportunities for engagement are opening up in the rapidly changing media landscape.

Strategies for institutions and researchers who want to bridge the double divide

Our research is focused on better understanding and improving relationships between academics and journalists. Due to space constraints and our role as academics, we focus here on strategies for academics engaging with journalists to translate research for diverse audiences. Media-training toolboxes that are sometimes made available to academics within their institutions often miss out on the specific challenges for those academics attempting to communicate across what we have been calling the double divide. Those whose research challenges common-sense beliefs, such as that society functions as a meritocracy or that schools are 'the great equalizer', need particular strategies for whether and how to engage with popular and other media to critique these dominant narratives and contribute to the development of counter-narratives. In this section, we attend to both specific and general strategies of academic–media engagement at multiple levels.

From the perspective of the individual academic contemplating media engagement, we outline here four broad recommendations, which are then followed by four strategies aimed at institutions. First: *assess the media landscape based on the communication goals and target the engagement accordingly.* The media system is not monolithic; it comprises corporate and government media (aka mainstream media), independent media outlets (e.g. e-zine news sites) and do-it-yourself media (such as blogs, vidcasts and podcasts). There are different forms of communication – most centrally, radio, television and print – as well as a range of ways to engage within each medium (e.g. acting as a news source, writing an 'op-ed' or opinion-editorial, issuing a press release or contributing to a blog). Each venue and means carries its own rules of engagement that shape opportunities and risks for academics. A guest appearance on corporate television news, for example, provides a wide audience, but very limited time to develop a complex argument and, often, a strong prior framing of the issue under discussion. Writing an opinion piece for the newspaper carries fewer risks of being misunderstood or placed within a frame of someone else's choosing, but the op-ed may not easily find a home within a high-circulation outlet (see Borer 2006). Thus, it's important to research the terrain, much as one would give careful thought to the best form and venue for communicating scholarly work.

Second, *understand the audience and frame the message with that audience in mind.* Once academics have a venue and a means of engagement in mind, they need to assess their audience, which includes the outlet's intended public and what will interest its viewers, readers or listeners. A related task is becoming aware of the zeitgeist. Academics can ask themselves questions like these, for example:

- Given what is going on and being discussed, what do you bring to the conversation?
- Can you tie your argument to current headlines and, if so, what specific expertise can you bring to bear on the subject?

Answering these questions will help academics arrive at their news 'hook', a term journalists use to indicate the critical bit of information or framing that makes something newsworthy. To arrive at a hook, academics need to think about what is at stake or why their targeted public would care about the message they hope to convey.

As discussed earlier, an important dimension of newsworthiness is providing a fresh perspective on an issue. Framing orients audiences (and media producers) to particular interpretations of issues and not others. Mainstream news reporters and editors, for example, often draw upon and reinforce the frames of 'troubled and troubling youth' (Kelly 2006), whereas critical scholars have tried to reframe the issues as youth 'at promise' (rather than 'at risk') or early school leavers as 'pushouts' (rather than 'dropouts'). Of course, such counter-frames call the status quo into question, and this dominant framing can be so powerful that speaking from a position that has been marginalized, ignored or belittled requires extra work.

Another key component of newsworthiness is timeliness. As an analytic tool for thinking through the best time to bring forth story prospects or to serve as a source for a media story, it helps to divide academic–journalist engagement into two types and phases. One type is proactive, where the academic approaches a journalist about a possible story. The story idea might be based on the academic's just-completed research project, or key off an annual event such as the beginning of the school year (e.g. findings related to children or schooling). The other type of engagement is reactive; the academic is contacted by a journalist for his or her expertise. This, in turn, can be broken into two phases (Cook 2005; Dimitrova and Strömbäck 2009). In the *news-discovery phase*, journalists might have a broad assignment, say on the sex education curriculum, with no particular angle developed yet. In the later *news-gathering phase*, journalists are usually on a tight deadline, have already developed a particular perspective (e.g. abstinence only) and are contacting an academic to serve as an 'objective' source to validate the journalist's framing of the story. In this latter phase, it is more difficult for an academic to introduce ideas that seem outside the realm of journalistic common sense.

Third, academics need to *assess their social location and perspective in relation to their targeted venue*. One resource for thinking through issues related to social location, power and representation is the work by feminist, postcolonial and other critical scholars on the concept of positionality. Alcoff (1988), for example, theorized a 'politics of positionality,' arguing that key aspects of people's identity – such as their gender, race, class, disability and age – 'are markers of relational positions rather than essential qualities. Their effects and implications change according to context' (Tetreault 1993: 139). Many of the challenges of being an insider and an outsider as a researcher vis-à-vis various communities (see e.g. Brayboy and Deyhle 2000) are analogous for academic–media engagement. Aboriginal scholars hoping to write for a mainstream outlet can anticipate pressures by mainstream editors to speak on behalf of an entire community or to speak only about Aboriginal issues, regardless of their research focus.

To give another example drawn from our own experiences with the media: a reporter writing a feature for a local corporate newspaper on the Spice Girls' reunion tour contacted Deirdre. She anticipated a polarized storytelling approach and sought to head off being framed as the 'no fun' feminist in two ways. First, she marshalled relevant facts from her interview-based study with girls, namely that two-thirds of the girls associated the phrase 'girl power' with the Spice Girls; and many had been fans but also critiqued the musical group as commercialized and overly body-focused. Second, she formulated a clear message: the Spice Girls do not challenge institutionalized gender inequities (they espouse feminism lite), but fans can simultaneously enjoy them and ask critical questions about what they stand for. In this way, Deirdre tried to avoid feeding into caricatures of feminism that currently circulate as common sense.

Fourth, *take the long view*. For each encounter with media, academics need to have one or two key messages. If writing an op-ed, for example, they should try to lead with the most provocative way of asserting the single, clear point they want the reader to take away. (Editors don't want 'Everything I know and have been thinking lately about the following subject.') If asked to be a source for a journalist on a topic within their area of expertise, they should choose their battle; too much critique of the dominant perspective or main-stream news coverage may be overwhelming and not allow them the time to develop their main points, with the result that their intended message gets diluted or ignored in the resulting story. If they are part of a group with a communication plan, they can draw on complementary strengths of different members and seek out other opportunities to get related arguments into the media.

Fifth, *develop a communication plan and revisit it on a regular basis*. A number of prominent scholars (Bourdieu 1996a; Ryan 2004; Altheide 2009) have suggested the need for academics to coordinate their efforts to disseminate their ideas and participate more effectively in mediated public discussions. A communication plan is a process of collectively thinking through how they want to explain research to diverse publics. The foundation for a communication plan is based in the four strategies discussed above.

Sixth, at the institutional level, *intervene in the academic reward structure*. We are not suggesting that universities do more to create academic media superstars; more could be done, however, to recognize scholars who participate in diverse ways and who take the risk of challenging the status quo. Universities might consider creating an award that showcases dissemination of research that has been ignored or frequently misrepresented.

Seventh, *implement procedures to protect academic freedom*. University admin-istrators might, for example, expand conflict-of-interest policies to include conflicts that the university (stemming from overly zealous concern over its brand) might have that infringe upon academic-media engagement.

Eighth, *challenge hidden assumptions about who should talk to the media*. Altheide (2009) and Bourdieu (1996a) both believe 'top scholars' (Altheide) or 'competent intellectuals' (Bourdieu) and professional organizations can rise above political bias. We need to be mindful, however, of how gender, race and disability, for example, filter who gets invited to participate on the 'ad hoc standing committee of top researchers . . . to provide informed press releases from academic organizations' (Altheide 2009: 21).

Conclusion

It is important that academics seek to share their insights and knowledge through media with publics beyond the academy. Academic–media engagement is often ignored or marginalized as a mode of knowledge exchange. We have argued that academics who care about public education as central to democracy must go beyond media critique to pursue strategies for intervention, including engaging with journalists. This is because media constitute a key arena where groups engage in discussions about research, educational policy and politics.

Within the fields of academe and journalism, there are people – dealing with the double divide – who have proved adept at crossing over in either direction. These individuals understand the challenges but have found spaces and means to intervene. We hope this chapter will prompt more interest in examining how academics, through their engagement with journalists, can deepen their understandings of how to communicate with large audiences of citizens.

References

Alcoff, L. (1988) 'Cultural feminism versus post-structuralism: the identity crisis in feminist theory', *Signs*, 13(3): 405–36.

Altheide, D.L. (2009) 'War and mass mediated evidence', *Cultural Studies – Critical Methodologies*, 9(1): 14–22.

Bennett, W.L., Lawrence, R.G. and Livingston, S. (2007) *When the Press Fails: Political Power and the News Media from Iraq to Katrina*, Chicago: University of Chicago Press.

Borer, D.A. (2006) 'Rejected by the New York Times? Why academics struggle to get published in national newspapers', *International Studies Perspectives*, 7(3): v–vi.

Bourdieu, P. (1990) *The Logic of Practice*, Stanford, CA: Stanford University Press.

—— (1996a) 'Intellectuals and the internationalization of ideas: an interview with Pierre Bourdieu', *International Journal of Contemporary Sociology*, 33(2): 237–54.

—— (1996b) *On Television*, trans. P.P. Ferguson, New York: New Press.

—— (2005 [1994]) 'The political field, the social science field and the journalistic field', in R. Benson and E. Neveu (eds), *Bourdieu and the Journalistic Field*, Cambridge: Polity.

Brass, K. and Rowe, D. (2009) 'Knowledge limited: public communication, risk and university media policy', *Continuum: Journal of Media and Cultural Studies*, 23(1): 53–76.

Brayboy, B.M. and Deyhle, D. (2000) 'Insider–outsider: researchers in American Indian communities', *Theory into Practice*, 39(3): 163–69.

Cook, T.E. (2005) *Governing with the News: The News Media as a Political Institution*, 2nd edn, Chicago: University of Chicago Press.

Dimitrova, D.V. and Strömbäck, J. (2009) 'Look who's talking', *Journalism Practice*, 3(1): 75–91.

El-Khawas, E. (2008) 'Emerging academic identities: a new research and policy agenda', in A. Amaral, I. Bleiklie and C. Musselin (eds), *From Governance to Identity*, Dordrecht: Springer.

Gardner, H., Csikszentmihalyi, M. and Damon, W. (2001) *Good Work: When Excellence and Ethics Meet*, New York: Basic Books.

Giroux, H.A. (2004) 'Public pedagogy and the politics of neo-liberalism: making the political more pedagogical', *Policy Futures in Education*, 2(3): 494–503.

Kelly, D.M. (2006) 'Frame work: helping youth counter their misrepresentation in media', *Canadian Journal of Education*, 29(1): 27–48.

—— (2010) 'Media representation and the case for critical media education', in M.C. Courtland and T. Gambell (eds), *Literature, Media, and Multiliteracies in Adolescent Language Arts*, Vancouver, BC: Pacific Education Press.

Kelly, D.M. and Stack, M. (2011) Lost in Translation? The possibilities and dilemmas of media-academic engagement, paper presented at American Educational Research Association, New Orleans, April 2011.

Kunelius, R. (2006) 'Good journalism', *Journalism Studies*, 7(5): 671–90.

Long-Scott, A. (2004) 'Understanding race, class and urban violence: why journalists can't do more to help us understand', *Race, Gender & Class*, 11(1): 6–22.

McLennan, G., Osborne, T. and Vaux, J. (2005) 'Universities in the "condition of publicity": how LSE engages with the wider world', *Globalisation, Societies & Education*, 3(3): 241–60.

Phaneuf, M.-R., Lomas, J., McCutcheon, C., John, C. and Douglas, W. (2007) 'Square pegs in round holes: the relative importance of traditional and nontraditional scholarship in Canadian universities', *Science Communication*, 28(4): 501–18.

Project for Excellence in Journalism (2010) *The State of the News Media 2010: An Annual Report on American Journalism*, New York: Columbia University Graduate School of Journalism. Online, available: www.stateofthemedia.org/2010/printable_overview_chapter.htm (accessed 3 June 2010).

Rowe, D. (2005) 'Working knowledge encounters: academics, journalists and the conditions of cultural labour', *Social Semiotics*, 15(3): 269–88.

Rowe, D. and Brass, K. (2008) 'The uses of academic knowledge: the university in the media', *Media, Culture & Society*, 30(5): 677–98.

Ryan, C. (2004) 'Can we be compañeros?' *Social Problems*, 51(1): 110–13.

Schor, J. (2004) 'From obscurity to *People Magazine*', *Social Problems*, 51(1): 121–24.

Schudson, M. (2002) 'The news media as political institutions', *Annual Review of Political Science*, 5(1): 249–69.

Stacey, J. (2004) 'Marital suitors court social science spin-sters: the unwittingly conservative effects of public sociology', *Social Problems*, 51(1): 131–45.

Stack, M. (2007) 'Constructing "common sense" policies for schools: the role of journalists', *International Journal of Leadership in Education*, 10(3): 247–64.

—— (2010) 'Spin as symbolic capital: the fields of journalism and education policy-making', *International Journal of Leadership in Education*, 13(2): 107–19.

Tetreault, M.K.T. (1993) 'Classrooms for diversity: rethinking curriculum and pedagogy', in J.A. Banks and C.A.M. Banks (eds), *Multicultural Education: Issues and Perspectives*, 2nd edn, Boston, MA: Allyn and Bacon.

Warner, M. (2002) 'Publics and counterpublics', *Public Culture*, 14(1): 49–90.

Zelizer, B. (2004) 'When facts, truth, and reality are God-terms: on journalism's uneasy place in cultural studies', *Communication and Critical/Cultural Studies*, 1(1): 100–19.

Chapter 10

Ethics and experiments with art in mobilizing educational research

Tara Fenwick

Knowledge mobilization of educational research is often discussed in terms of finding creative ways to engage diverse public users in research. The use of art forms to both produce and represent research knowledge has attracted considerable interest in my field of adult education (see e.g. Butterwick and Selman 2003; Clover and Stalker 2007), perhaps particularly in the service of engaging and representing those who have experienced marginalization or oppression. Of course, art-based educational research is by now a well-developed field. Debates about purposes and approaches have been wide-ranging since Eisner's (1981) first promotions of 'artistic' inquiry as distinct from 'scientific', but equally powerful. The practices of art and of research are often seen as enacting very different worlds, with different and sometimes conflicting languages, criteria, and audiences. Mixing these practices – or, more funda-mentally, these ways of knowing – opens tensions and ethical questions that ultimately double back to challenge central assumptions about what comprises research, and what is most valuable in educational research. This chapter tells the story of what can happen when researchers who describe themselves as non-artists attempt to work with art forms for purposes of knowledge mobilization.

Arts-based educational researchers have argued that, through their aesthetic languages, the arts can illuminate particular insights in the study of educational phenomena (Barone and Eisner 2006; Eisner 2006). Inquiry working with art typically incorporates design elements, such as plot, images, and expressive language, to stimulate imagination. Much debate has focused upon different approaches, and how different artistic modalities illuminate unique 'ineffable' educational phenomena and affect audiences (Barone and Eisner 2006). New forms continually arise, such as the increasingly popular a/r/tography (see Irwin 2004), which attends to the spaces in-between research, art, and education, focuses on the complexity of relations among people, things and meanings, and highlights shifts in new awareness. As the field has grown and developed, it has deepened its own questions to theorize arts-based research. O'Donoghue (2009), for example, argues for moving beyond questions about how research might both include artwork and produce substantive, useful results, towards questions about the relations of arts-based research with professional fields of art and artists.

In the story that unfolds below it will become clear that the educational researchers, myself and my colleagues, were not much aware of these rich issues when we first thought to use art as a way to engage the public in our study. Nor were we working with art as part of the actual inquiry process (and therefore we are not claiming here that what we did was 'arts-based educational research'). Our study had explored the experiences of women garment workers in Canada. The use of art in knowledge mobilization activities for this study was not developed until the data gathering and analysis were nearly complete. The art form that we chose to employ was theatre. Ours was an example of performed theatre, not participatory theatre such as has been used in other studies of workplace practices to engage research participants in producing knowledge. For example, Quinlan (2010) explored workplace bullying practices using theatre processes that engaged health care workers in reflecting on the history and structure of such practices, and developing alternate solutions. However, in our case, the theatre was assembled for an audience outside the research participants: we attempted to represent some themes and even participant voices from our study in the form of a short play. We added songs and sounds recorded in the garment factory, and backcloth projections of work in the factory, then presented the play to various academic and practitioner audiences. The results were sometimes puzzling, sometimes painful, but always provocative. For us, it was an experience not only of learning something of the specific problems of working with art as non-art specialists, but of grappling with important questions at stake in all activities purposed as knowledge mobilization: questions that have for many years now been central in debates about the politics of representation in qualitative research. The following discussion briefly describes the study, then tells our story of preparing and presenting the drama, with all its troubling remembrances and questions that continue to haunt.

Women's learning in garment work

The research project focused on work and learning experiences of immigrant women garment workers at a large jeans-making factory, both on the job and in English language training programs offered at the plant. The plant was the GWG (Great Western Garment) Company, which opened in 1911 in Edmonton, Alberta. Acquired by Levi-Strauss in 1961, the plant was closed permanently and operations moved to Haiti in December 2004. Our team not only interviewed workers, managers, union stewards, and plant-based educators, but also videotaped garment production operations at the plant, and studied historic archives including hundreds of photographs depicting the factory's activities throughout the twentieth century, old advertisements, union records, and different garments produced over the years. Interviews with the workers, mostly seamstresses, explored their worklife at GWG/Levi's, their relationships, the nature of the work community, and their responses to the many plant changes, including learning opportunities over time. Many had been employed by GWG/Levi's for two or three decades, sometimes performing the same task for years at a time (one woman introduced herself as, 'I'm buttonhole').

By way of brief context, studies of the Canadian garment industry have shown it to be a job ghetto of low wages and status for women (Steedman 1997). In Canada, about 50% of garment workers traditionally have been new immigrants, and this category of immigrant women has served to commodify them to employers, reinforcing their class position in providing cheap, docile labor in exploitive conditions often permeated with racism and sexism (Ng 2002). While many Canadian garment factories became unionized by the mid-twentieth century to offer stable employment and decent wages and working conditions, globalization brought a widespread closure of these plants in the 1990s, with a loss of 33,000 jobs in Canada between 1989–93. Garment workers after years of employment in garment piecework lacked training to do little else, and thus often were forced into precarious employment as home-based sewers dependent upon an unregulated network of 'jobbers' that supplied large clothing distributors.

As we spoke with the workers, many of whom had immigrated directly from China, Vietnam, India, Eastern Europe, and parts of Africa, we were moved by their personal identifications with the GWG/Levi's plant. Many spoke about the strong bonds they had formed with the other women. They learned instrumental skills of managing big industrial machines and the labor structure of piecework of course, but more important to them was learning to survive and support one another at the plant. They shared vivid stories about strategies they had learned to outwit supervisors and piecework structures, but also to adapt to the grinding conditions by turning their bodies into machines. They experienced what some might call political or 'critical' learning about their rights and the power of solidarity, while simultaneously learning to be compliant with the company's hierarchies, even bearing allegiance to the firm and its managers. Several articles were published from this study in 'traditional' academic disseminatory fashion about the difficult conditions and exploitative potential of garment piecework, the solidarity and sociality among these women, the balancing act of plant educators, and the contradictory learning threads woven through the women's tales of survival (Fenwick 2007a, b).

Experiments with 'art'

However, our research group wanted to go further to invite our academic audiences as well as the public into the close personal power of these workers' stories. We obtained a bit of funding to create a large free-standing display of the historic photos overlaid with participant quotes, which was developed by a professional media company. This was mounted at various locations such as May Week events (celebrating labor history) and City Hall. While the display looked impressive, it could not convey more than a gloss of the study's context and the workers' tales. We were unsure of its impact or relevance to casual passers-by, or the sense they made of it.

So we also decided to make it into a play to present to the Congress of Learned Societies in Canada. This 'play' was a very modest reader's theatre script, which we thought might be a straightforward art form suitable for non-dramatists like ourselves. That is, we read the script aloud while seated, in the voices of the workers. The reading was supplemented by bits of action that we invented, sound effects from the plant, and historic plant photos projected onto a screen behind us. The script was entirely constructed from the actual words of the workers in the interview transcripts, and grounded in the themes of learning, struggle, solidarity, contradiction, and the role of plant educators that were identified through academic analysis of the interviews.

We first showed the play to the people we had interviewed, mainly for their approval and corrections. This event turned into perhaps the most unexpected reward of our study. The workers and educators seemed delighted: laughing, pointing out themselves and their friends in the portrayals, elaborating the stories, sharing different meanings and emotional responses to the portrayals. The next performance was for education scholars at the Congress conference, after which we were invited to present the play to various community educators and immigrant service agencies. The community responses were also compelling and immediate: audience members appeared to identify closely with the portrayals and the issues, and the drama launched discussions around workers' learning, educators' roles and agency supports. Finally we recorded the presentation on DVD to make it more easily available to such audiences. In other words, I believe we were engaging the spirit of 'knowledge mobilization', or thought we were: attempting to communicate research findings in creative ways that truly engage public hearts and minds, and possibly inspire action around important social issues.

However, several messy issues lurked in this mobilizing process. A fuller explanation was published in *Labour/Le Travail* (Fenwick 2007b), but a few are useful to highlight here. First are the difficulties encountered in simply borrowing art forms to represent research findings. Art does not exist as a neutral form into which substance can be poured, and art forms such as theatre have deep integrities that texture the conception of the content. In our case, the dramatic script was developed after the formal research analyses were complete. What we did not fully appreciate were the challenges involved in constructing coherent story lines and engaging, consistent characters. Five character voices were created to present composites of the GWG/Levi workers and educators: excerpts from various transcripts were collapsed into each one of the five voices. Incidents from different time periods were juxtaposed to focus on the workers' personal experiences of these events, rather than on chronological plant developments. However, as was pointed out by arts-based educational researchers to whom we presented, the jumping timeline was confusing and the characters appeared contrived: structural faults that tended to obscure the power of the original experiences. Further, the action we had inserted violated the form of readers' theatre in ways that ultimately were somewhat incoherent. One dramatist at this gathering suggested that the presentation was 'only about 10% art'. This comment invites a host of considerations. The judgment of good or bad art must be located against criteria of technique, aesthetics, and theme appropriate to the form and purposes of art. Are these criteria equally appropriate when judging knowledge mobilization that begins from research findings and draws from art forms? And to what extent ought we to apply such criteria, presumably alongside criteria of rigor, validity, significance, and so on that, for many, characterize 'good' research? The application of percentage suggests that art-mediated research representation may be part art and part research, perhaps to be adjudicated proportionately in either field. Such judgments still do not broach issues of impact through mobilizing knowledge: how can such impact be understood and assessed in activities such as this little drama, whether or not it was bad art? Barone and Eisner (2006: 102) suggest criteria for appraising arts-based educational research that move more closely to this issue of impact: its 'illuminating effect', its 'generativity', or capacity to stimulate questions, and its incisiveness, addressing educationally significant issues.

Second are the practical difficulties in adopting unfamiliar formats to communicate research findings. The performers were not trained actors, but myself alongside volunteer education graduate students. We were surprised by the amount of rehearsal required to attain even a modest level of performance quality. The successful coordination of music, sound effects, and photo slides with our reading was also far more difficult to achieve than we had realized.

Third, we made the mistake of producing the DVD by simply hiring a video production company to film our live readers' theatre. We did not understand the different nuanced distinctions and demands of theatre and film, and we ended up using what some may consider rather banal tropes of docudrama in assembling the final product. The result was a little static, to be truthful, and, without the intimate power of live performance, the DVD amplified our rather naïve readings.

One important lesson was that we had neglected to collaborate closely with performance artists. We didn't know how much we didn't know—about art and art forms, about the tremendous labor required to develop such representations, about audience and the mirrors of interplay set into motion through art presentations, and about the multiple effects of representation when woven with research. These issues and their lack of recognition perhaps arise in much 'knowledge mobilization' activity more broadly.

Considering ethical questions

But there are further important issues, ethical ones, haunting our experiment with art and research. The first has to do with what happens to collective and individual histories and their tensions when they become structured according to the genre demands of theatre. The women workers made it clear that they wanted the play presented as widely as possible, to show their stories to others. Yet whose collective story were we showing, and for what ends? A troubling part of the script-assembling process was choosing those pieces of transcript that seemed to 'play' best, dramatically. As Barone and Eisner (2006: 100) point out, in arts-based representation of research, 'meaning is achieved and enhanced as portions of the world are construed, organized and disclosed [and] . . . may take liberties with the world as it is seen'. An example is one scene where the women shut down all the sewing machines in protest over equipment that would not handle the new thin fabric, forcing endless seam rippings that slowed down their piece production and cost them wages. Although this was only a small story in terms of the women's remembrances of factory life, it was more powerful and easy to invoke with a few quotes than the significant long-term and subtle resistances that they began to incorporate into their daily routines as they learned English. Conversely, some important issues were omitted entirely. One was (most) women's enthusiasm for the oppressive factory and its managers, citing the annual picnics and a sense of 'family' that they associated with the plant. These complexities seemed far more difficult to broach effectively through drama than through more familiar modes like expository critical discourse.

The script began to take a shape of its own. This narrative arc became driven by the more dramatic conflicts involved in the women's work lives, perhaps in ways that arguably distorted them. For example, we sometimes chose a broader sweep of vocal juxtapositions rather than a deeper focus on one nuanced aspect. To illustrate this (see Figure 10.1), the play's opening is a series of decontextualized, layered voices uttering different women's descriptions of the factory. These descriptions seemed particularly moving in their matter-of-fact inevitability, invoking the profoundly numbing conditions better than would have a close exploration of one woman's journey into that life serving a sewing machine. Yet even in scholarly articles about this research, the women's stories were subjected to an interpretive process of data reduction and selection, and each article focused upon small bits of story. Of course, this process, including the problematic practice of representing participant 'voices' through snippets of quotations, has been widely debated among qualitative researchers, and most endeavour to find representational approaches that honor participants' tales without becoming captured within their worldview. These activities of compression and re-construction became uncomfortably visible when the women's voices become embodied in a literary recreation.

Actors stand facing audience, in front of stools.

*Four are in a row in middle, in two pairs. The fifth is Down Right
(Woman 4 – educator). All except Woman 4 wear aprons.*

*Silence. Then bell – all except Educator whirl around, sit on stool, heads down,
back to audience. Educator goes over to her stool and sits, facing audience.
Machine sounds up.*

*Projected on large screen behind actors – photos of factory, early days.
Projected photos continue to change throughout the presentation, showing
sewing workers at the machines, at lunch, at company picnics, union activities,
from 1930s to present, etc.)*

Actors turn around quickly to face audience only when speaking.

Woman 1: I walk to there. When I get there, punch the timecard, punch these
papers, punch those papers, then I go closer to sew station to wait
for bell.

Woman 2: Of course you couldn't go up until the bell went and you got to
your machines and you got your work. A bundle girl would bring
the work. We would get quite upset if the bundle girl didn't bring
the work on time because you just wanted to work.

Woman 1: I sew clothes, sew till coffee time and then I stop, go to washroom
15 minutes. Go back to work then until 12 PM. Eat lunch.
Afternoon 3 PM again is coffee time. Drink something, go to
washroom. Then work again. 4:30 work is done.

Woman 2: You went by the bells.

Woman 5: My first day at work was a revelation. All I could see was a sea of
sewing machines. At each one a bent over operator was working
as if her life depended on it. All the operators were women. No one
was saying anything.

Woman 4: Mass assembly operations are mind-numbing. You cannot afford
to think of anything but one, get it done right get it done fast, two
don't hurt yourself. And you cannot afford to let your mind
wander. And so the mind loses its ability to think.

Woman 1: The first day, standing there, the feet were all swollen. I didn't
know how – after work – didn't know how to walk.

Woman 3: Everything was dark, the floor was dark, the walls were dark, there
was no daylight, artificial light. You didn't get out of your chair,

Woman 5: And I remember being hot in there, there was no air-conditioning I
know that. I hated it, it was an awful place. I just couldn't be shut
up like that, it was like being in jail almost. Because I was sitting at
a, at a, at a machine.

Woman 2: I remember it being stuffy. You would see layers of dust every day,
layers of – well not dust, but you know the dust from the sewing.
. . . Fuzz, yeah that's it. And it would cover everything. Even your
clothes.

Figure 10.1 Scene one

However, there is also a new space and new possibilities opened when researchers begin to engage their data afresh through an art form. The data becomes re-enfleshed, after having been stripped from the workers' bodies and enactments, and frozen in digital moments in transcripts hoarded in our hard drives. The re-encounter of researcher and researched enables multiple recognitions, such as our first discomfort at hearing the interview participants' words come out of our own mouths – and releases, from notions of validity and rigorous analysis into creative emergence with the data. Not only did we as researchers re-learn the (re)search, we re-searched what truths were at play, what truths held sway, to whom, and for what purposes. Obviously, in terms of knowledge mobilization, the questions of which/whose truth and what truth of mobility (in what direction) is judged in representation are rather more complex than existing definitions may allow.

A second ethical issue has to do with the obligations of the researcher/artists to participants when representing their experience. For example, while our academic audience appeared appreciative, some felt that the play needed to present a more robust critique of the labor process, the garment company, and educators' complicity in the exploitation of garment work. Not untypically, very little of this critique was extant in the interview transcripts. We had already inserted text into the final slides of the presentation that told about the plant shut-down in 2004, throwing 450 garment workers out of work, including all of the interviewees. The company moved operations to Haiti where a subsequent workers' strike was violently quelled by hired militants. Thus our final scene of the play, where the women workers claimed that working for this company was like being part of a family, was juxtaposed against slides telling the larger story. But the women interviewees asked for all of this text to be taken out. They wanted the play to end showing how much they loved their jobs and the plant. The interpretive tension here between participant and researcher perspectives on the stories is a familiar one in many qualitative studies employing critical social theory, where the so-called truth of oppression wielded by researchers embedded in hegemonic research relations constitutes an additional act of oppression. In our case, we ultimately decided to retain the slide text in our live performances. We also held follow-up discussions with audiences to explain the women's unhappiness with this text, the problematics of critical analysis, and our own conflicted allegiance to both their personal tales as well as the wider collective tale of their location in the political economy. In the DVD representation of our performance, we finally eliminated the text. We felt that, without the possibility of engaging viewers in dialogue about these tensions, we could not simply refuse the women's insistence to own at least part of the truths at play. This struggle illuminates the complex considerations in choosing a vehicle for knowledge mobilization: different modes invite different forms of engagement, with different ethical obligations – obligations to audience and researchers as well as to the research participants.

In considering our next steps, we found ourselves acknowledging the capacity of a play, even a problematic and modest venture like ours, to exhort strong audience identification and response. The ethical question of whose authority should be allowed most influence on the story/stories circulating amidst such heightened response becomes critical, but it will be answered differently according to the governing logic and its languages – whether of art and aesthetics, critical social science, narrative, ethnomethodology, reflective dialogue, or many others that have been invoked throughout this discussion. Moving beyond issues of epistemic authority and assessment, a question more to the point in the very activity of knowledge mobilization ought to focus upon what new spaces for connecting people to learn from each other, and what new forms of human engagement in knowledge, are enabled through the entanglements of 'art' and 'research'. In exploring this question, we found that the boundary separating these domains folds in upon itself – but not to the point of dissolving distinct realms of thought and expression. Amidst the folds, hybrid forms of inquiry and knowledge engagement may be possible that cross realms of imagination, aesthetics, and social science without distorting or reducing them.

Re-considering knowledge mobilization

Knowledge mobilization in action surely must form a circulation of multiple meanings and responsibilities, in multiple directions – not just for diverse users, but also for the knowledge producers. For us, the whole experience of constructing the drama provided a unique interpretive pathway into the data, yielding fresh insights about the workers' learning. We learned that a drama can engage viewers with an emotional power and immediacy that moves quickly into dialogue of key issues. Vastly different audience responses can be stimulated, and these oppositions opened new questions and perspectives for us. Indeed, our experience of performing these workers' voices, reading their words aloud again and again, brings a new appreciation for the subjective worlds within these words. In this way, researchers, research participants, and audience members participated at various times as both users and producers of knowledge.

However, we also learned through these experiences of knowledge mobilization that aesthetic creation is a field of its own. Our presentation to the arts-based researchers helped us to realize that we had focused all of our efforts on the social science of our research, and had turned to art forms only in the most superficial ways to provide a vehicle of communication. For some of them, at least, we had produced 'bad art', but still our play had managed to rouse intense and emotional responses to the garment workers' experiences – and not only among academic audiences desperate for respite from talking-head presentations. One lesson that may be derived from artists justifiably defending their expertise is that researchers who aspire to incorporate arts media into their dissemination of findings, while avoiding bad art, need to develop knowledge of fine arts. Or better yet, we might collaborate directly with artists in the conception and conduct, as well as the representation, of research, as Butterwick and Selman (2003) did in their research using participatory theatre. Indeed, in considering knowledge mobilization, we might do much more to build collaboration not only with artists and study participants, but also with others working in diverse realms of public engagement (social activists, journalists, graphic designers, chefs, therapists, gardeners), with whom we might explore new hybrids of both knowledge development processes and representational forms.

These issues ultimately foreground important questions about all activities of knowledge mobilization and its injunctions, which tend to encourage alternative modes and media of communication that can reach out to diverse public audiences in ways that academic publications may not. Such communication practices, whether arts-based, technology-enhanced, or workshop-oriented, require highly specialized expertise in various domains – copy-writing, graphics design, marketing, various fine arts, digital media production, etc. Social science researchers cannot be expected to develop such specialized skills, or perhaps even to understand them sufficiently to recruit and manage effectively in the research process. Further, even simple uses of these alternate forms are expensive in time, equipment, and funding, particularly when we figure in the lengthy collaborative time required. Finally, the effective representation, communication, even 'mobilization' of research through alternate forms is not a novelty to be tacked onto the end of a research process, but must be woven throughout the conception and conduct of research. In other words, if taken seriously, knowledge mobilization will require dedicated time in design, development, and collaboration, by networks of individuals bringing various specialized expertise. One can even imagine the influx of new 'knowledge mobilization consultants' who are skilled at pulling together teams of communication/ graphics specialists and liaising with researchers to weave processes of research and its mobilization. The prospect of this weaving inevitably should make us pause: what then is educational research, and how does the knowledge mobilization process affect systematic inquiry? Who decides which representation is the most truthful? Even more daunting are familiar ethical questions in research that acquire new significance when we understand how activities of knowledge mobilization and the inevitable interdisciplinarity they entail erase old distinctions between knowledge 'producers' and 'users': *What* knowledge is ultimately mobilized? Whose knowledge? For whose purposes? And what of knowledge unknown to the researchers that becomes mobilized, among themselves as well as other participants and audiences? This is not to refuse a serious consideration of knowledge mobilization working with art and other media. But we must acknowledge the new worlds we are entering when we do, their complex languages, and the ethical issues that arise. As O'Donoghue (2009: 366) concludes,

> A commitment to the arts as an approach to educational research brings many challenges, but equally it brings responsibilities. It requires us to think deeply about how we understand, articulate, and engage in educational research; how we ask and hope to answer questions, as well as the types of questions we might ask.

Acknowledgements

Contributions to this research were made by Edmonton Community Foundation, Provincial Archives of Alberta, Joan Schiebelbein, Catherine Cole, Lan Chan Marples, Don Bouzek, and Melanie Wong. I am indebted to the women garment workers, and to those who helped present the drama.

This chapter is revised and updated from an article, 'Considering knowledge mobilization in educational research: what knowledge, what mobilities, what responsibilities?' published in *Educational Insights*, 2008, 12(2). Comments by Rita Irwin and Lynne Fels on an earlier draft are gratefully acknowledged.

References

Barone, T. & Eisner, E. (2006) 'Arts-based educational research', in J. Green, G. Camilli and P. Elmore (eds), *Handbook of Complementary Methods in Education Research*, New York: Lawrence Erlbaum Associates, pp. 93–107.

Butterwick, S. and Selman, J. (2003) 'Deep listening in a feminist popular theatre project: upsetting the position of audience in participatory education', *Adult Education Quarterly*, 54 (1): 7–22.

Clover, D. and Stalker, J. (eds) (2007) *The Arts and Social Justice: re-crafting adult education and community cultural leadership*, London: National Institute of Adult Continuing Education.

Eisner, E.W. (1981) 'On the differences between scientific and artistic approaches to qualitative research', *Educational Researcher*, 10 (4): 5–9.

Eisner, E. (2006) 'Does arts-based research have a future?' *Studies in Art Education*, 48 (1): 9–18.

Fenwick, T. (2008) 'Women learning in garment work: solidarity and sociality', *Adult Education Quarterly*, 58 (2): 110–28.

—— (2007a) 'Tightrope walkers and solidarity sisters: critical educators in the garment industry', *International Journal of Lifelong Education*, 26 (3): 315–28l.

—— (2007b) 'Learning on the line: voices of garment workers at GWG', *Labour/ Le Travail*, 59: 215–40.

Irwin, R. L., (2004) 'A/r/tography as metonymic, metonymic, metissage', in R. L. Irwin and A. deCosson (eds), *A/r/tography: Rendering Self Through Arts Based Living Inquiry*, Vancouver, BC: Pacific Educational Press, pp. 27–38.

Ng, R. (2002) 'Freedom for whom? Globalization and trade from the standpoint of garment workers', *Canadian Women Studies*, 4: 74–82.

O'Donoghue, D. (2009) 'Are we asking the wrong questions in arts-based research?', *Studies in Art Education*, 50 (4): 352–68.

Quinlan, E. (2010) 'New action research techniques: using participatory theatre with health care workers', *Action Research*, 8: 117–33.

Steedman, M, (1997) *Angels of the Workplace: women and the construction of gender relations in the Canadian clothing industry, 1890–1940*, Toronto, ON: University of Toronto Press.

Chapter 11

Balancing knowledge management and knowledge mobility in the connected university

Chris Chesher and Sarah Howard

Since universities began adopting computers and the internet, there have been constant struggles to balance knowledge mobility and knowledge management. Some forces within universities embrace openness and connectivity, while others prioritize reducing risks and managing knowledge. This chapter examines three cases in which tensions emerged as universities adopted particular digital media, and contestations arose between practices of openness and closure, democracy and authority, intellectual autonomy and centralized management. The learning management systems (LMSs) Moodle and WebCT, the citation management tools EndNote and Zotero, and the journal databases Directory of Open Access Journals and Web of Knowledge embody contesting paradigms in digital politics of knowledge.

Information technologies have two key capacities that make them attractive mediators of knowledge in the university. First, they offer efficient means of generating, circulating, collecting and presenting all kinds of data. Second, they have capacities to impose selective control over knowledge: restricting access, and monitoring and managing user activities. Knowledge mobility extends knowledge, while knowledge management helps privileged actors control it. These two features of the new knowledge environment are not dichotomous: they are simultaneous.

Recent changes in teaching and research platforms have contributed to transformations in intellectual work, many reducing the autonomy of knowledge workers. The case studies we have chosen illustrate how configurations in knowledge-mediating technologies have political implications. Academics and universities have traditionally had authority based in expertise in managing knowledge. They can legitimize knowledge through peer review, working in disciplines and drawing on the institutional support of schools and faculties. Some uses of the internet enhance the capacity and authority of academics, offering new ways of producing and sharing knowledge and changing scholarly roles. On the other hand, many new services, such as centrally managed LMSs, ask academics to forfeit their control in the interests of standardization and accountability. Any piece of software tends to encourage certain styles of working, and even thinking. With coercive infrastructures, researchers and the knowledge they produce have become subject to unkind interfaces, obsolescence and unwanted constant change. These changes are not only changes in tools. They affect career paths, intellectual property rights, liability, reputation and collegiality.

Changes to knowledge environments present universities and intellectuals with ethical challenges as they negotiate balances between knowledge management and knowledge mobility. In a global environment of diversified knowledge vectors, intellectuals and universities tend not to be central authorities in knowledge, but more or less powerful nodes in knowledge networks. It is not yet clear the extent to which the adoption of the internet will be a new knowledge paradigm or a modification of existing experiences. It is unlikely that patterns of change will be consistent or universal.

Literacies, affordances and vectors of knowledge mobility

Universities were among the first major institutions to develop and use the internet, establishing a distinctive culture of technology years before the first e-commerce boom of the mid-1990s. Internet pioneers favoured open technologies, fostering an ethos of unrestricted connectivity, often with an agenda for social change (Turner 2008). By the early 1990s, the internet emerged into the mainstream as an irresistible and relatively unregulated vector for knowledge mobility. It allowed seamless connections within, between and outside organizations, permeating traditional barriers.

As the internet became more familiar, however, institutions began to impose upon its use new forms of control. In this chapter we employ three concepts to understand what is at stake in these knowledge environments: literacies, affordances and vectors. In combination, these concepts capture something about the changes in the mediation of knowledge mobility associated with digital technologies.

The first concept, digital literacy, refers to the dominant norms about people's capacity to create and communicate. The need to develop, maintain and teach digital literacy places new pressures on academics, while also offering new opportunities. The skills and habits of computer-mediated communication have become as important to functioning well socially and professionally as conventional literacies of reading and writing (Gilster 1998; Lankshear and Knobel 2008; Hartley 2009). Digital literacies involve not only technical skills, but also applying these skills critically in ways appropriate to a profession or a discipline. Digital literacies are multiple and constantly changing. They involve developing a critical awareness of hardware, software and uses, as well as generic skills. The complex competencies of digital literacy are always interconnected, embedded in social, economic and institutional contexts (Gee 2007). Ideally, digitally literate people are innovators in their preferred medium, extending their capacity to work in their discipline (Lankshear and

Knobel 2008). Institutions often intervene in digital literacy, providing training for financial and research administration systems. While learning a new system represents a significant time investment, users are motivated to learn by the advantages that this knowledge opens up.

The second concept, the affordance, refers to the perceived and actual properties of an artefact that establish the limits for all its possible interactions (Graves 2007; Hutchby 2001; Norman 2002). Typical system affordances are comprised of a keyboard for entering text, a software interface for performing a database search, and a sequence of components for publishing a document or for sending a message. Each of these affordance components helps establish the scope of possibilities of user–artefact interaction. Affordances are deeply bound up with digital literacies, because learning is inseparable from knowledge-mediating artefacts. For example, an LMS offers teachers and students a particular suite of affordances supporting online interaction, sharing of artefacts (e.g. academic articles, assignments, etc.), participation in forums, and so on. When teachers develop learning activities, the choice of available affordances in a platform often biases learning design. Some platforms, such as blogs and wikis, are open to learners' connections with each other, and even with those outside the classroom or the university. In some learning environments, teaching becomes a tightly managed practice, with monitoring and control of content delivery becoming the dominant affordances. The economic contexts of software production can also be apparent in the complex differences between open source and commercial software, such as between Moodle and Blackboard, and between the reference managers EndNote and Zotero.

The third theme, the vector, refers to forces that catalyse and channel movement and communication. As previously suggested, digital technologies have particular capacities to connect classrooms and researchers' offices with the outside. The term vector originated in geometry, meaning 'a line of fixed length and direction but having no fixed location' (Wark 1994: 11). Extending this meaning offers a powerful concept to examine how new media change the speed and direction of communication. In universities, digital vectors both allow and restrict knowledge flows. From the slower but authoritative vector of a refereed journal, to a fleeting discussion on Skype, vectors are not mere conduits. Vectors carry structuring force and authority. The internet gave many inside and outside universities unprecedented potential to mobilize knowledge. However, the internet's vectoral openness prompted great uncertainties around legitimacy, privacy and intellectual property, leading to a variety of regulatory responses.

The rise of knowledge management

The idea that *knowledge* can and should be *managed* first appeared in the early 1970s in the information management discipline. Alavi and Leidner (2001:

109) identify six common conceptions of knowledge: data and information; a state of mind; an object; a process; a question of access to information; and a capability. Each implies a different organizational approach to knowledge management. A common approach to online resources in universities, facing the impossible complexity of disciplinary diversity, is to treat knowledge and learning resources as objects. Making this pragmatic move turns knowledge into a collection of objects that can be gathered, stored, reused, manipulated and transferred. Digital literacies can be standardized as universal 'best practices'. Affordances can be simplified and smoothed. Vectors can be partitioned and controlled.

It has increasingly become a commonplace to see 'knowledge' as a primary economic resource (Carlsson 2003). Historically, universities have had 'authority' over knowledge, but with relatively little social or economic power. As knowledge became more culturally important, and technology increased knowledge mobility, some of universities' authority translated into power (Stehr 1994). Ironically, developments such as the internet have diversified sources of knowledge, leaving the university as no longer the predominant producer of knowledge (Barnett 2000). What power it has had has come into question.

Knowledge generation in the university can be grouped into two activities: the production of knowledge and the production of qualified knowledge workers. The internet makes knowledge-work of universities more visible. At the same time, new internet platforms become vectors for other knowledge creators, each with its own claims to legitimacy and influence, such as blogs, social networking and Wikipedia. Some see this competition as a challenge to the validity and legitimacy of knowledge produced by the university (Barnett 2000). When universities respond by introducing centralized and standardized systems to staff they risk imposing monolithic affordances and closed vectors. The university's consciousness of the value of knowledge as an asset and a technocratically controllable commodity threatens to undermine traditional values of openness and enquiry.

Scholars have begun to explore the nature of knowledge and its distinctions from data and information, as well as outputs of knowledge management practices as intellectual capital (Jashapara 2005: 138). For knowledge to be tradeable as a commodity, it must be transformed into data or information that others can use; in other words, it must take on forms that are culturally visible and comprehensible. The value of existing knowledge practices in universities has come into question (Barnett 2000: 410–11):

- What happens when the university is not the only supplier of knowledge?
- How is the university's accountability for the quality of knowledge produced?
- How should the university position itself in the market (academic capitalism)?

- How are the criteria and validation of knowledge changing?
- Are skills of the university necessarily tied to knowledge (e.g. production)?

In a more diverse environment of knowledge producers, many have greater capacity to commoditize knowledge than universities. Organizations such as consulting firms, 'earn revenue by applying the expertise held by (or accessible to) their professional consulting staff' (McQueen 1998: 610). The translation and management of tacit knowledge as a commodity has created an 'academic capitalism' (Barnett 2000: 410–11). Organizations often create 'repositories of electronic communication', attempting to capture, manage and transmit tacit knowledge. Universities also attempt to capture and quantify knowledge produced and used by academic staff through academic dissemination (e.g. the use of databases to rank peer-reviewed articles and citations, etc.) and teaching resources (e.g. recorded lectures, LMSs, etc.).

The remainder of this chapter focuses on three case study genres of knowledge systems: LMSs, citation management and publication databases. These illustrate alternative ways of balancing mobility and management of knowledge in universities, as the organization attempts to maintain access, validity and legitimacy of knowledge produced by academics and students.

Systems for the management of learning

The implementation of LMSs across universities embodies some of the tensions around digital literacies, affordances of internet tools and control over vectors of knowledge. LMSs emerged in the late 1990s into e-learning environments characterized by a diversity of local solutions. They tended to follow upgrades of organizational networks, administrative databases and communication systems (Hengehold 2001). They have become among the most ubiquitous internet tools in higher education instruction today, and one of the most contentious. One of the most controversial aspects of LMSs is that they tend to standardize and homogenize teaching and content delivery across the faculties. They systematize student engagements with content and offer a limited range of learning activities.

The goal of a true LMS – the primary affordance – is to handle all aspects of the learning process, from development of course materials to reporting results (Watson and Watson 2007). Digital literacies, affordances and vectors are aligned. Content fits the digital tool, rather than teachers structuring appropriate tools to support teaching and learning. This object-oriented pedagogy is not a new trend in higher education. Trow (1974: 8) outlined that, as higher education moves from educating the elite, to mass education, curriculum becomes 'more modular, marked by semi-structured sequences of courses . . . allowing flexible combinations of courses and easier access and movement between major fields and indeed among institutions'. This idea is embodied in the uniform nature of content delivery through the LMS. Assessments, discussions, resources, etc. are all slotted into the designed space in the online tool's interface. This standardized interface often lacks the nuanced specialization of the different disciplines. For example, Physics would be presented in the same manner as History (e.g. asynchronous discussions, synchronous chat, resource uploads, etc.), but these two disciplines would have very different instructional practices. The impact of this phenomenon on content delivery varies in intensity depending on the rigidity and closure of the digital system, as well as levels of user access and customizability. To illustrate these differences, the following discussion will examine two different LMSs: Blackboard, a commercial software package, and Moodle, which is open source.

Blackboard is the globally dominant for-profit licensed commercial LMS, sold to universities and other educational institutions. The functionality and structure of Blackboard provides some customizability for the client organization, but very little for the end user. Blackboard is marketed as 'helping institutions at all levels drive learner achievement . . .'. It promises 'big and measurable change in learning outcomes' (Blackboard Inc. 2010a). Historically, Blackboard has been highly acquisitive, buying competitors including WebCT, Elluminate and Wimba. It uses its patents strategically, including threatening to enforce 'Internet-based education support systems', which would have excluded the open source use of eLearning tools such as discussion boards, content editing, etc. (Blackboard Inc. 2010b).

Moodle, on the other hand, is a free-to-licence, open source LMS developed by a global community of developers. The company's description of the LMS states that it helps learners to 'tinker' and be 'creative', and that it supports a 'social constructivist framework of education' (Moodle 2010).

In 2008, the average Blackboard contract with an educational institution was USD 50,300 (Blackboard Inc. 2009), while there is no fee for using Moodle. Further, research has shown that 71% of students feel Moodle is easier to use, and 75% of student respondents would prefer to use Moodle in a future course (van Rooij 2009: 5). This said, Blackboard held the majority (80–90%) of the secondary school and higher education markets (Machado and Tao 2007). These trends suggest that the choice to use Blackboard is not necessarily related to cost or ease of use, but potentially comes from a priority to manage course content and knowledge.

One of the primary affordances of LMSs desired by universities is the ability to centrally manage the tool. This allows the organization to secure control of instructional and content knowledge vectors across faculties and disciplines. Considering this institutional requirement, the choice of using Blackboard is not illogical. Blackboard affords more security and highly structured content management, supporting the modularization and standardization of courses across the university. Alternatives such as Moodle, which may be highly customizable, flexible and attractive for academics and students, are not as desirable to administrations, as the affordance of flexibility reduces centralized knowledge management. Interestingly, while academics may desire flexibility and mobility in teaching and learning content, they often voluntarily regulate their own knowledge use in their writing through their choice of reference managers.

Reference and knowledge managers

Among the strongest norms of universities is the convention that academic writers reference all their sources. Plagiarism is among the most serious academic transgressions. Citations are also ritual performances of academic competency, shared resources for the community of peers and contributions to economies of influence. Therefore it is not surprising that specialized software that embeds the conventional academic literacies of 'proper' referencing has been developed. Reference-managing software has the affordance of providing mobility through access to bibliographic details from databases, managing references in a database and including references within writing and bibliographies. At the same time, the conventions of referencing, and the nature of the software, have constraining properties designed to manage and standardize the referencing process. However, there are differences between the reference managers. Their design reveals traces of negotiations around academic norms and practices, decisions over software affordances, and contexts of technology production and consumption. The following discussion will examine knowledge mobility and management in referencing practices through two softwares: EndNote and Zotero.

EndNote was one of the earliest commercial reference managers, first released for the Macintosh in 1988 by Niles and Associates. The story is of a company founded by a mathematician working in a Berkeley, California basement. The product was very successful, with over 200,000 users by 1999. EndNote remains the dominant incumbent in personal academic reference management, with millions of licensed users and an estimated 90% of the market (Muldrow and Yoder 2009). As a legacy of the PC era, the software affordances suit individual users rather than groups or scholarly communities. Users generally input, import and manage their own references, insert citations into documents and generate bibliographies. Even with the recent addition of an online supplement called EndNote Web, online vectoral features are limited, and available only to licensed users. While EndNote is expensive, many universities buy site licences. Providing students with this software is a practical initiative, a statement about the importance of proper academic conduct, and it provides a valuable and managed vector through Thomson Reuters.

In the 'Web 2.0' era of the mid-2000s a number of new free and open source reference management services emerged, including Connotea (2004), CiteULike (2004), Zotero (2006) and Mendeley (2007). Some of these drew inspiration from widely used online bookmarking services like delicious, diigo, and so on, which offer users free accounts to keep annotated records of sites they have visited. These records could be easily shared with others online, and lists became resources for groups and communities.

Comparing EndNote with Zotero reveals the differences between user-centred and network-connected generations of reference management software. Zotero is a browser plug-in that users download free and install in Mozilla Firefox. It is an open source GPL-licensed product made by the Centre for History and New Media (CHNM) at George Mason University (GMU), funded by government and philanthropic sources. Like EndNote, Zotero allows users to manage categorized lists of references and manage bibliographies in word processors with different referencing styles. One notable difference in Zotero is how references can be imported, through site translators. Whenever a webpage contains or links to bibliographic metadata, an icon appears in the browser bar. Clicking on the icon begins the download of the reference information into a library. This import process is much quicker than with EndNote. Once they have assembled a collection of references, users can easily share them with other Zotero users.

The competition between these generations of referencing software blew up into public conflict when EndNote owners Thomson Reuters sued George Mason University in September 2008. They claimed that the CHNM had breached the university's software licence by reverse-engineering the proprietary '.ens' files that encoded the different referencing styles (Harvard, APA, etc; Nunes 2008). This legal move, which seemed to have little basis, created some outcry in the academic community: 'Thomson/Reuters is transparent in its effort to use a software license to suppress a competitor in a product market and to interfere with the production and distribution of knowledge' (Madison 2008). Ultimately a Virginia court dismissed the suit in June 2009.

The intrusion of legal threats into scholarly practices is a good example of how activities within university environments are increasingly open to external vectors. Many software affordances align to some extent with conventional academic literacies, such as gathering references and choosing where in the text to include citations. However, they necessarily require competencies of working with proprietary systems, managing files or network connections, performing effective searches, and problem solving. Scholarly/technical practices become more network-connected, and everyday academic practice has become more exposed to external influences. Some of these offer new capacities, such as modes of publication in blogs and e-journals or the ability to download new tools. At the same time, these changes can expose academics to the implications of legal confrontations or economic changes.

With the mediation of the internet, knowledge can certainly become more mobile, but it also becomes governed by the affordances of digital toolsets and their vectoral configurations. Traditional principles of academic freedom are compatible with values of open source software and open access, but these projects often struggle for resources, offer over-complex affordances and are dominated by technical disciplines and subcultures. Commercial information vectors, from academic publishers to information services, operate to serve, complement and exploit academic production. These differences are apparent in the affordances that proprietary software such as EndNote and Zotero offer developers. Like other open source projects, Zotero invites independent developers to build applications that connect with their application. Endnote invites suggestions for new features, but promises centralized quality control and support. Universities have overwhelmingly chosen EndNote, which belongs to the dominant vector of Thomson Reuters' managed knowledge. The strong influence of Thomson Reuters' knowledge vector is not restricted to EndNote: it flows in other products supporting practices by which academics and institutions validate and legitimize knowledge.

Making publications 'legitimate' and discoverable

The standard peer-reviewed commercial academic journal is no longer considered the only outlet for dissemination of research, but many newer publications struggle for acceptance. Online academic publications are typically produced more quickly and made available more extensively than print journals. However, they face two challenges beyond assuring quality: securing symbolic legitimacy, and being included in the right databases. Some new platforms, such as blogs and research group wikis, do not meet conventional standards for academic publication. Some publications, such as refereed and open access electronic journals, meet these standards, but are not always recognized by relevant scholarly communities. Some open publishing platforms are unconventional in style, lack a track record or are perceived to have inadequate peer review. On the other hand, these new vectors have greater speed of dissemination, high mobility of knowledge and democratization of access to research findings. Some claim that open access journals generate more citations and have greater impact (Antelman 2004), but this claim is contested (Craig *et al.* 2007). New vectors are not sufficient to change academic publishing.

Thomson Reuters, which sells EndNote, is also one of the largest indexers of commercial journals. They claim that their database Web of Science actively covers 11,261 high impact journals (Thomson Reuters 2011). In contrast, there are currently 5,446 peer-reviewed or editorially controlled journals listed in the Directory of Open Access Journals (2010). While not as large as the ISI database, the open access database represents a significant number of peer-reviewed publications under a different knowledge economy. Despite its size and reach, this alternative measure of publications has questionable validity and applicability to many fields of research. There is the thought that, without consistent peer review and publication in an accepted academic journal, how will academics know if knowledge is legitimate?

In parallel with the growth of open access publications, as if in response, there has been a growing insistence that citation rankings should be measured, and stand in for quality. Rankings are based on measuring the number of citations per article, journal impact factors and journal rankings. These data sources are not necessarily new, but increased computing power and the development of journal and article citation databases has made these resources available to the research public. Unfortunately, the vectors of citation rankings are slow, as they are often based on subscriptions, and the rankings have a year or two's lag (e.g. rankings for 2009 were released in 2010). It is important to note that the data is often only gathered from vectors controlled by certain publishers. One of the biggest, and most 'valued', sources for this type of information is the Thomson Web of Knowledge. Researchers are encouraged by the university to look to the Thomson Reuters Journal Citation Reports (JCR) to determine where they should be submitting scholarly work. Many academics make the economic decision to choose journals with the highest influence and presumed value in the academic marketplace.

Academic publishing practices tend towards a self-reinforcing dynamic, in which universities prefer the journals that publishers rank as high impact, so that more researchers try to publish in these journals, and these journals continue to rank highly. In this relationship, journals in new fields, unranked journals and many open source journals do not receive the same exposure or marketing and therefore are less likely to be indexed. This practice biases towards the hard sciences, which publish at a much faster rate than the social sciences, arts or humanities. Further, as the same high 'impact' journals are targeted by more academics, a homogenization of the market occurs. The smaller, more specialized, and possibly cutting-edge publication outlets become risky options for dissemination, irrespective of their quality or value.

The aggregation of dominant publishing data sets creates a cultural desire and financial imperative for academics to publish through 'ranked' outlets. The legitimacy of this knowledge, particularly research dissemination, becomes increasingly important as governments and funding agencies look to the 'quality' and 'ranking' of scholarly works, such as the citation rankings of peer-reviewed articles and books, as benchmarks for providing funding. At a time when knowledge produced at the universities is being questioned, knowledge management and standardization operate as self-validating systems for the organization. As previously outlined, Trow (1974) has argued that, as universities come under greater scrutiny in times of social growth, there is a universalization of the sector. The recent turn to citation metrics and validated 'quality' publication outlets provides a way by which institutions can be measured against one another, in their own national market and internationally. While universities cannot usually mandate which journals academics should publish in, the organization can reward individuals for selecting channels of dissemination recognized by the university as 'high quality' and of 'value.'

Moreover, these trends represent additional ways in which universities and governments undermine academic autonomy in choosing the most appropriate outlet for publication. Academics can be coerced to choose publication outlets based on their career and financial impact more than on appropriateness to the research.

Conclusion

Knowledge mobility in universities is increasingly mediated through computer and internet technologies. Digital literacies are now among the norms of scholarly subjectivity and practice. However, digital literacy is necessarily bound up in a complex politics of technology. In using software, academics are constrained by affordances aligned with particular practices. In teaching, teachers and students are negotiating centralized and homogenizing LMSs. In research, software tools carry different feature sets, reflecting different philosophies, historical legacies, economic models and vectoral dimensions. In publishing, quantified influence and impact are becoming a powerful measure of reputation, even when these measures are often problematic. Standardized platforms and universalizing metrics risk effacing differences between disciplines and closing off the diversity of practices so important to the university. Digital literacies should be critical literacies, bringing in readings of the politics of technology. When institutions choose new platforms they should recognize the value of a diversity of affordances and vectors, including those offered by FLOSS (free/libre/open-source software), open publishing and open education that align with and enhance the culture and economy of universities.

References

Alavi, M., and Leidner, D. E. (2001) 'Review: knowledge management and knowledge management systems: conceptual foundations and research issues', *MIS Quarterly*, 25(1): 107–36.

Antelman, K. (2004) 'Do open-access articles have a greater research impact?', *College and Research Libraries*, 65(5): 372–82.

Barnett, R. (2000) 'University knowledge in an age of supercomplexity', *Higher Education*, 40(4): 409–22.

Blackboard Inc. (2009) *Blackboard, Inc. Q4 2008 Earnings Call Transcript*.

——— (2010a) *Blackboard*. Online, available: www.blackboard.com (accessed 14 August 2010).

——— (2010b) *The Blackboard Patent Pledge*. Online, available: www.blackboard.com/Company/Patents/Patent-Pledge.aspx. (accessed 29 September 2010).

Carlsson, S. A. (2003) 'Knowledge managing and knowledge management systems in inter-organizational networks', *Knowledge and Process Management*, 10(3): 194.

CiteULike (2004) *CiteULike: Everyone's Library*. Online, available: http://citeulike.com (accessed 14 August 2010).

Connotea (2004) *Connotea: free online reference management for clinicians and scientists*. Online, available: www.connotea.org (accessed 14 August 2010).

Craig, I. D., Plume, A. M., McVeigh, M. E., Pringle, J. and Amin, M. (2007) 'Do open access articles have greater citation impact? A critical review of the literature', *Journal of Informetrics*, 1(3): 239–48. Online, available: doi:10.1016/j.joi.2007.04.001 (accessed 19 October 2010).

Directory of Open Access Journals (2010). Online, available: www.doaj.org/ (accessed 19 October 2010).

Gee, J.P., (2007) *New Digital Media and Learning as an Emerging Area and 'Worked Examples' as One Way Forward*, Cambridge, MA: MIT Press.

Gilster, P. (1998) *Digital Literacy*, San Francisco: John Wiley & Sons.

Graves, L. (2007) 'The affordances of blogging', *Journal of Communication Inquiry*, 31(4): 331–46.

Hartley, J. (2009) *The Uses of Digital Literacy*, St Lucia, Qld: University of Queensland Press.

Hengehold, L. (2001) 'Going the last mile: connecting Virginia's community colleges', *Community College Journal*, 72(2): 50–54.

Hutchby, I. (2001) 'Technologies, texts and affordances', *Sociology*, 35(02): 441–56.

Jashapara, A. (2005) 'The emerging discourse of knowledge management: a new dawn for information science research?' *Journal of Information Science*, 31(2): 136–48.

Lankshear, C. and Knobel, M. (eds) (2008) *Digital Literacies: Concepts, Policies and Practices*, New York: Peter Lang.

Machado, M., and Tao, E. (2007) 'Blackboard vs. Moodle: comparing user experience of learning management systems', paper presented at the 37th ASEE/IEEE Frontiers in Education Conference.

McQueen, R. J. (1998) 'Four views of knowledge and knowledge management', paper presented at the Proceedings of the Fourth Americas Conference on Information Systems.

Madison, M. (2008) 'EndNote v. Zotero', *Madisonian.net: Law, technology, society*. Online, available: http://madisonian.net/2008/09/28/endnote-v-zotero/ (accessed 16 September 2010).

Mendeley (2007) *Mendeley* [Software] Online, available: www.mendeley.com/ (accessed 10 September 2010).

Moodle (2010) *Moodle*. Online, available: http://moodle.org/ (accessed 14 August 2010).

Muldrow, J., and Yoder, S. (2009) 'Out of cite! how reference managers are taking research to the next level', *Political Science and Politics*, 42(01): 167–72.

Norman, D.A. (2002) 'The psychopathology of everyday things', D. J. Levitin (ed.), *Foundations of Cognitive Psychology: Core Readings*, Cambridge, MA: MIT Press, 417–42.

Nunes, G. (2008) *Thomson Reuters (Scientific) Inc. Plaintiff v. David A. Von Moll*, Comptroller of the Commonwealth of Virginia and George Mason University Defendants.

Stehr, N. (1994) *Knowledge Societies*, London: Sage Publications.

Thomson Reuters (2011) 'Quality and Quantity: Science, Thomson Reuters'. Online, available: http://workinfo.com/realfacts/qualityandquantity/. Accessed 21 June 2011.

Trow, M. (1974) *Problems in the Transition from Elite to Mass Higher Education*, Berkeley, CA: Carnegie Commission on Higher Education.

Turner, F. (2008) *From Counterculture to Cyberculture: Stewart Brand, the Whole Earth Network, and the Rise of Digital Utopianism*, Chicago: University of Chicago Press.

van Rooij, S. W. (2009) 'Adopting open-source software applications in U.S. higher education: cross-disciplinary review of the literature', *Review of Educational Research*, 79(2): 682–701.

Wark, M. (1994) *Virtual Geography: Living with Global Media Events*, Bloomington: Indiana University Press.

Watson, W. R., and Watson, S. L. (2007) 'An argument for clarity: what are learning management systems, what are they not, and what should they become?' *TechTrends*, 51(2): 28–34.

Zotero (2006) *Zotero: The Next Generation Research Tool* [Software] Online, available: www.zotero.org/ (accessed 4 August 2010).

Part IV

Responsibilities and rights in mobilizing knowledge

Chapter 12

Regulating knowledge as intellectual property in the global knowledge economy

Michael Fraser

Introduction

Since prehistoric times valuable objects have been bartered across great distances. From these beginnings, international transport and digital communications networks have grown to carry a global trade in goods and services. Intellectual property law has always been crafted in response to advancements in distribution and communications technology. The first copyright law, the Statute of Anne (Copyright Act 1709), was enacted in response to new technology, the printing press, 'For the encouragement of learning' and to control pirate printers (Defoe 1709).

Global knowledge mobilization depends on stable markets for intellectual property, and intellectual property law is being developed in response to technological developments today.

Globalization

The concept of globalization is itself controversial. What is globalization? Three schools of thought have been identified:

> Hyperglobalists who look forward to a global market and new social structures which will supersede the nation state;
>
> Sceptics who consider globalization to be a myth because the international flows of capital, goods and labour have historically been relatively greater than at present;
>
> Transformationists who consider that the current unprecedented global changes are transforming the foundations of power and authority in the nation state. The new modes of accelerated communication and network connection are driving a qualitative change in social interaction which is reshaping societies.
>
> (Held *et al.* 1999)

The development of a global knowledge economy is indeed unprecedented and presents us with a transformative challenge to our assumptions about the social structures and processes that support nation states.

Origins of intellectual property rights

Land

In early agrarian societies communal ownership of land was based on mutual obligations of kinship and loyalty. Absolute concepts of ownership that applied to possessions, such as the Roman concept of *res in rem*, did not exist in ownership of land.

Feudal tenure of land was a system of rights that expressed political, social and economic relationships. Tenure was the bridge between ancient communal ownership and modern property law.

The industrial revolution and the ascendancy of capitalism depended on the destruction of functional feudal property relationships and the enclosures that excluded peasants from common land. Common land was closed, consolidated and taken into exclusive private ownership.

Patents, copyright and designs

The Statute of Monopolies, in 1623, the first English patent statute, granted a patent to an inventor for 14 years, which time the inventor was given to teach the art of his invention to his apprentices (Statute of Monopolies 1623: Jac. 1, c.3).

The Statute of Anne was the first copyright law, 'An Act for the Encouragement of Learning' (Copyright Act 1709), which protected the commercial interests of authors and publishers.

Designs were protected for a period of two months from the date of first publication by the Calico Printers Act (1787: 27 Geo.III, c.38).

Registration of trademarks confers a right in an indicative mark of origin for goods and services, which grew out of the tort of passing off (Trademark Registration Act 1875: c.17).

Common law

The common law action of *passing off* prevents a trader from freeriding on another's reputation by misrepresenting his own goods or services as being related to someone else.

Another common law doctrine called breach of confidence (*Prince Albert v Strange* 1849) was developed in the mid-nineteenth century to protect against unauthorized use of confidential information such as trade secrets at a time when the mass market for newspapers was emerging.

All these particular utilitarian regimes protected certain interests, but such interests were not initially conceived of as property rights. The modern development of these interests as intellectual property has extended the rights of the owners of intellectual property.

Modern intellectual property rights

The concept of property rights expresses the relationship of individuals and the state to tangible and intangible objects.

In modern law, there are three types of property:

- real property, for example property in land and buildings and associated rights;
- personal property, for example personal possessions like a watch or a hat; and
- intellectual property, which refers to works of the mind, for example copyright, patents and trademarks.

Rights in real property endure, but rights in intellectual property are of limited duration and, when they expire, the rights revert to the public domain.

In a market economy intellectual property is the legal and economic framework that has been established to protect works of the mind. It rewards investment of creative effort and capital by the creators and producers of original work.

Intellectual property as a human right

Article 27 of the Universal Declaration of Human Rights (United Nations 1948) states:

(1) Everyone has the right freely to participate in the cultural life of the community, to enjoy the arts and to share in scientific advancement and its benefits.

(2) Everyone has the right to the protection of the moral and material interests resulting from any scientific, literary or artistic production of which he is the author.

The two parts of Article 27 set out inseparable rights, each of which supports and complements the other. These rights have been carried into other normative international instruments such as Article 15 of the International Covenant an Economic, Social and Cultural Rights (United Nations 1966):

1. The States Parties to the present Covenant recognize the right of everyone:

   (a) To take part in cultural life;
   (b) To enjoy the benefits of scientific progress and its applications;
   (c) To benefit from the protection of the moral and material interests resulting from any scientific, literary or artistic production of which he is the author.

2. The steps to be taken by the States Parties to the present Covenant to achieve the full realization of this right shall include those necessary

for the conservation, the development and the diffusion of science and culture.

3. The States Parties to the present Covenant undertake to respect the freedom indispensable for scientific research and creative activity.

4. The States Parties to the present Covenant recognize the benefits to be derived from the encouragement and development of international contacts and cooperation in the scientific and cultural fields.

Article 27 of the Universal Declaration of Human Rights was the basis for the foundation of the World Intellectual Property Organization (WIPO):

WIPO is a specialized agency of the United Nations. It is dedicated to developing a balanced and accessible international intellectual property (IP) system, which rewards creativity, stimulates innovation and contributes to economic development while safeguarding the public interest.

WIPO was established by the WIPO Convention, 1967 with a mandate from its Member States to promote the protection of IP throughout the world through cooperation among states and in collaboration with other international organizations. Its headquarters are in Geneva, Switzerland.

(WIPO Homepage 2010)

The European Convention on Human Rights and Fundamental Freedoms (2009) also protects the right to property. The European Court of Human Rights has interpreted Article 1 of the first Protocol to the Convention to include trademarks, giving the intellectual property in a trademark a human right dimension (Carpenter 2009).

Intellectual property rights are human rights. They are rights that benefit the individual and the community in which they are respected.

Intellectual property treaties

There is a well-developed and highly elaborated framework of treaties and conventions for the protection of intellectual property.

The Paris Convention for the Protection of Industrial Property (1883) was the first major international treaty to protect inventions (patents), trademarks and industrial designs.

In 1886 the Berne Convention for the Protection of Literary and Artistic Works aimed to secure international protection for copyright owners to control, and receive payment for, the use of their creative works.

WIPO now administers 24 intellectual property treaties. In 1996 WIPO reinforced intellectual property rights management in global trade by entering into a cooperation agreement with the World Trade Organization (WTO). National intellectual property laws must conform to the requirements of international treaties, such as the intellectual property treaties and trade agreements to which a nation is signatory.

International trade in intellectual property

International trade is the basis on which international law has developed. The forum of the General Agreement on Tariffs and Trade (GATT) came into force in 1948 to meet and exchange trading concessions, and then to provide for dispute resolution as a response to the tragedies of the twentieth-century World Wars. These wars were caused in part by the consequences of national trade tariff protectionism and the lack of international trading agreements.

During the eighth round of GATT negotiations known as the Uruguay round (1986–94) the World Trade Organization was established under the Marrakech Agreement (1994) and in 1995 it began work to liberalize and regulate more integrated global trade. The Agreement on Trade-Related Aspects of Intellectual Property Rights (TRIPS) is Annex 1C of the Marrakech Agreement. TRIPS ties intellectual property to international trade rules for the first time. TRIPS's copyright provisions import Berne Convention standards of copyright protection for creative works into the GATT. TRIPS provisions on trademarks and patents also import Paris Convention standards of protection for industrial intellectual property into GATT trade regulation. The TRIPS Agreement requires states to have strong intellectual property rights protection, and states that do not protect and enforce intellectual property can be disciplined through a juridical process in the WTO's dispute settlement mechanism.

The Dispute Settlement Body (DSB) of the WTO makes decisions on trade disputes between governments on the recommendation of a Dispute Panel. The DSB may direct a Member State to bring its laws into conformity with WTO Agreements, failing which the DSB may authorize a state whose complaint has been upheld to take retaliatory trade measures.

TRIPS made it a requirement for WTO member nations to have and to enforce intellectual property law effectively, to international standards, as a condition for participation in the international trading system. Nations in breach of TRIPS standards may ultimately be brought by a complainant state to a juridical process in the WTO that can lead ultimately to trade sanctions being imposed on the state that is in breach.

Developing countries that are net importers of intellectual property have agreed in effect to increase protection of intellectual property under TRIPS in exchange for better access to global agricultural and textile markets under the WTO liberalized trade rules.

The Doha round of GATT negotiations that commenced in 2001 has yet to be concluded. Many nations, not waiting for a result from the multilateral negotiations, have entered into bilateral trade treaties in the meantime. Bilateral treaties such as the Australia–United States Free Trade Agreement (2005) include 'TRIPS-plus' provisions that have extended intellectual property protection beyond the requirements of the TRIPS Agreement and tie the requirements of national intellectual property regulation to bilateral trade.

National intellectual property policies

National policies toward intellectual property agreements are conditioned by the value of intellectual property to national gross domestic product (GDP). Nations that have valuable intellectual property-based industries and services and that are net exporters of intellectual property ensure better protection for intellectual property rights in their territories and promote international protection for intellectual property through treaties and conventions and in trade agreements. Nations with fewer valuable intellectual property industries and services, and that are net importers of intellectual property, opt for less protection for intellectual property in the national and international spheres.

National intellectual property policies, laws and enforcement practices reflect international deals in which each nation attempts to achieve national benefits and interests as a whole and wherein intellectual property is one bargaining chip.

In each nation it is an important national policy consideration in shaping an intellectual property law and enforcement framework that it should be seen to be sufficient to attract international intellectual property resources by foreign direct investment. Intellectual property protection must also be sufficient to qualify the national territory as a market for high-quality foreign intellectual property goods and services, including copyright works and knowledge products and services that are valuable in the national interest and for the public benefit.

These considerations result in each nation trying to match its intellectual property practices with its specific stage of development. Developing countries try to mitigate the effect of intellectual property rights on the nation insofar as they are seen to be in the foreign interest and against the national interest. Within every nation, intellectual property rights policy is characterized as a balance of interests among rights owners, users of rights and the general public.

In countries that are net importers of intellectual property, TRIPS and TRIPS-plus bilateral trade agreements have provoked loud public controversies over whether these trade agreements, while protecting intellectual property rights, also protect the national public interest. National intellectual property law is territorial and it is difficult for national legislatures to reform intellectual property laws to conform to international treaty standards when many consumers resent acknowledging and paying for intellectual property in knowledge products and services.

Developed countries that are net exporters of intellectual property have benefitted from increased revenues as less developed countries that are net importers of intellectual property have had to pay more for imported intellectual property, while the dismantling of European and United States farm subsidies has so far been inconsistent.

Works of the mind are the most valuable commodity in the world today. In every nation local creators are not viable and creative industries cannot exist and cannot grow without secure national protection for intellectual property. Weak national protection for intellectual property harms local creators more than foreign rights owners. In the long term it is in the interests of developing countries to have strong copyright law and practice in their territories. It is only by protecting and enforcing intellectual property rights that developing countries can create the conditions to establish and grow their own national intellectual property-based industries. It is these local creative industries that are the drivers of a knowledge economy in each nation.

China

China is the target of global efforts to enforce intellectual property rights. The trade imbalance between China and the USA is the major trade issue underlying the global economy. The size of the trade imbalance in favour of China has also increased because to date China has not been paying for all the intellectual property it uses, and this has caused tensions in its trading relations, notably with the USA. In times past, when Britain was faced with a severe trade deficit with China, Britain reduced the deficit by selling opium, grown in India, to China, over the objections of China itself. That historic trade confrontation led to the opium wars, and trade disputes throughout history have led to dangerous confrontations.

The Office of the United States Trade Representative released a report to the US Congress on 23 December 2009 about China's compliance with its obligations under the World Trade Organization as required by the US–China Relations Act of 2000.

The report states that in 2009 two IP decisions under the WTO dispute settlement process were made in favour of the USA, concerning China's copyright and trademarks laws, and market access for copyright music, movies and print media. The report says that IP rights enforcement is a key priority area for US relations with China (United States Trade Representative Report 2009).

The US Senate Finance Committee has sought a US government investigation into the effects of China's intellectual property rights infringement on American jobs and the American economy, which it says cost hundreds of thousands of American jobs every year (US Senate Finance Committee Press Release 2010).

On one view, the intellectual property infringements and counterfeiting in China that rights owners complain of is simply a reflection of Chinese culture that is leading to a clash of cultures over knowledge. According to this account, Confucian education practice lays emphasis on recitation and rote learning. Confucian pedagogy stresses the importance of following and copying a role model, absorbing and retelling the great man's ideas in tribute to him. But this rationale, which refers to Confucian culture as the reason for breaches of intellectual property in China, is clearly baseless. Most copying of copyright content and counterfeiting takes place carelessly or with disregard for the rights of the intellectual property owners at best, and in secrecy at worst. Certainly the infringing copying and counterfeiting is not in tribute to a great man. Bill Gates would certainly prefer more sales and fewer such acknowledgements by copyright users and pirates. Indeed a true interpretation of Confucian philosophy would recognize its steadfast insistence on private and public morality and justice, and thus it cannot be the basis for the disrespect for intellectual property in China. The more likely basis for the lack of intellectual property enforcement in China is a still-developing appreciation of private property rights, including intellectual property rights and laws, as China moves to a market economy, as well as a lingering sense of resentment of foreign imperialism, which consumers may feel excuses taking foreign intellectual property without paying for the rights.

The right to own private property was introduced into the Chinese Constitution in 2004 and a property law went into effect in 2007. This law divides property rights into three types – ownership, use and security rights – and it forbids the expropriation of private property, except in the public interest. This concept of property is based on the German civil concept of usufruct.

Intellectual property rights have been protected in Chinese law since 1979, but, absent private property and the rule of law, there was little recognition or compliance by the general population or the authorities. The national policy agenda also meant that intellectual property enforcement was not given priority. It is clear that China's national intellectual property policy is opportunistic in serving the national interest. Respect for intellectual property in China is growing in proportion to the growth of China's intellectual property industries (State Council of the People's Republic of China 2008). In this regard China is acting in its own national self interest, in the way that all nations do, to protect what is valuable to them.

The example of China's experience, however, illustrates that weighing intellectual property rights *against* the nation's public is misconceived. There is no dichotomy between protection for intellectual property and the public interest. Respecting and valuing intellectual property drives creativity and innovation. Intellectual property rights provide a framework in which those who invest their time, talent, work and capital in works of the mind can be rewarded for their work. Creators and inventors are given limited property rights so that they can, to a degree, control and may commercially profit by their work for a certain period. These property rights encourage creativity, innovation, production and distribution of creative and innovative works, so that they will be marketed and made available to the public. Creators can earn a commercial reward for their new work and the public benefits from using the new work. After a period the property rights in these works expire and they enter the public domain. Reasonable statutory copyright exceptions that comply with the standard in the Berne Convention ensure that the public interest in access is protected (Berne Convention 1979, Article 9). Highly protecting and valuing intellectual property is not only in the interest of creators and innovators but it is in the wider public interest in every nation.

In 2007 a Chinese company, General Protecht Group, Inc., was sued in the USA for patent infringement. The Federal Court of Appeals for the Federal Circuit ruled in favour of the Chinese company for the first time in a patent infringement case (*General Protecht Group, Inc. v. International Trade Commission* 2010). That decision had an impact in China by demonstrating that foreign intellectual property law could protect the intellectual property of China as well as foreign rights. China is now improving its capacity to create, and so at the same time it is improving its ability to protect and administer intellectual property.

Digital content access models

Intellectual property is regarded as a non-rival good because it is not destroyed when it is used. It has been suggested, however, that intellectual property can be 'overgrazed' (Landes and Posner 2002) because of the 'tragedy of the commons' (Hardin 1968). For example, Landes and Posner consider that the value of the intellectual property in Mickey Mouse would plummet through overuse if the character were in the public domain. Disney carefully manages the exposure and exploitation of its characters to maintain their value to Disney while they are still in copyright.

Traditional creative industries produced and distributed creative works such as books, journals and records or CDs as physical products. The production and distribution of copyright works required expensive production machinery and distribution and marketing supply chains, for example publishing presses, warehouses, and wholesale and retail distribution and transportation networks to bookstores and libraries. This type of intellectual property business model was built on industrial production technology, which is expensive to build and operate. The producers of intellectual property such as book publishers and record companies enjoyed the benefits of exclusive ownership of the means of production and distribution, which require major investments of capital. While producers alone could undertake high-volume reproduction of creative works as physical products such as books, the intellectual property business model followed the law of supply and demand, because there were a limited number of copies of works produced, for example a print run of 5,000 copies of a book title. In a networked digital communications environment anyone with access to digital information and communications technology can make and communicate copies of creative works without physical limitation. The marginal cost of copying and distributing creative content in knowledge products and services online is close to zero. The digital knowledge economy does not follow the laws of supply and demand of a limited number of copies. Rights owners use technical protection measures and digital rights management technologies to manage copying of their content, but they cannot control access to their creative content in a digital environment. Consumers of intellectual property use web technologies and personal communications devices for easy access to digital content, and with this technological ease of access to content, consumers have assumed a sense of entitlement to it. The intellectual property rights owners have turned to legal remedies to protect their income. Enforcement measures have not proven to be effective as a means to manage intellectual property rights. In a borderless international communications network intellectual property protection is only as strong as its weakest link and the focus of rights owners and users has turned to the international agreements that are the basis for the legislation and enforcement in each jurisdiction.

Access to the web is growing rapidly. In 2007, Australia – a developed country of more than 20 million people – spent nearly USD 23 billion on information technology (IT): 3.0% of GDP. There are over 1.7 billion people online, 26% of the world's population, and this number has grown 380% since 2000 (Miniwatts Marketing Group 2010). Over the next five years, 460 million people in emerging countries will go online. The growth will be highest among consumers and small businesses. The current pattern of unlawful use of content online demonstrates the scope of the challenge for intellectual property owners as more consumers connect to the web and mobile devices.

World Wide Web

- 40 billion file shares a year are illegal uses worldwide.
- About 50% of the ISP (internet service provider) *iiNet*'s traffic is BitTorrent (a protocol for sharing large files) traffic (both these facts: *Roadshow Films Pty Ltd v iiNet Limited (No.3)* 2010).

Text

- One-third of *Publishers Weekly*'s 2009 top 15 best-selling fiction books were available for illicit download (Spring 2009).
- 10,000–13,000 copies of every book published are downloaded for free, a loss of up to USD 1 million per book (Boutlin 2010).
- In a review of 913 digital books in 2009, the titles were pirated online 9 million times in the year, equal to a loss of USD 3 billion (Mokoto 2010).
- The book piracy market is valued at over USD 660 million (Association of American Publishers 2007).
- Less than 24 hours after the release of Dan Brown's *The Lost Symbol* over 100,000 pirated copies were downloaded on file-sharing sites (Cabot 2010).

- News is going online. Eighty regional newspapers in the UK went bankrupt or closed their doors in the last 12 months (WIPO 2009). Online news aggregators do not pay for the professional journalism that makes content and take revenue from the newspapers that do.

Music

- 20% of the music market is legitimate sales.
- 95% of online exchanges of music are illegal.
- 20 billion tracks were illegally swapped or downloaded on the internet in 2005 (IFPI Digital Music Report 2010).
- Illegal file-sharing and online piracy are major factors in the 30% global market decline in music sales (IFPI Digital Music Report 2010).
- There has been a five-year decline in major record industry revenues from USD 13.5 billion to USD 8 billion p.a.

Film

- 4% of the film market is legitimate sales.
- According to the BBC News, one in four people on the internet have illegally downloaded a film (BBC 2004).
- A survey on Physorg estimates losses incurred by the film industry due to the illicit downloads at around USD 8.4 billion worldwide (Physorg 2010).

Former EC Commissioner for Telecommunications Viviane Reding has said 'growing internet piracy is a vote of no confidence in existing business models' (Willis 2009). The Pirate Party has two seats in the European Union Parliament and is the third largest party in Sweden.

The general public expects that creative content is free and has lost its sense of responsibility for property rights in copyright content. Peer-to-peer piracy is the norm. Copyright has become more and more ineffective because it does not provide a reliable remedy for the commonplace violation of a vested legal right. At the same time it continues to be the case that to make high-quality content takes investments of time, talent and capital. Books, films, music cannot come for free in a market economy in the way that many consumers have now come to expect.

In these circumstances some authors are able to make their livelihood by support from wealthy organizations. Some authors earn a salary from employers, others win grants and other forms of patronage, and some types of authors generate income from advertisements that companies attach to their work. But these third parties support those creators whose content serves their interests. To rely on them alone to support creativity would limit the range of professional creativity. They do not by themselves support the *diversity of independent creativity* and the full range of free expression that is essential to a democracy. Only a market for copyright content where copyright owners are paid directly for their work by their audience can support the diverse range of individual, original voices.

But copyright is no longer generating value for independent, professional creators to maintain the production of quality and diversity of work for consumers.

How, then, can creators and producers fund their work of cultural expression and knowledge production in the digital environment?

Digital content business models

The pattern of unlawful access to content online undermines the economic foundations of the knowledge industries. Copyright industries are in decline. Inflexible mass media content business models are not delivering to consumers what they want and are not returning value to creators.

Online content business models that have not adapted to the web do not meet consumer demand. These models are alienating consumers and provoking general consumer complicity with online piracy. They are barriers to a knowledge economy.

Lawful copyright content supply models cannot succeed online until the legitimate content services are at least as easy and attractive to consumers as the pirate services. Moreover, enforcement by rights owners through civil litigation and criminal prosecutions will continue to provoke hostile reactions from consumers while legitimate content access models are inferior to the pirates.

Scholarly communications paradox

The scholarly communications paradigm is supported by the taxpayer and, as the volume of knowledge production and publication grows, the scholarly content publication model has become unsustainable.

Salaried academic authors write and peer review articles for journal publishers. There are no direct payments to the authors and peer reviewers and no royalties. Universities donate their academics' content to the publishers and then, through their libraries, buy that content from the publishers. Academics gain advancement through publication, but many articles in academic journals on university library shelves are never read.

There is no direct market incentive for authors of successful articles and no market signals from consumers. An author whose content is in demand and an author whose content is never read receive the same zero return from the market for their works, while commercial publishers that publish them profit from each alike.

In the digital environment universities have responded to the growing cost of library subscriptions to journals by establishing institutional e-repositories for articles. Some universities fund the entire cost of their repositories, while other repositories require the academic authors to pay to have their articles published in them. Institutional repositories are an attempt to address some of the problems confronting scholarly communications, but the repositories do not have a sustainable publishing model. They do not generate revenue and so they must depend on rounds of grant funding for their continued existence. Nor do they provide any economic or reputational incentive for the authors of the content by rewarding quality or demand for an article.

Sustainable digital content paradigm

Access to knowledge is the basis of an educated, civil society. In a global market economy each nation must establish real security of individual intellectual property rights to engender an information society.

Access to high-quality and diverse content can only be sustained in a functioning copyright market. A content market depends not only on intellectual property rights but also on lawful business models that empower consumers. Viable online copyright content models must offer consumers instant, direct access to high volumes of content at a reasonable price and return fair payments to creators and producers, according to the use of their work. It is these copyright content utility services that will lower the barriers to making content available, offer equality of access to content and improve information equity.

Copyright infrastructure that fosters original independent creativity also enables content to flow online in a fair, efficient and viable marketplace.

Advanced economies depend on stable market frameworks for key assets and commodities. Secure utility markets for intellectual property online will improve access and attract talent and investment in digital knowledge creation and content services. A secure copyright market framework will fund sustainable cultural and knowledge services, which are the catalyst for a productive global knowledge economy.

Conclusion

Intellectual property forms the backbone of innovation, which drives a knowledge economy. The challenge facing the international community is to establish norms that support and reward individual creativity and communication of new ideas in a digital environment.

References

Association of American Publishers (2007) 'Publishers Welcome USTR's Annual "Special 301" Report and Results of China Provincial Review,' 30 April 2007. Online, available: www.publishers.org (accessed 25 September 2007).

BBC (2004) 'Online film piracy "set to rise"', *BBC News* 9 July 2004. Online, available: http://news.bbc.co.uk/2/hi/technology/3879519.stm (accessed 7 September 2010).

Boutlin, P. (2010) 'E-book piracy costs U.S. publishers $3 billion, says study', *Venturebeat*, 2 March. Online, available: http://venturebeat.com/2010/03/02/book-piracy-costs-u-s-publishers-3b-says-study (accessed 27 April 2011).

Cabot, M. (2010) Interview, 'e-book Piracy With Author Meg Cabot'. Online, available: www.australianwomenonline.com/e book piracy with-author-meg-cabot/ (accessed 11 Jan 2010).

Carpenter, M. M. (2009) 'Trademarks and human rights: oil and water? or chocolate and peanut butter?', *The Trademark Reporter*, 99(4). Online, available: http://ssrn.com/abstract=1562791 (accessed 10 January 2011).

Defoe, D. (1709), *A Review*, 26 November.

Hardin, G. (1968) 'The tragedy of the commons', *Science*, 162: 1243–48. Online, available: www.interworldstats.com/stats.htm (accessed 23 Mar 2010).

Held, D., McGrew, A., Goldblatt, D. and Perraton, J. (1999) *Global Transformations*, Stanford, CA: Stanford University Press.

IFPI Digital Music Report (2010) 'Music how, when, where you want it'. Online, available: www.ifpi.org/content/library/DMR2010.pdf (accessed 6 May 2011).

Landes, W. M. and Posner, R. A. (2002) 'Indefinitely renewable copyright', University of Chicago Law and Economics, Olin Working Paper No. 154. Online, available: http://ssrn.com/abstract=319321 or doi:10.2139/ssrn.319321 (accessed 27 April 2011).

Miniwatts Marketing Group (2010) Internet World Stats, Usage and Population Statistics www.internetworldstats.com/stats.htm (accessed 23 March 2010).

Mokoto, R. (2010) 'Report finds 9 million illegal downloads of e-books', *New York Times*, Online, available: http://artsbeat.blogs.nytimes.com/2010/01/14/report-finds-9-million-illegal-downloads-of-e-books (accessed 25 October 2010).

Physorg (2010) '49 servers shut in Euro police raid on online piracy network', *Physorg* (AFP). Online, available: www.physorg.com/news203095727.html (accessed 11 Jan 2011).

Spring, T. (2009) 'E-book piracy: the publishing industry's next epic saga?' Online, available: www.computerworld.com.au/article/330902/e-book_piracy_publishing_industry_next_epic_saga_ (accessed 23 March 2010).

State Council of the People's Republic of China (2008) 'Outline of the National Intellectual Property Strategy', issued 5 June 2008 *State Council of the People's Republic of China*. Online, available: www.sipo.gov.cn/sipo_English/laws/developing/200906/t20090616_465239.html (accessed 11 Jan 2011).

US Senate Finance Committee (2010) 'Baucus, Grassley seek ITC investigation into the effect of China's intellectual property rights infringement on the U.S. economy and job growth', press release. Online, available: http://finance.senate.gov/newsroom/chairman/release/?id=d48e7053-ddc1–476b–9599–14dd68710836 (accessed 19 April 2010).

United States Trade Representative (2009) *2009 Report to Congress on China's WTO Compliance*, December 2009. Online, available: (accessed 11 Jan 2011) www.ustr. gov/webfm_send/1572.

Willis, A. (2009) 'Brussels claims failed business model is causing online piracy', *EU Observer*. Online, available: http://euobserver.com/9/28438 (accessed 7 Sept 2009).

WIPO (World Intellectual Property Organization) (2009) Address by Dr Francis Gurry, Director General, to the National Press Club, Canberra, 4 August. Online, available: www.wipo.int/export/sites/www/about-wipo/en/dgo/speeches/pdf/dg_np_au_09.pdf.

——— . Online, available: www.wipo.int/about-wipo/en/what_is_wipo.html, www.wipo. int/treaties/en/general (accessed 29 January 2011).

Cases

Prince Albert v Strange [1849] EWHC Ch J20.

General Protecht Group, Inc. v. International Trade Commission, Nos. 09–1378, –1387, –1434 (Fed. Cir. Aug. 27, 2010).

Roadshow Films Pty Ltd v iiNet Limited (No. 3) [2010] FCA 24. Online, available: www.austlii.edu.au/au/cases/cth/FCA/2010/24.html (accessed 27 April 2011).

Legislation, International Conventions and Treaties

Statute of Monopolies 1623, 21 Jac. 1, c. 3.

Copyright Act 1709 8 Anne c.19.

Calico Printers' Act, An Act for the Encouragement of the Arts of designing and printing Linens, Cottons, Callicoes and Muslins by vesting the Properties thereof in the Designers, Printers, Proprietors for a limited Time 1787, 27 Geo.III, c.38.

Trade Mark Registration Act (UK) 1875, c.17.

Paris Convention for the Protection of Industrial Property 1883. Online, available: www.wipo.int/treaties/en/ip/paris/trtdocs_wo020.html (accessed 27 April 2011).

United Nations (1948) *The Universal Declaration of Human Rights*. Online, available: www.un.org/en/documents/udhr/index.shtml#a27 (accessed 27 April 2011).

——— (1966) *International Covenant on Economic, Social and Cultural Rights*. Online, available: http://www2.ohchr.org/english/law/cescr.htm (accessed 27 April 2011).

Berne Convention for the Protection of Literary and Artistic Works of September 9, 1886, as amended on September 28, 1979, Article 9 (2) the 'three step test'.

Agreement Between the World Intellectual Property Organization and the World Trade Organization 1995, WIPO.

US–China Relations Act (2000). Online, available: www.govtrack.us/congress/billtext. xpd?bill=h106-4444 (accessed 11 Jan 2011).

Australia–United States Free Trade Agreement 2005, Chapter 17. Online, available: www.dfat.gov.au/trade/negotiations/us_fta/final-text/index.html (accessed 11 Jan 2011).

The European Convention on Human Rights and Fundamental Freedoms, Article 1 of the First Protocol, 2009. Online, available: www.echr.coe.int/NR/rdonlyres/D5CC24A7-DC13-4318-B457-5C9014916D7A/0/ENG_CONV.pdf (accessed 11 Jan 2011).

Chapter 13

Scholarly publishing, knowledge mobility and internationalization of Chinese universities

Rui Yang

Introduction

Scholarly publication is a significant instance of the way in which academic knowledge is 'mobilized' in the global network. Scholarly communities understand themselves to transcend national borders, engaging in the collective production of scientific knowledge for its own sake and the collective good of humanity. The global mobility of scientific knowledge is often taken for granted. However, there exists a powerful yet unequal global knowledge system featuring a centre–periphery divide among nations, resulting from historical factors and enhanced by globalization. The centres take charge of the means of communication of knowledge, including major scholarly journals and publishers, to monopolize the resources and exclude the peripheries. The peripheries need to participate in the system in order to be able to access the knowledge produced by the centres and produce their own knowledge that can be recognized in the system (Altbach 1998). This global division of labour reveals a stratified nature among cultures and the existing global inequality of knowledge creation and application, functioning to perpetuate academic dependency (Alatas 2003).

This chapter looks at scholarly publishing in the Chinese mainland as a principal means of knowledge dissemination in a context of the global knowledge network. Beginning with the latest developments, it discusses some specific issues facing Chinese scholarly publishing, with particular regard to China's ambition of importing the world into China while bringing China to the world. It explores the effectiveness of using Chinese indigenous publishing houses and journals as an act of liberation to break Western control and examines the problems faced by Chinese institutions and scholars in scholarly publishing as an example of the non-Western world.

Book-based education has long been 'global'. The advent of the book accelerated both standardization and the international exchange of knowledge (Eisenstein 1980; Febvre and Martin 1976). With a rich and lengthy historical record of printed culture, China produced the world's first printed book in the ninth century (Bodde 1952). The number of books published in China until the end of the fifteenth century was more than the total in the rest of the world (Wang 2004). China invented the technology upon which publishing depended until quite recently (McGowan 1999). The invention has been seen as one of the greatest contributions in the history of humankind (McDermott 2006).

China's current research capacity in sciences is developing remarkably. The number of peer-reviewed papers published by Chinese researchers rose 64-fold over the past 30 years. China's growth as a scientific powerhouse has been unprecedented: it ranked 18th and 12th in 1992 and 1998, respectively (Donovan 2000) and overtook Japan and the United Kingdom in 2006 to become the world's second largest producer of research papers. Chinese scientists have increased their output at a far faster rate than counterparts in rival 'emerging' nations such as India, Russia and Brazil. Jonathan Adams, a research evaluation director at Thomson Reuters, calls China's growth 'awe-inspiring' (Moore 2010).

According to Marginson (2008), China is 'remaking the knowledge economy landscape': between 1995 and 2005, the annual number of scientific papers produced in China rose from 9,061 to 41,596, with an annual output of papers rising by 16.5% in contrast to South Korea (15.7%), Singapore (12.2%), Taiwan (8.6%), the EU (1.8%) and the USA (0.6%), while in the UK the number did not rise at all. In 2008, China produced 112,000 scientific papers, and the number of papers by Chinese researchers in five top research journals – *Nature*, *Science*, *Cell*, the *Lancet* and the *New England Journal of Medicine* – tripled to 21 papers a year. China is set to take first place within ten years (Moore 2010).

Furthermore, China's demography suggests vast long-term research potential. By 2010, 90% of all PhDs in the physical sciences and engineering were held by Asians living in Asia, most of them produced by China. Chinese science and technology (S&T) workers are becoming stronger and younger. According to the latest national survey by the China Association for Science and Technology (CAST) and the China Institute for Development Strategy of Science and Technology, China's S&T workers had grown rapidly from 29.56 million in 2002 to 51.60 million by 2007, rising by 74%. Among them, 37 million are under the age of 40, accounting for more than two-thirds of the total (CAST 2009).

Scholarly publishing reflects the scientific and technological strength of a country (Baensch 2004). With one of the largest publishing industries in the world, China's scholarly publishing deserves serious attention. In 1999, over 140,000 titles were published, 7,329 million volumes were sold and total sales reached USD 4.3 billion. The number of publishing houses increased from 105 in 1979, to 214 in 1981 and to 566 in 2000. By the early 2000s, the industry employed 46,390 people, with 73,898 bookstore retailers and over 240,000 people working to distribute books (Yu 2004). In line with China's submissions to Western publishers is its massive growth in the purchasing of foreign language publications. China will take its full place in the international publishing scene, and is strategically positioning itself as a leader in the global arena. Its publishing industry is too important for the rest of the world to ignore. While major international publishers have become aware of China's great potential and set their policies accordingly (Stanley and Yan 2007), little research has been done.

Administration of Chinese publishing

The former president of the Chinese Academy of Science once compared academic publications to a dragon's head and tail of academic research, meaning that research projects begin with study of the already published literature and end with the publication of the results of the research project in question. Because of its significance to the development of science and technology, the Chinese government always places great importance on academic publishing (Wang 1994). Each publisher submits an annual list of proposed new projects for approval by the General Administration of Press and Publications (GAPP), which is responsible to the State Council for supervision of all publishing in China and directs all activities of Chinese registered publishing houses (McGowan 1999). GAPP is also responsible for the administration of publishing and distributing magazines and newspapers throughout the country, and is the central office that administers and assigns the ISBN (International Standard Book Numbers) and ISSN (International Standard Series Numbers) to all new publications in China (Baensch 2004).

Until recently, Chinese publishing houses were established by ministries and other government organizations to produce books in particular subject areas or for particular purposes, or by provinces or municipalities to produce books for local sale. Publications were priced by number of pages and category of book (Fang and Xu 2005). According to the Ministry of Culture, books published in 1956 were divided into 11 classes, and then further into 26 subdivisions. Each type had a fixed price range per printed sheet, which remained valid until the 1980s. The pricing system took almost no account of either the cost of a publication or of the market demand for it. The presses did not have to worry about bankruptcy. During the entire planned economy period, there were some slight modifications to this system, while its fundamentals remained untouched.

Such a system was undoubtedly detrimental to academic publications, which are always published with high unit costs and short print runs – although most heads of presses would choose to publish those titles that could break even at least, to minimize the allocation of funds from the government. After the mid-1980s, the fixing of prices without reference to unit cost inevitably led to those publications with a small market showing heavy losses. For example, Science Press, one of China's largest STM (scientific, technical and medical) publishing houses, published 522 titles in 1987, of which 489 (93.7%) lost money. Among the 101 journals that it published, 92 (91%) lost money, which resulted in a total loss of 3,990,000 RMB that year. The publishing of academic works thus became a huge burden for the industry and academia (Xu *et al.* 2007).

With the implementation of the open-door policy and the introduction of the market since the late 1970s, China's publishing industry has been in a period of fundamental transition, from a preoccupation with socialist propaganda to increasing market orientation. For example, Jilin General Publishing House gained approval from the Jilin Price Bureau in April 1987 to try pricing academic works by cost. In December, the State Price Bureau permitted Science Press to price by cost within certain types of their books. In March 1988, GAPP transmitted the State Price Bureau's reply to the Chinese Academy of Science and gave approval to publishing houses to price by cost those academic and professional works for which the market was small, shifting the right to set prices of academic publications to publishers (Fang and Yao 1998).

After three decades of reforms, the impact of the market on China's publishing industry is becoming increasingly evident, although it remains a self-contained market to a high degree (McGowan 1999). Due to the political significance attached to it by the communist government, deregulation is unlikely to go as far or as fast as in other consumer industries and services (Drury 1998). It operates with ideological reservations about the free flow of ideas and remains state-controlled. However, new publishing business models are being investigated and in some cases implemented. It is becoming an increasingly dynamic market (Buckwallter 2004).

Learned journals

China produces many journals. The total number printed reached 401.38 million issues in 2001, 1.37 times that of 1988 and 1.76 times that of 1978 (Tian 2003). The number of Chinese journals reported has varied across the years, due to different methodologies employed. Dai (2004) noted that there were 8,889 periodicals in 2001, including 520 integrated journals, 2,252 philosophy and social science journals, 4,420 science and technological journals, 947 culture and education journals, 545 literature and art journals, 141 magazines for children, and 64 pictorials. Zhang (2006) reported over 9,000 journals published in mainland China in 2004, with a total of 280 million copies and an average of 2.32 copies for each mainland Chinese resident. Academic journals form the main body of these periodicals and account for nearly 80% of the total. Guo *et al.* (2006) reported 5,387 STM journals in China in 2005. Among them, 3,685 were academic/scholarly journals, 1,090 were technological, 235 covered popular science, 214 were general and policy, and 163 were indexing/abstracting journals (Stanley and Yan 2007). Chinese learned journals exhibit a number of unique features, demonstrating challenges as well as opportunities.

Quality and impact

Using the citation index as a prime criterion, Chinese scientific journals have little international impact. By 2003, less than 1% of publications within China were included in major international indexing databases (Dai 2004). In 1999, China's top-cited journal, *Mining and Geologica Sinica*, had an impact factor (IF) of 1.487. The average number of citations per article published in the Chinese journals catalogued by the Science Citation Index (SCI) was 0.326 (Lu 2004). According to the Journal Citation Report 2003 of the Institute for Scientific Information (ISI), the highest IF of the 12 journals financed by China's National Natural Science Foundation (NNSF) was 1.095, with the highest citation frequency of 2,391. The two values were far lower than the equivalent overseas journals, which had a highest IF of 28.172 and total citations of 212,938.

China's low global scientific influence is partially due to the fact that English has become the preferred language of international communication in science. The Chinese consider that their research findings are neglected by the international community (Donovan 2000). One means to improve their situation is to publish in English to foster the inclusion of Chinese journals in international abstracting and indexing databases. China has 199 scientific journals published in English. Most articles published in these journals are catalogued by major international indexing systems such as the SCI and EI (Engineering Index) (Lu 2004). Most Chinese scholarly journals are only published in Chinese, and China's latest scientific developments are not readily available to non-Chinese-speaking scientists. In 1999, only 13, 96, 110, 117, 132, and 193 Chinese journals were respectively indexed by the SCI, EI, Index of Science and Technology Programs, Science Abstracts, Centre for Biophotonics, Science and Technology, and Abstract Journal. By June 2001, 62 Chinese journals (44 in English) were indexed in the Science Citation Index–Expanded (SCI-E) (Wu *et al.* 2002).

Chinese journals' small international impact reflects China's far less impressive domestic research capacity (Lo 2010) and the quality of domestic academic journals. This is firstly because many Chinese researchers are not fully aware of the requirements and standards expected in the international academic community, lacking the required familiarity with the extant literature (Wang and Weldon 2006). They cite few references in their publications, with an average of 6.6 per article (Tian 2003). Secondly, publishing in journals catalogued by major international indexing systems has become a yardstick in many Chinese institutions of learning, where SCI papers mean not only promotions but also hefty monetary rewards (Cao 2010). Chinese scientists prefer to publish their best papers in international English language journals.

However, it is fair to point out that the quality of Chinese domestic journals is increasing. Some journals have even gained international respect. By 2003, 64 journals were listed by the SCI. *Geology Journal* (English version) has become one of the most influential journals in its field (Wang 2004). One direct drive has been the prominence given to the so-called citation index by librarians, abstracting and indexing services, administrators and others, despite its many defects (Donovan 2000).

University journals

Chinese university journals are designated to report the achievements in teaching and research of their host institutions (Stanley and Yan 2007). They account for a quarter of China's periodicals. China had 2,263 regular higher learning institutions by 2008 (China Education and Research Network 2010). Each has at least one journal. Some universities publish different versions by discipline. Chinese university journals are edited, published and distributed by their own editorial departments or staff, with similar contents based mainly on the work of their staff. They are inevitably integrative (Wang and Wang 2004) and inconvenient for readers and libraries. Such diversity in contents acts against the trend toward specialization of content (Donovan 2000), discourages the circulation of articles and fails to attract readers.

Some 30 university journals are published entirely in English. Of the rest, almost all have English translations of abstracts, titles and sometimes key words to increase their international impact. Some have gradually been included in international database systems. In 1996–98, 10 university journals were among the 40 Chinese academic journals indexed in the Current Bibliography on Science and Technology (CBST) of Japan, 4 (3 in English and 1 in Chinese) were among the 63 in SCI or SCI-E in 2000, and 37 were among the 133 indexed by EI in 2003. However, a general feature of China's university journals is low quality papers. The *Chinese Scientific and Technical Journal Citation Reports 2001* reported that the impact factor and citation frequency of university journals were lower than those for journals of the Chinese Academy of Science (Wang and Wang 2004). While Chinese universities are becoming the driving force of national basic research (during the ninth Five-Year Plan, SCI papers published by researchers in universities accounted for 70% of all papers from China indexed by SCI, and 75% of those from China in EI), university journals do not reflect this. University researchers prefer to send their papers to international journals.

There have been some measures to upgrade the status of university journals and provide a route for their entry to the SCI. Since 2001, the Ministry of Education has urged university journals to merge and cooperate to create specialized high-level journals, has reviewed the responsibilities of editors-in-chief and the terms of employment of editors, and has called for a mechanism to encourage broader activities of editors. In 2002, the Ministry hosted discussions specifically on the improvement of the philosophy and social science edition of university journals. In 2003, the Ministry initiated the Fame-Journal Project to develop 10–20 high-status social science and philosophy journals to reflect the academic strengths of Chinese universities in these areas. At the Ninth Annual Meeting of the Natural Sciences Edition of University Journals in 2003, the development and reform of university journals were placed high on the agenda. The Higher Education Press (HEP) and the University Journal Institute jointly launched the Chinese University Journal Abstract Program in 2003 to build up a database of high-quality material by selecting the best papers published in university journals yet not indexed by the SCI and providing abstracts of these papers.

Scholarly publishers

According to GAPP, China had 562 publishing houses in 2001 (Li 2004). Wang (2004) reported 141 scholarly publishers in China that produced 4,420 journal titles and 34,126 new book titles in 2002. Most Chinese scholarly publishers were established after 1982. They are concentrated in major cities. Science Press, formed by the consolidation of the Pre-Edit and Translation Bureau of the Chinese Academy of Science and Longman United Book Company, which was established in the 1930s, is the largest comprehensive scientific, technical and professional publishing institute. Previously, distribution was entirely represented by the state-owned Xinhua bookstores around China. With the introduction of the market, other kinds of enterprises are rapidly developing. A new pattern of book distribution system has taken shape in China. State-owned bookstores remain the main part of the system, but are complemented by non-state-owned bookstores that have become an important component of China's book market (Yang 2004).

China's first university publisher, People's University Press, was set up in 1955. Most Chinese university presses were established in the 1980s. By 2008, China had 103 university presses, accounted for 17.7% of Chinese publishing houses (Peking University 2009). They cover high-level academic publishing in the fields of humanities, social sciences, science and technology. In 2003, 45 titles by university presses (6% of all the prize winners) won the national book prize, the highest honour in Chinese publishing, conducted every two years (Wang 2005). Although based at their affiliated university campuses, they serve the national book market, which is distinguished by the fact that students are the major customers. With their central task being to publish educational books, their efforts are usually directed to the cultural needs of society, while national regulations require them always to put social benefits first.

Most academic works have a narrow market and small sales. Scholarly publishing is rarely viable commercially. It is inevitably an unprofitable undertaking that requires a direct or indirect subsidy (Altbach 1978). Many Chinese scholarly publishers establish funds to provide financial support for academic publication. In 1988, Shandong Science and Technology Publishing House set up the Taishan Fund specifically to subsidize the publication of scientific and technological works. In 1994, 321 scholars from the Chinese Academy of

Science wrote to the State Council to appeal for help in solving the financial problems of publishing academic works. This led to more publication funds for academic publications with a dramatic increase in both number and size of works.

By 2003, 80% of China's 96 university presses had such funds established by organizations at varying levels (Jin 2003). Those set up by the central government are usually large, while most funds set up by local government only support academic works by local writers or works by writers from other places that are closely connected with regional economic and cultural development. Funds run by universities are for the publication of academic works or textbooks by their own staff. Many state or provincial scientific research institutes set up specialized funds for academic publication.

In 2006, a new phenomenon emerged. Some university presses began to receive support from foreign scholarly publishers to set up funds for academic publication. For example, Zhejiang University Press and Springer-Verlag set up a fund for publication of science and technology, with 1 million RMB (about USD 125,000) from Zhejing University Press and EUR 50,000 from Springer-Verlag. Their aim is to encourage and finance Chinese scientists to publish their academic and research results in the form of academic books to be promoted in the international academic publishing market (Xu *et al.* 2007).

Issues and observations

Chinese scholarly publishing has shown a series of paradoxical developments, with both remarkable achievements and daunting tasks. While the scenario shares much with many non-Western societies, China's response is unique and salutary.

Language: Chinese or English?

China is a country with 56 indigenous nationalities. Besides the official *Putonghua*, 33 scientific journals are published in Tibetan, Korean, Mongolian, Uygur and Kazak. By 2004, China had 196 English language academic journals. The number of papers by Chinese scientists published in English is increasing rapidly (Stanley and Yan 2007). Back in 2000, of the papers from China indexed in the SCI, over 80% were in English, while the remainder were chiefly in Chinese, with just a few in other languages such as Japanese, French and German.

The number of journals published in English is increasing rapidly. The Chinese regard English academic journals as an important tool for international scientific communication in many non-English speaking countries (Jia 2006). Based on the report by Qiu *et al.* (2009) on the evaluation of Chinese academic journals, there are 199 academic journals published in English in mainland China. Among them 55 and 31 are indexed by the SCI/SCI-E and EI, respectively.

English has become the dominant language of scientific discourse (Ammon 2001). Unlike many non-Western countries, China sees this as a historical fact. Instead of resisting the fact, China has initiated various policies to adapt to it. For instance, in order to accelerate internationalization of Chinese academic journals, the NNSF set up the Key Academic Journals Fund Project in 1999, applicants for which have to show that they are indexed by the SCI, SCI-E or SCI-Search, or that the total citation frequency of their journals is in the top 50 of those listed in *Chinese Scientific and Technical Journal Citation Reports*.

The bias of the international indexing systems towards the English language has strongly encouraged a move towards more use of English in Chinese scholarly publishing (Wang and Wang 2004). The use of English instead of Chinese as the language of publication, however, greatly limits the readership within China. International recognition thus may run counter to the interests of academics within China (Donovan 2000).

Purpose: domestic or international?

A long-standing dilemma in the internationalization of higher education in non-Western societies exists between domestic needs and international orientation. For more than a decade, Chinese scientific policy-makers, universities and research institutes have been encouraging publication in foreign journals. This has helped to increase China's international academic position and promotes the top research done within China. Policies have been developed at various levels to offer substantial financial awards to papers catalogued by major international indexing systems, especially the SCI, and much more for those published in top-tier international journals. Those in domestic SCI-indexed journals are treated very differently. The Ministry of Education and the Ministry of Science and Technology survey the number of papers published in international journals and those indexed by the SCI, EI and ISTP (International Scientific and Technological Proceedings, an ISI product) annually. Such numbers are used in the evaluation of national awards for scientific and technological progress, the selection of the best PhD theses and the promotion of academic staff (Stanley and Yan 2007).

The aim is to serve domestic needs while simultaneously enhancing international visibility. In June 2005, Elsevier initiated a new project to collaborate with some university journals such as the *Journal of Tsinghua University* and the *Journal of University of Science and Technology Beijing*. Elsevier selects and republishes some papers from these journals on their ScienceDirect website, and asks the Chinese journals to recommend high-quality Chinese papers to be published simultaneously in Elsevier's English journals. More recently, in 2006, Springer began to co-publish a series of 27 journals with HEP. Covering 24 fields, the series is called *Frontiers in China – Selected Publications from Chinese Universities*. The editorial team selects papers already published in Chinese from Chinese journals and asks the authors to translate them into

English. The *Frontiers* editors then check both the content and language. While HEP does the typesetting and printing and provides financial aid for editing, Springer is responsible for English language quality and overseas distribution. Throughout the process, the editorial teams on both sides work with Chinese authors. A Western publisher and Chinese partners share experiences and promote science in a global arena. Springer gets additional content for its aggregation and is able to build relationships with the authors and the Chinese community, while the authors' papers are read and cited internationally.

Initiative: individual or governmental?

Scholarly publishing remains highly centralized in China. The Chinese government is keen to improve the nation's scientific capability and has taken a series of measures. China's scholarly publishers and journals are supported by governments at different levels. Those supported by the central government are usually regarded as highly prestigious, and authors preferentially select them for their best work. Top-tier academic journals are indexed by major domestic indexing services (Lu 2004) and are heavily dependent on finance from the government. Increasingly, the money offered by the government can hardly guarantee their basic editing and printing. There appears to be a movement towards a market-economy mode. Many publishers and journals are trying to be self-financing, and charging publication fees is their main approach. Usually authors have to pay a publication fee before their work can be published. This pushes some authors further away to overseas submissions (Wang and Weldon 2006).

One way for the government to increase China's international academic position is to encourage scientists to publish their work with international major publishers and in high-level foreign journals. As noted earlier, China's policy of awarding money has led to high-quality manuscripts being published in foreign journals and greater difficulty for domestic journals to obtain submissions from indigenous researchers. In 2000, a total of 30,499 articles by Chinese authors were indexed by the SCI. They appeared in 2,081 journals within 38 countries. Among them, 4,676 were in 720 journals in the USA and, respectively, 3,117 and 510 were in the UK and 2,899 and 310 in the Netherlands (Dai 2004). In 2000–2003, Chinese scientific and technical papers published in domestic SCI-indexed journals fell by 8 percentage points to 32.7%, whereas papers published in foreign journals increased by 8 percentage points to 67.3% (Institute of Scientific and Technical Information of China 2004). While government monetary reward has effectively boosted researchers' incentive to publish overseas, a sustainable development depends on motivated individuals doing creative research. An academic culture that is based on merit-based norms and competition for advancement and research funds is vitally necessary.

Conclusion

Chinese higher education is fast integrating with the international community. China is now witnessing massive growth both in the purchasing of foreign language journals by Chinese authors and in the submission of articles written by Chinese scholars to Western journals. With policies of financial rewards for international publication at all levels from national higher education assessment to individual academics' promotion and the completion of postgraduate studies, research publications in international journals are seen as the most important indicator of internationalization. The Chinese scientific community has demonstrated greater openness to ideas and co-operates with overseas publishers. Chinese scholarly publishing has been developing rapidly to take its place in the international scene, in line with China's general developments in science and technology. It is a sign of China's positioning itself for leadership in the knowledge-based economies of the coming era.

Recently, there has been a growing realization that the production of indigenous scientific research and analysis is important. In the social sciences and humanities, indigenous scholarship has been emphasized. While links to an international scientific community remain to be prioritized, efforts are underway to provide an independent base for research and scholarship. Quoted in *Folio* magazine, Thomas D. Gorman, a leading publishing authority in the market and Hong Kong-based chairman of CCI Asia-Pacific Ltd., licensees of Time Inc.'s *Fortune* in China, states, 'If you have the right outlook, do your homework carefully, and especially if you take a long-term view, there is tremendous opportunity here' (Buckwallter 2004: 26).

International publishing and China's conforming of domestic scholarly publishing to international norms have many implications. As international publications produced by Chinese scholars increase rapidly, scientific and technical papers published in domestic SCI-indexed journals fall remarkably. Chinese publishers, distributors and the intellectual public still look to the major Western societies for their intellectual needs, and domestic products are not considered prestigious. This is necessarily related to the global knowledge network dominated by Western countries and operating predominantly in English. It reminds us that real/proper knowledge is only produced by some particular countries in a particular way, and that the Western educational system and structures continue to define education for the rest of the world, and, by extension, they define what knowledge is and who may claim competence in it.

References

Alatas, S.F. (2003) 'Academic dependency and the global division of labour in the social sciences', *Current Sociology*, 51(6): 599–613.

Altbach, P.G. (1978) 'Scholarly publishing in the Third World', *Library Trends*, Spring: 489–503.

—— (1998) *Comparative Higher Education: knowledge, the university and development*, Hong Kong: Comparative Education Research Centre, University of Hong Kong.

Ammon, U. (2001) *The Dominance of English as a Language of Science*, New York: Mouton de Gruyter.

Baensch, R.E. (2004) 'Introduction', in R.E. Baensch (ed.) *The Publishing Industry in China*, New Brunswick: Transaction Publishers.

Bodde, D. (1952) 'Translator's preface', in Y.L. Fung, *A History of Chinese Philosophy*, vol. I, Princeton: Princeton University Press.

Buckwallter, C. (2004) 'Guidelines for magazine publishing in China', in R.E. Baensch (ed.) *The Publishing Industry in China*, New Brunswick: Transaction Publishers.

Cao, C. (2010) 'China's "Great Leap Forward" in scientific papers'. Available: www.upiasia.com/Society_Culture/2010/01/05 (accessed 23 April 2010).

China Education and Research Network (2010) 'National educational expenditure announcements'. Available: www.edu.cn/jiao_yu_fa_zhan_498/20090720/t2009 0720_392038.shtml (accessed 23 May 2010).

Dai, W.M. (2004) 'An analysis of international influence of the Chinese academic periodicals', *Fudan Journal* (Social Sciences), 17(1): 111–18.

Department of Policy Research and Publicity, China Association for Science and Technology (2009) 'China investigation on the status of scientific and technological workers of China in 2008', *Science and Technology Review*, 27(13): 19–26.

Donovan, B. (2000) 'A glimpse of journals in China', *Learned Publishing*, 13(2): 128–29.

Drury, R. (1998) 'Publishing in China: development since 1992', *Asian Library*, 7(5): 111–18.

Eisenstein, E. (1980) *The Printing Press as an Agent of Change* (vols 1–2), New York: Cambridge University Press.

Fang, Q. and Xu, L.F. (2005) 'A brief history of non-state-owned book business on mainland China', *Publishing Research Quarterly*, 4: 39–45.

Fang, Q. and Yao, Y.C. (1998) *Book Marketing*, Taiyuan: Shanxi Economic Press.

Febvre, L. and Martin, H.J. (1976) *The Coming of the Book: the impact of printing 1450–1800*, Norfolk, UK: Lower & Brydone.

Guo, Y., Zhao, X.L., Pan, Y.T., Zhang, Y.H., Zhu, X.D. and Song, P.Y. (2006) 'Analyses and basic statistics of Chinese sci-tech periodicals', *Acta Editologica*, 18(1): 1–3.

Institute of Scientific and Technical Information of China (ISTIC) (2004) *Chinese Scientific and Technical Statistics and Analysis 2003*, Beijing: Scientific and Technical Documents Publishing House.

Jia, X. (2006) 'English language academic journals from China: a great opportunity', *Learned Publishing*, 19: 9–13.

Jin, M. (2003) 'A brief analysis on college publication and college textbook compilation'. Available: www.tbook.com.cn/news_display/news_template.jsp?news_id=118&fid= 111&sid=113 (accessed 12 May 2006).

Li, Y.J. (2004) 'A growing children's book publishing industry in China', in R.E. Baensch (ed.) *The Publishing Industry in China*, New Brunswick: Transaction Publishers.

Lo, A. (2010) 'Quality control', *South China Morning Post*, March 18, A15.

Lu, J.X. (2004) 'Scientific publication in China: an overview and some thoughts on improvement', *Scientific Editor*, 27(4): 120–21.

McDermott, J.P. (2006) *A Social History of the Chinese Book*, Hong Kong: Hong Kong University Press.

McGowan, I. (1999) 'Publishing in China', *Publishing Research Quarterly*, 15(1): 20–32.

Marginson, S. (2008) 'China: rise of research in the Middle Kingdom'. Available: www.universityworldnews.com/article.php?story=20080814152535508 (accessed 23 April 2010).

Moore, M. (2010) 'China to lead world scientific research by 2020'. Available: www.telegraph.co.uk/news/worldnews/asia/china/7075698/C (accessed 23 April 2010).

Peking University (2009) 'University press development in China: advantages and difficulties', Available: http://cbs.pku.edu.cn/nw/newsdetail.cfm?iCntno=3223 (accessed 3 May 2010).

Qiu, J.P., Yan, J.W. and Zhou, M.H. (2009) *A Report on Chinese Academic Journals Evaluation*, Beijing: Science Press.

Stanley, A. and Yan, S. (2007) 'China opening up: Chinese university journals and research-today and tomorrow', *Learner Publishing*, 20(1): 43–49.

Tian, Z.Y. (2003) 'Thoughts on Chinese scholarly journals' current condition and development', *Journal of Liaoning Technical University* (Social Science Edition), 5(1):107–9.

Wang, J.X. (2004) 'Scientific, technical, medical and professional publishing', in R.E. Baensch (ed.) *The Publishing Industry in China*, New Brunswick: Transaction Publishers.

Wang, L.P. (2005) 'Challenges and opportunities: China's university presses in transition', *Learned Publishing*, 18(4): 271–74.

Wang, S.H. and Wang, H.J. (2004) Challenges and strategies for Chinese university journals', *Learned Publishing*, 17(4): 326–30.

Wang, S.H. and Weldon, P.R. (2006) 'Chinese academic journals: quality, issues and solutions', *Learned Publishing*, 19(1): 97–105.

Wang, W.Z. (1994) 'The implication of Taishan Funds for publication of scientific and technological monographs', *Study of Publication*, 5: 16–17.

Wu, Q., Zhang, G.H. and Zhu, X. (2002) 'Evaluation of scientific journals and analysis of scientific publication by natural scientists at Beijing University', *Scientific Research Management*, 23(6): 113–18.

Xu, L.F., Fang, Q. and Lian, X.C. (2007) 'Scholarly publishing funds in China', *Learned Publishing*, 20(1): 36–42.

Yang, D.Y. (2004) 'The reform of the book distribution industry and the development of non-state-owned bookstores in China', in R.E. Baensch (ed.) *The Publishing Industry in China*, New Brunswick: Transaction Publishers.

Yu, H.M. (2004) 'Publishing education of China faces the challenge of development', in R.E. Baensch (ed.) *The Publishing Industry in China*, New Brunswick: Transaction Publishers.

Zhang, Y.M. (2006) 'China's academic journals: development and problems', *Journal of Tsinghua University* (Philosophy and Social Sciences) 21(2): 28–35.

Chapter 14

Explicating a shared truth about a colonial past

Knowledge mobilization, coalition building, Aboriginal literature and pedagogy

Dolores van der Wey

Introduction

A host of issues related to 'responsibility' can seem overwhelming when, at least for critical Indigenous[1] educators, a goal is to mobilize knowledge about Indigenous epistemologies and our shared colonial legacy. Among the most significant of the multitude of federal policies that subjugated Indigenous people was the establishment of residential schools, which operated from the late nineteenth century well into the latter half of the twentieth century. Children were removed from their parents and denied traditional intergenerational relationships, their languages were slain,[2] and their rituals and spiritual beliefs were maligned. In addition, at these schools children were delivered a poor-quality education, one designed to relegate students to the lowest rung of society (Barman 1995; Milloy 1999 among others). The implications of such policies continue today.

The challenges inherent when making explicit that Indigenous people should not bear the sole responsibility for addressing a shared legacy that was not of our making are formidable and often subject to hostile resistance. So, too, is the disruption of the master narrative, the myth of the Canadian nation state that valorizes settlers while often misrepresenting or erasing Indigenous peoples (Episkenew 2009; Mackey 2002). Episkenew argues that Indigenous literary genres validate Indigenous peoples and their experiences while helping to fill the gaps and falsehoods in this master narrative. The body of Indigenous literature constitutes a 'counterstory' to the myths and serves to resist the oppressive identity that has been assigned to Indigenous people. It attempts to replace those stories with accurate ones that command respect. But is immersion in Indigenous literature sufficient, most particularly in university classrooms? The issue of understanding pedagogy as a process of knowledge mobilization, especially in mobilizing difficult knowledge, is particularly complex in a classroom where at least two epistemic worlds are colliding. And how might coalition politics theory inform practice when navigating potentially volatile spaces of difference?

This chapter explores these questions in the context of graduate and under-graduate courses on Indigenous education that enroll both Indigenous and non-Indigenous students. First, I argue that Indigenous peoples and settler society must coalesce. I draw on Indigenous scholars and writers as well as Black feminist scholarship to support this assertion. In the next section, I discuss pedagogical possibilities to address these questions through use of Indigenous literature. The risks, considerations and possibilities in daring to invoke Indigenous narratives in university classrooms will be addressed in the light of Episkenew's (2009) assertion that such texts serve a 'socio-pedagogical function' (p. 17): their objective is to change society by educating the settler readers about Indigenous perspectives of society. Next, I provide details of the methods of enquiry used to mobilize such potentially disruptive knowledge through pedagogy. Then, I argue the importance of examining or re-examining one's relationship with Aboriginal people, as previously held beliefs and attitudes are disrupted, tensions are moved through, and space is created for new knowledge, new truths and new relationships with Aboriginal people. Ultimately, I return to my argument about the imperative of coalescing between and among Indigenous people.

Coalition politics, knowledge mobilization and Indigenous education

Knowledge mobilization has been defined as ' . . . moving knowledge into active service for the broadest possible good', with knowledge 'understood to mean any or all of (1) findings from specific social sciences and humanities research, (2) the accumulated knowledge and experience of social sciences and humanities researchers, and (3) the accumulated knowledge and experience of stakeholders concerned with social, cultural, economic and related issues' (OISE 2008, citing SSHRC's knowledge mobilization strategy, the most recent of which is SSHRC (2009)). The definition prompts the question, whose 'accumulated knowledge and experience . . . ' is considered valid and worthy of consideration? I argue that, if we are to collectively move Indigenous knowledge into active service through institutions of higher education, and if together we are to begin to address the long-term implications of the colonial legacy for the 'broadest possible good', we must coalesce. In order to do so it is essential to understand what it means to coalesce and actively commit to engaging in the process of coalescing, despite its inherent tensions, while simultaneously becoming knowledgeable of the colonial legacy.

Black feminist scholar Cynthia Burack (2004) defines coalitions as the 'joint activity of autonomous groups, either for a single purpose, or to pursue long-term social, economic or political goals' (pp. 150–51). As such, coalitions are places of discourse where participants actively and persistently engage in discussion of the ubiquity of difference. In these spaces the imperative of ongoing intellectual, emotional, and political work across difference is recognized as imperative to achieving stated goals. Burack theorizes three coalitional frames that correspond to levels of difference: with the self, within the group, and between groups. Coalition building cannot take place in intergroup contexts in the absence of vigorous engagement with difference within the self, and within intragroup contexts; that is, in groups that come together for the express purpose of pursuing particular goals. I have found this frame helpful when working with undergraduate and graduate students registered in Indigenous education courses that enroll both Indigenous and non-Indigenous students. It was a useful tool as well when analysing group relations in Indigenous graduate cohorts, where my findings revealed that significant intragroup differences, assumptions and biases impacted group relations (van der Wey 2007). It is made clear to students that, if reparative relations are to be realized, each must be willing to unpack their own assumptions, biases and stereotypical views, and each must be willing to embrace and work through the tensions that are inevitable when undertaking such work. Through this process conflict and power may be discursively negotiated to facilitate reparative politics; however, the emotional drain on group members that accompanies such negotiation within the self and others must be acknowledged. To engage purposefully in coalition politics, then, requires a genuine willingness to disrupt the status quo, to be vulnerable and to let go of any stance of innocence in relations with others. That is a challenging and oftentimes disturbing task for all, whether Indigenous or non-Indigenous.

Black culture historian Bernice Johnson Reagon (1983) also recognizes that coalition work is seldom comfortable. Like Indigenous Hawaiian scholar Huanani-Kay Trask (1991) she works in coalitions because there is no alternative. Regardless of context, when people are oppressed and have been exploited, they have little choice but to join with other activists if their respective common ends are to be reached. There will inevitably come a time when groups must interact with non-members or must open up to members whose differences disrupt comfortable assumptions of homogeneity within the group. Varying experiences and perspectives of differently situated members require collective and ongoing recognition and negotiation. Even if there is a desire for sameness for political or social reasons, differences are enmeshed with likenesses of identity. Therefore, because group members' multiplicitous identities cause them to occupy different positions, or to point out intersections in subjectivity and power that trouble an accepted group identity, the first and second frames (self and intragroup) are inextricably linked (Burack 2004).

There are risks for marginalized groups in acknowledging intragroup difference. Doing so may destabilize a desire to present a 'united front,' a counter-discourse to power, as a result of what may be perceived as an 'airing of the dirty laundry.' Regardless, it is essential for both groups to take such risks if the foundation for reparative processes with other groups is to be built. However, because of the asymmetrical relationship in coalitions, doing so is less than an ideal choice for those with less political power, and oftentimes the agendas of the marginalized groups may slip off the table (Burack 2004; Trask 1991). But what are the prospects, processes and possibilities of coalitions in mobilizing knowledge across Indigenous and non-Indigenous peoples in Indigenous education classrooms?

A pedagogy of disruption

Aboriginal literature and pedagogy: possibilities and pitfalls

Episkenew has posited that Indigenous literature responds to and critiques Canadian government policies and, further, it helps cure the colonial contagion by healing communities that have been injured. It does so, she argues, by challenging the stories that embody the settlers' 'socially shared understanding' of the settlement of what is now called Canada (Episkenew 2009: 2). The notion that communities are necessarily healed through Aboriginal literature is contestable, but I concur with Episkenew that multiple generations of Indigenous people live with intergenerational post-traumatic stress response, which may be directly attributed to multiple generations of being impacted by colonial policies and historical trauma. Regardless, I argue that Aboriginal literature can be empowering for Aboriginal people, and informative, intellectually stimulating and accessible for both Aboriginal and non-Aboriginal people, depending on the text, the context and the pedagogical approaches that are employed, and depending on students' receptivity to the mobilization of alternate knowledge. However, not all students are willing to engage with issues beyond sanctioned textbooks and perspectives of history. Disrupting the dominant Western narrative with students who have accepted as normative its hegemonic properties while in the same classroom as those who have been 'othered' by it adds both a racial and political dimension to our classrooms that mainstream scholars do not, generally speaking, have to encounter (Larocque 2002).

I, too, have experienced student resistance to Indigenous perspectives of history and immersion in a centre/periphery reversal, which is the case when syllabi reflect almost exclusively the literary works and scholarship of Indigenous writers. As Larocque (2002) asserts, many students have come to expect and are comfortable with a focus on 'cultural portraiture'[3] and are put off by the critical work necessary in addressing Canada as a colonial project. She adds, 'good scholarship dictates that we not teach with one eye closed' (Larocque 2002: 215). Daring to engage with students in the process of reversing the master narratives requires more than just reading from a body of Aboriginal literature that constitutes a counterstory to the myths. Indigenous experiences and knowledge must be validated and gaps must be filled. It is imperative that falsehoods embedded within the master narrative be explicated. Further, it requires more than introducing students to a coalition frame, strategically returning recursively to it throughout the course. It calls for engaging students in pedagogical practices that facilitate students' reflective and reflexive relationship with Aboriginal people where they may come to recognize themselves as a product of the historical process, as Dion (2007) proposes.

Methods of enquiry in mobilizing knowledge through pedagogy

In my teaching practice, where my syllabi include extensive use of Aboriginal literature, I have adopted and adapted Sumara's (2002) pedagogical approaches. He has asserted that literary engagements can be important sites for thinking and that classrooms may function as significant sites where insights about human experience may be created. Creating pedagogical structures that include interpretations of literary texts is imperative if assumptions about truth are to be disrupted. Following Sumara, students in my classes are encouraged to apply literary anthropological research methods.[4] In order to reveal truths and to serve as locations for insights about Aboriginal peoples' experiences, carefully selected novels, poems and short stories by Indigenous writers are used strategically in course syllabi. These texts, which are authored primarily but not exclusively by Indigenous scholars, are read through the lens of relevant historical, philosophical and theoretical literatures (including literary criticism). The intent is to have students analyse the relationship between (for some) their newfound knowledge of/or introduction to Aboriginal history, memory (their own relationship with Aboriginal people), culture (Aboriginal philosophy and epistemology), geography, language and identity.

Adapting literary anthropological methods, students in the class on which this chapter is primarily based[5] were asked to annotate their copies of the primary text. They added their questions, interpretations and insights to passages that prompted a response. In small groups students then shared their most provocative passages and annotations, followed by whole group discussion. Students wrote one-page journal entries and later a concluding paper or presentation that was informed by their readings of the text, their journal entries, classroom discourses and other relevant course readings. This paper was to be reflective of students' evolving perceptions and interpretations. These 'spaces' afford the manifestations of their thinking evident in the annotations, group discourses, subsequent recursive passes over the text and their journals and papers. Within these spaces readers have opportunities to review past, present and imagined interpretations of themselves and of others and the contexts of experience (Sumara 2002: 29). In effect, students, whether they identify as Aboriginal or non-Aboriginal, may build new relationships and coalesce with Aboriginal people through literary engagements with the text.

To further inform students' reading of Aboriginal literature and to bring a heightened awareness of their respective ideologies, which may otherwise be imposed on their interpretation of texts rather than opening themselves to alternate ideologies, students read Episkenew's (2002) 'Socially Responsible Criticism: Aboriginal literature, Ideology, and the Literary Canon.' We then discuss its implications before immersing in the reading of Aboriginal literature. Regardless of students' prior knowledge of Aboriginal peoples, they are more likely to analyse their respective interpretations of literary texts with a consciousness of how much their assumptions, biases and attitudes influence their interpretations. They are also conscious of how that process of analysis may impact their perceptions of their relationship with Aboriginal people. Students are then more inclined to recognize the import of historical, philosophical and theoretical readings in informing their interpretations of Aboriginal literary works.

To recognize oneself as a product of the historical process as it impacted Aboriginal people, and to understand one's relationship with Aboriginal people, of course requires knowledge of our history, globally, nationally and locally. Hawaiian scholar Trask implicitly concurs with this argument, as she provides an in-depth backdrop of the history of colonization in Hawaii in her paper on coalition building. While Indigenous peoples' experiences with the excesses of European colonialism and imperialism globally share disturbing similarities, it is imperative to avoid essentializing Indigenous peoples by ignoring the uniqueness of context, varying epistemologies and ways of knowing. Thus, the specific historical backdrop provided by Trask is essential to understanding the coalitions she has entered into to address land use, women's issues and tourism issues in a Hawaiian context. Membership in such coalitions is, as she suggests, comprised largely of people who lack knowledge of Hawaiian history and present-day land claims. Accordingly, informed decisions cannot be made in the absence of the Hawaiian historical record from native Hawaiian perspectives, particularly as it relates to land use and land rights (Trask 1991).

Similarly, the literature that provides the lens through which any literary text is interpreted must be chosen carefully and strategically and, amidst those readings, an historical backdrop must be introduced. However, context will determine just what readings are chosen. In the case of the graduate course, readings included, as an example, Anishinaabe poet and essayist Armand Ruffo's (1994) 'Inside looking out: Reading *Tracks* from a native perspective.' His essay provided students with insider (that is, Anishinaabe) knowledge with which to inform, analyse and interpret mixed blood (German/Anishnaabe) writer Louise Erdrich's (1988) novel *Tracks*, which all students in the class read. The novel is rooted in Anishinaabe culture and explicates the early clashes between traditional Anishinaabe ways and the Catholic Church. This is not to suggest, however, that any one author holds the definitive knowledge of a culture or lens though which a literary piece may be read. It is simply one perspective. Students may seek out or draw upon prior knowledge to inform their analysis and classroom discussions.

It is beyond the scope of this chapter to list and discuss many of the readings from this course. However, Smith's (1999) arguments in chapter one of her book, which she titled 'Imperialism, History, Writing and Theory', are central to the topic of this chapter and, in particular, to informing my arguments with respect to interpretations of Aboriginal literature and Aboriginal research in general. From an Indigenous perspective, Smith states, the four words in the chapter title are provocative; they stir up feelings, attitudes and values:

> They are words which draw attention to the thousands of ways in which indigenous languages, knowledges and cultures have been silenced or misrepresented, ridiculed or condemned in academic and popular discourses. . . . Decolonization is a process which engages with imperialism and colonialism at multiple levels. For researchers, one of those levels is concerned with having a more critical understanding of the underlying assumptions, motivations and values which inform practices.
>
> (Smith 1999: 20)

Smith's concluding sentence in the quote above resonates with my arguments about the imperative of adopting a coalition frame and opening oneself up to disruption of the status quo if we are to facilitate reparative politics between Indigenous and non-Indigenous people. And discerningly chosen Aboriginal literary genres, analysed in relation to relevant theoretical readings, hold the promise of such coalescing, as theoretical arguments are critiqued and applied in specific contexts. The reader's prior assumptions and perceptions regarding Indigenous knowledge and cultures, and how they have been misrepresented and silenced both historically and in a contemporary sense, may be examined.

(Re)-examining relationships with Aboriginal people and existing 'truths'

Dion (2007) effectively applies coalescing strategies in her work with grade school teachers and their handling of Indigenous subject material. She argues that the majority of teachers, like the majority of Canadians, have limited understanding of Aboriginal peoples of Canada, their history or their culture; rather, their understanding is informed by dominant discourses. In order for Aboriginal peoples to live, to be seen as real, dominant discourses must be disrupted. For that to occur, teachers must have the opportunity to investigate and transform their understanding of Aboriginal people and the history of the relationship between Aboriginal and non-Aboriginal people. Dion asserts that many teachers claim the position of 'perfect stranger' to Aboriginal people with ease and argues that such a stance is informed by what teachers know, what they do not know and what they refuse to know. For many, it is a view premised on a range of experiences with stereotypical representations shaped by media, textbooks and their everyday worlds. Further, there is a fear and silence involved in addressing stereotypical content – fear of offending, of introducing controversial subject material and of challenging students' understanding of dominant discourses of Canadian history, excuses that I hear from teacher educators on a regular basis. All of these factors contribute to supporting teachers' claims for the position of perfect stranger (Dion 2007).

Following Dion (2007) I have asked students at the beginning of Indigenous education courses that I teach to free-write in response to the question, 'What is your relationship with Aboriginal people?' They are free to interpret the question in any way they like. Then students are asked for a written reflection on how their knowledge of Aboriginal people has been informed. I collect their responses and enter them anonymously in bullet form into a word file, although I do cluster their respective points together. Then I circulate the file to all students prior to the next class, where we open the class by discussing observations and insights based on reading peers' responses.

Responses to question one vary a great deal. One student in my undergraduate class, for example, found it a 'funny question' and likened it to asking about one's 'relationship with Chinese people or gay people'. The student added, 'we are all human . . . and because of that we are all brothers and sisters'. Another revealed how his/her relationships, or lack thereof, have been shaped by observations of Aboriginal people as being 'intoxicated on the streets'. Another student imagined 'how Aboriginals conquered the tall mountains, rapid waters and deep forests' and therefore she felt a connection to Aboriginal people. Yet another expressed her 'frustration at the amount of extra support afforded students who identify as Aboriginal . . . when other students could benefit from such support'. Students are often willing to reveal their Aboriginal identity through this anonymous process, but are reticent to do so in class. For example, 'I have relatives on one side of my family who are Aboriginal but I have met few of them.' This student effectively explained her reticence to identify publicly as of Aboriginal descent by adding, 'I always felt growing up that being an Aboriginal person was never good enough.' Inevitably a few students indicate their desire to be a 'helper' for Aboriginal students who struggle in school. Some students who openly identify as Aboriginal do so with pride and in the process highlight the importance for them of a 'sense of belonging' in Aboriginal communities, as well as the experience of being able to meet another Aboriginal person and strike up a conversation 'whether I know them or not.'

Typical responses to the second question (how their knowledge of Aboriginal people was informed) include recollections from grade school, books they have read, courses taken, films they have watched, lived experiences, and the like. I have found this to be a productive strategy to help students, whether native or not, begin to uncover the relationship that may structure teachers' and prospective teachers' approaches to teaching Aboriginal content. What is revealed are the dominant stories that Dion alludes to, those 'that position

Aboriginal people as romanticized, mythical, victimized, or militant Other, [the stories that] enable non-Aboriginal people to position themselves as respectful, moral helper, protector of law and order' (Dion 2007: 331). She asserts that teachers and students take up these discourses to protect themselves from having to recognize their own implication in knowledge of the history of the relationship between Aboriginal and non-Aboriginal people in Canada.

Students' interrogation of each other's responses and the processes of critical self-reflection they immerse in foster what for many may be the beginning of an investigation of the origins of their belief systems, including what might explain why they have gone unquestioned, and how they have become internalized. Teachers' prior reliance on dominant discourses that gave structure to their teaching approach, without their having questioned the effects of those discourses, may be opened to close scrutiny for the first time. The students themselves prompt these investigations during this process. For example, when an Aboriginal student in my undergraduate class read the response of the student who expressed frustration at the amount of extra support afforded to Aboriginal students in the school where she worked, she came to class prepared to address the issue, to inform the class of inaccuracies and assumptions that were evident in the response; she also provided some background information about the impact of historical policies that impacted Aboriginal peoples. An in-depth discussion of that issue as well as others ensued in class, informed further by course readings, including Aboriginal literature. Such pedagogical processes enable students to 'call into question existing "truths" and imposed limits on what they know, while simultaneously envisioning new possibilities for both themselves and their ways of teaching' (Simon 1992: 141, cited in Dion 2007: 334).

Dion calls upon students to position themselves in relationship to the work of artists. They draw upon Aboriginal ways of knowing, experiences of colonization, history and culture to create works that reflect their relationship with Aboriginal peoples and their evolving understanding of what it is to be Aboriginal in contemporary times. My practice draws extensively on Aboriginal literature for similar purposes. Whether students are doing so in response to cultural artefacts that may include family photos, postcards or Aboriginal literature, pedagogical strategies must be geared to specifically draw students' attention to how their participation in particular practices may inscribe ways of knowing. These processes increase the likelihood that students will see themselves as shaped by the colonial process. Aligned with Burack's (2004) coalition frame, then, students came to recognize that it is about an examination of the self rather than about 'fixing them'. Yet, it is at once about considering the intragroup dynamics, as students become increasingly informed about critical issues in Indigenous education.

Discussion

At times the tension in the graduate class was palpable, depending on what we were reading and discussing. Despite use of coalition building strategies and attempts to create an intellectually stimulating yet mutually respectful environment, not surprisingly, many students struggled with the disruption of previously held views that was seemingly taking place. It takes time to move into and through such a process, depending on the prior knowledge and experiences students have with such content and pedagogy and on willingness to examine prior assumptions and biases.

Clarissa was one student who seemed to struggle with the Indigenous perspectives that permeated the course. At the end of the term she sought a deferred grade for reasons that we found reasonable. Six weeks later we received all assignments, some of which had been revised. Clarissa had reread and reinterpreted a book she had first read a year earlier, Shirley Sterling's (1992) novel *My Name is Seepeetza*, which is based on the author's childhood experiences in an Indian residential school. She had been quite vocal about her distaste for Sterling's approach in writing the book upon first read. The humour that permeated the book, to her mind, served to shift the focus away from the devastating, long-term impact of residential school on attendees and subsequent generations. However, her final paper revealed that her views about the book had been transformed, a process of critical knowledge mobilization that she attributed to the intertextual connections, pedagogical approaches and personal reflection that she had been immersed in. Aboriginal scholars' insights about Aboriginal peoples' ways of knowing and being and knowledge of history (which she acknowledged she lacked) were instrumental to her new insights as she immersed in a recreation of aspects of her cultural identity. So, too, were the literary anthropological methods she employed in reading and re-reading the text. When Clarissa dropped by my office a month or so later accompanied by a new student to whom she had recommended the course, I was convinced that Clarissa's attitude about Indigenous people and Indigenous issues had been significantly impacted. This act suggested that not only had she immersed in a process where she examined her own assumptions and biases (the first coalition frame), but her having done so was also impacting her intergroup relations (the third frame).

For others in the class the centre/periphery reversal implicit with respect to course content, where Indigenous voices predominated, proved to be challenging. Comments such as, 'They [Indigenous students] have an unfair advantage in this course. They have the knowledge' were heard well into the course from a few students. It seemed not to matter when we reminded them that Indigenous knowledge, perspectives and students were rarely positioned as such, that content and pedagogy by and about Indigenous peoples, knowledge and history are typically scant, if at all in evidence in most course syllabi. As Margaret, an Aboriginal student, stated,

It is important to acknowledge the importance of having access to resources such as Lee Maracle and Jo-Ann Episkenew [Aboriginal novelist and literary critic, respectively, who were both guests during the course]. The discussions brought so much to my understanding of not only the literature but also of the process involved in the creation of their texts. To have the input of Aboriginal writers and scholars brings added perspective to Aboriginal education in the world of academia.

(Journal entry, 24 July 2009)

Another student of immigrant parents revealed through her writing that the course content was striking a little too close to home for comfort. She had struggled with her identity, her relationship with her parents and her desire to be accepted in Canadian society. That desire for acceptance, she wrote, had led her to take up a stance, which required her to forsake her traditional cultures; that is, to not stand out as different. Immersion in this class brought this student face to face with the application of the theoretical frame of coalition politics in her personal life. She was immersed in a process of examining the self, the intragroup context of the class and her world beyond the class, as the process does not begin and end within the confines of the classroom. That is tough to reconcile. Awareness of the frame does not necessarily mean that one is prepared to embrace the ongoing reflexive practices necessary to coalesce. In these moments of tension it is important to remind all that coalition work is hard work but it is a necessary choice if we are to reconcile differences, and it is seldom comfortable.

The response of a student in my undergraduate class on Indigenous Education resonates in relation to Guinier and Torres's (2002) argument that problems of racially marginalized people are symptoms that we are all at risk, not just people of colour. The student wrote:

Reading Hogan's (2000) article 'A Different Yield' alongside Dion's (2007) 'Disrupting Molded Images' makes evident an important link in regards to the relationship between Euro-Western society and Aboriginal peoples; both challenge the reader to thoroughly examine their own patterns of thinking, and the likely result of such examination will reveal that colonization has had, and continues to have a destructive effect on all of us.

(Breanne's journal entry, 31 January 2010)

Not all students will come to terms with the disruption inherent in mobilizing Indigenous knowledge and experience more fully into active service within the duration of one course. But Breanne's poignant and frank response when students were asked to reflect in writing on the course through the lens of the three coalition frames offers hope to those of us who engage in coalition work. She wrote about how she had been impacted on a personal level, how she had come to recognize her own truth as she investigates the history of colonization. Breanna noted that each of us must recognize that there have been consequences for Aboriginal people and non-Aboriginal people alike. Colonization had shaped her worldview, her 'ways of seeing, hearing, perceiving and being'. Breanna added:

> Also, until recently, I was unaware that Aboriginal peoples had worldviews that are so distinct from those of Euro-Western societies. I must shamefully admit that I considered it most acceptable that I focus on sameness when evaluating myself in relation to other human beings – I believed this meant I was not a racist.
>
> (Journal entry, 6 April 2010)

Clearly, there is much work yet to be done in our classrooms. Yet, I am convinced that, by immersing students in pedagogical practices, including the principles of coalition building, rather than just theorizing about it we can increase the likelihood that knowledge mobilization towards building difficult understandings across epistemological worlds may take place. Group members may come to recognize that we must collectively, continually, and consciously lay and build on the foundations for reparative processes within and between groups.

Notes

1   The terms Indigenous and Aboriginal are used interchangeably in this chapter, depending on the context. Indigenous is used when alluding to Indigenous peoples globally and Aboriginal when referring collectively to Canada's Indigenous people who include First Nations, Métis and Inuit.
2   St. Denis (2007) takes exception to describing Aboriginal people as having *lost* their Indigenous language, given that Aboriginal people were punished, shamed and sometimes tortured for speaking their language.
3   Larocque (2002) uses the term 'cultural portraiture' to refer to cultural programmes that include a focus on Native spirituality, ceremonial practice or the practice of replicating crafts.
4   Iser (1989, 1993, cited in Sumara 2002: 29) coined the phrase 'literary anthropology' to describe the interpretive practices associated with the reader/text relationship. It suggests that the interpretation of the text impacts the reader's ongoing self-identity.
5   The graduate class was 'Writing from the Margins: Pedagogical Possibilities in Indigenous and Other Peoples' Literature.' It was co-taught by the author and another Indigenous instructor.

References

Barman, J. (1995) 'Schooled for inequality: The education of British Columbia Aboriginal children', in J. Barman, N. Sutherland and J. D. Wilson (eds) *Children, Teachers and Schools in the History of British Columbia*, Calgary: Detselig Enterprises, 57–80.

Burack, C. (2004) *Healing Identities: Black feminist thought and the politics of groups,* Ithaca, NY: Cornell University Press.

Dion, S. (2007) 'Disrupting molded images: identities, responsibilities and relationships – teachers and Indigenous subject material', *Teaching Education,* 18: 329–42.

Episkenew, J. (2009) *Taking Back our Spirits: Indigenous literature, public policy, and healing,* Winnipeg, MAN: University of Manitoba Press.

—— (2002) 'Socially responsible criticism: Aboriginal literature, ideology, and the literary canon', in R. Eigenbrod and J. Episkenew (eds) *Creating Community: A roundtable of Aboriginal literatures,* Penticton, BC: Theytus Press, 51–67.

Erdrich, L. (1988) *Tracks,* New York: Harper & Row.

Guinier, L. & Torres, G. (2002) *The Miner's Canary: enlisting race, resisting power, transforming democracy,* Cambridge, MA: Harvard University Press.

Hogan, L. (2000) 'A different yield', in M. Battiste (ed.) *Reclaiming Indigenous Voice and Vision,* Vancouver: UBC Press, pp. 115–23.

Iser, W. (1993) *The Fictive and the Imaginary: charting literary anthropology,* Baltimore, MD: The John Hopkins University Press.

—— (1989) *Prospecting: from reader response to literary anthropology,* Baltimore, MD: John Hopkins University Press.

Larocque, E. (2002) 'Teaching Aboriginal literature: the discourse of margins and mainstreams', in R. Eigenbrod and J. Episkenew (eds) *Creating Community: a roundtable of Aboriginal literatures,* Penticton, BC: Theytus Press, 209–34.

Mackey, E. (2002) *The House of Difference: cultural politics and national identity in Canada,* Toronto: University of Toronto Press.

Milloy, J. (1999) *'A National Crime': the Canadian government and the residential school system, 1879 to 1986,* Winnipeg: University of Manitoba Press.

Reagon, B. J. (1983) 'Coalition politics: turning the century', in B. Smith (ed.) *Home Girls: a black feminist anthology,* New York: Kitchen Table: Women of Color Press, pp. 356–68.

OISE (2008) *Research Supporting Practice in Education: linking research and practice,* Ontario Institute for Studies in Education, University of Toronto (accessed on January 2 2011 from www.oise.utoronto.ca/rspe/KM_Products/Terminology/index.html).

Ruffo, A. (1994) *Inside Looking Out: reading* Tracks *from a native perspective,* Penticton, BC: Theytus Books.

Simon, R. (1992) *Teaching against the Grain,* Toronto: OISE Press.

Smith, L. T. (1999) *Decolonizing Methodologies: research and Indigenous peoples,* New York: Zed Books.

SSHRC (2009) SSHRC's Knowledge Mobilization Strategy 2009–2011. www.sshrc-crsh.gc.ca/about-au_sujet/publications/kMbPI_FinalE.pdf.

St Denis, V. (2007) 'Uniting Aboriginal education with anti-racist education: building alliances across cultural and racial identity politics, *Canadian Journal of Education,* 30: 1068-91.

Sterling, S. (1992) *My Name is Seepeetza,* Vancouver: Groundwood Books.

Sumara, D. (2002) *Why Reading Literature in School Still Matters: imagination, interpretation, insight,* Mahwah, NJ: Lawrence Erlbaum.

Trask, H. K. (1991) 'Coalition-building between Natives and non-Natives', *Stanford Law Review,* 43: 1197–1213.

van der Wey (2007) 'Coalescing in cohorts: building coalitions in First Nations education', *Canadian Journal of Education,* 30: 989–1014.

Chapter 15

Deparochializing educational research

Three critical, illustrative narratives

Bob Lingard, Ian Hardy and Stephen Heimans

Introduction

We live and work today in globalized spaces and places and need to recognize this in our theorizing, pedagogies and educational research within the academy. This use of the term 'educational research' rather than 'education research' is significant: the former suggests a commitment through research to progressive improvements in educational policy and practices, necessarily within these globalized settings, while the latter simply names the focus or topic of research subject to the application of social science theories and methodologies (Lingard and Gale 2010). Educational research involves the application of social science theories and methodologies, but with a commitment to improvement to both policy and practice. Implicit in this definition is the researcher's desire for what approximates universal knowledge, but applied to specific, contingent circumstances, which always mean rearticulation through teacher professional knowledge and reading of specific situations. Yet today, these specific contexts of practice are intimately interconnected and imbricated with global educational policy discourses.

Given the globalized spaces and places in which we do educational research today, we need to challenge any taken-for-granted assumptions of a society/ nation homology in research and theorizing, yet also recognize the specificities of local and national educational systems. We need to be wary of making universal knowledge claims that are derived from a non-acknowledged location, usually nations of the Global North. Today, society is in some ways simultaneously local, national, regional and global in terms of effects, experience, politics and imaginaries. This is true of schooling systems, which, while still seemingly national institutions, are now also embedded in global policy framings and discourses. Further, these spaces are situated within unequal power relations, which reflect both contemporary geopolitics and past political struggles. Residual, dominant and emergent geographies of power, including those of the colonial past and postcolonial present, are at play across these global spaces and manifest in vernacular ways in the local and the national. Western 'meta-culture' (Fisher and Mosquera 2004: 5) relates to these cartographies and geographies of power and includes academic theories, epistemologies and research methodologies in the social sciences and in educational research specifically. Recognition of theoretician, researcher and teacher positionality within Western universities and of their relationships to these cartographies of power is a central beginning for challenging the silent (and sometimes, not so silent) valorization of Western epistemologies and ontologies underpinning in a non-reflexive way much educational research. Western metaculture needs to be challenged. A specific step is the need to recognize some universal knowledge claims as specifically Northern knowledge claims, as Raewyn Connell (2007) would put it.

Such recognition and challenge are also imperative for moving towards what Arjun Appadurai (2001b) calls the deparochialization of research and a strong internationalization of the Western academy, in light of enhanced global flows of students and academics as part of the ethnoscapes, mobilities and networks of globalization. Connell (2007: vii–viii) in *Southern Theory* argues similarly that most social science theory 'embeds the viewpoints, perspectives and problems of metropolitan society, while presenting itself as universal knowledge'. Connell also argues that this remains the case with much globalization theory, which fails to recognize the geopolitics of knowledge production of all kinds, including educational research, and regards the periphery as simply the site of empirical data informed by theory developed in the metropoles of the Global North. In this way, Connell (2007: 56–60) suggests that the antinomies of most globalization theory, namely, global versus local, homogeneity versus difference, and dispersed versus concentrated power, reflect concerns of intellectuals located in the metropoles of the Global North and at the same time conceal the conditions and the limitations of the development of such theory. Connell (2007: 221) also notes the need to reject a 'conceptual style in which theory is monological, declaring one truth in one voice', which has been the case with Northern theory masquerading as universal.

Appadurai and Connell are both challenging the contemporary geopolitics of academic work that sees theory as only produced in the high-status universities of the Global North and suggesting the need to redress this situation and encourage theory development in multiple sites across the globe, across the Global North–Global South divide. Connell also makes the point about subjugated knowledges of Indigenous peoples within many nations of the Global North. There are important challenges here for the social sciences and for educational research as a category of social science.

This chapter utilizes postcolonial theory and Pierre Bourdieu's work to draw attention to these usually overlooked matters in respect of educational research. It does so through three illustrative, critical and somewhat granular narratives, specifically, the changing nature of policy studies in education, teaching educational policy studies to travelling non-Western students studying within Western universities, and the use of journal ranking as an accountability mechanism to monitor and measure Australian academics.

The perhaps contentious conjoining of Bourdieu and postcolonial theory, including the work of Gayatri Spivak, Edward Said, Linda Tuhiwai Smith and Appadurai, is justified in terms of Bourdieu's (2003) recognition that contemporary globalization read performatively as neo-liberal politics and economics has been a political project with a history, and that the effects of globalization within nations are in some ways contingent upon the extent of 'national capital' held and developed by them historically. This seems to complement the postcolonial recognition of the colonial past forever haunting the postcolonial present and the politics involved in challenges from postcolonial aspirations to these resistant residues in an attempt to strengthen 'national capital' for a more autonomous postcolonial politics.

There are also evident complementarities between Bourdieu *et al.*'s rejection of an epistemological 'state of perfect innocence' (1999: 608) and Appadurai's (2001b) postcolonial call for 'epistemological diffidence', both of which recognize the constructedness and positionality of knowledge and thus potential disfiguring through failure to acknowledge this. Rejecting epistemological innocence through revealing the position of the researcher/theorist in knowledge production and acknowledging the potential disfiguring of knowledge and theory claims are central to better social science and educational research and to deparochializing both. In this way Connell's (2007) work on 'Southern Theory' might also be seen as part of a postcolonial project, even though she argues that the project functions more in respect of literary theory, and in the work of Edward Said more in relation to the humanities, rather than the social sciences per se. We would argue for the need to add educational research. Connell argues her case in relation to the social sciences more generally.

The chapter specifically works in dialogue with Arjun Appadurai's (2001b) paper, 'Grassroots globalization and the research imagination', and to a lesser extent also draws on Connell's (2007) *Southern Theory*, to challenge the silent ways in which the geopolitics of knowledge production and representation in educational research fail to encourage theory building in dialogues across the Global North and Global South, a necessary step towards educational research in a context where globalizations of various kinds are remaking what Connell refers to as 'planetary society'.

Appadurai (2001b: 15) suggests the need to deconstruct in both an anthropological and pragmatic sense the 'taken for granteds' of the contemporary system of research in the context of globalization and its flows of capital, people, ideas, images and technologies, and disjunctions and related asymmetries of power. Specifically, he calls for a 'deparochialization of the research ethic' and a strong internationalization of research. This is necessary to the globalization of the knowledge of globalization and for challenging globalization as simply neo-liberal economics. This is in opposition to the performative usage of globalization that Bourdieu wrote about, where globalization is taken to mean simply neo-liberal globalization and the necessity of adaptation to that reality.

Connell (2007) argues that much globalization theory is about such adaptation, perhaps reflecting its source in management theory.

The arument of this chapter is that deparochialization and strong internationalization are required of educational research; in Connell's (2007) terms, we need to encourage the possibility of Southern Theory. To this end, the chapter provides three narratives regarding the pressing need for the deparochialization of research in education. Narrative one draws on Bob Lingard's educational policy research trajectory from a national policy focus to researching the effects of globalization (Rizvi and Lingard 2010) and proffers an argument that a new imaginary is imperative as factors affecting national systems of education, educational policy and local pedagogies now extend well beyond the nation. This is part of the larger project that suggests that the mobilities associated with globalization demand a rethinking of implicit taken-for-granteds in social theory that regard society as simply a nationally bounded space (Urry 2000, 2002; Beck 2000). The work of Bourdieu (1996, 2003) on fields will be utilized to suggest an emergent global educational policy field with the extent of national autonomy mediated by the strength of specific national capitals (Lingard and Rawolle 2010), thus recognizing, as Connell (2007) demands, the inequalities of power associated with the residues of the colonial past and the realities of the colonial present on a world scale.

Narrative two draws on Bob Lingard's experiences teaching and directing a doctoral programme in the Caribbean for the University of Sheffield, and teaching about globalization and educational policy on a Sheffield-based MA course in educational policy and research. This narrative also references Bob's teaching on a similar degree at the University of Edinburgh, where most students were from China. These experiences have raised awareness of those elements that need to be considered and traversed as part of Appadurai's (2001b) desired move towards a stronger definition of what the internationalization of research in education might entail and Connell's call for more pluralist theory building and dialogues across the globe.

The third narrative draws on research conducted by the three authors, Bob, Ian and Stephen, on the system of journal rankings across all disciplines (including educational research) created recently by the Australian Research Council for research accountability purposes in Australian universities (Hardy, Heimans and Lingard forthcoming). This might be seen as part of the audit culture of the restructured neo-liberal state (Power 1997) and recognition that academic work plays out both within and beyond this state. This case demonstrates how such ranking legitimates current geopolitics in knowledge production and circulation, failing to recognize the need for the deparochializing agenda that is the focus of this chapter. As Connell (2007: 219) has noted with respect to systems of academic knowledge circulation more generally, 'the ways in which the production and circulation of knowledge are organized generally produce metropolitan dominance and peripheral marginality in social science'. In its valorization of existing status hierarchies, the Australian Research Council's ranking of journals reinforces and solidifies extant power differentials and, for Australian educational researchers, encourages them to publish in journals produced and edited outside Australia, with implications for research, theory and styles of research reporting. As Lyn Yates (2010: 11) has argued, 'One effect of emphasizing journal ranking as a codified assessment of quality is to drive and to reproduce a narrowness about what kinds of research and what kinds of questions matter.' This ranking system can also be seen as part of the valorization of English as the language of academic publishing globally.

Appadurai (2001b) suggests a number of ways in which the dominant research ethic might be challenged; he argues for a reconnection with earlier pre-research paradigm thinking premised on a strong moral position, reconnection with the style of argumentation of public intellectuals, and consideration of research linked to policy-making and state functions in a range of nations, particularly the developing world. This chapter endeavours to engage in this necessary work.

Deparochializing research

Appadurai (2001b) postulates that 'epistemological diffidence' is necessary to the project of deparochialization of research, and suggests that this can be contrasted with the epistemological certainty of dominant forms of modernization theory of the 1950s and 1960s and its effects, particularly in what was then called the 'Third World' and is now usually referred to as the Global South. Modernization theory accepted without question that theory and research were metropolitan, modern and Western, while the rest of the world – in this case the developing world, now the Global South – was simply a research site to test and confirm such theory. Here relations of researcher and researched paralleled relations of colonizer and colonized, even within decolonizing and postcolonial politics and aspirations. As an aside, as a university student in Australia in the 1960s and 1970s, Bob Lingard had similar experiences where theory was something that Australian academics and researchers utilized and applied, but did not develop. The same dependency is evident in contemporary Australian academe, when international recognition is utilized to evaluate research output; here 'international' sometimes is read as 'non-Australian but English-speaking', a very different reading from that in the United Kingdom or United States of America, where it is read as high-quality with large impact, while potentially remaining deeply parochial.[1] Indeed, Connell (2007) in a brief history of Australian sociology has argued that in the late nineteenth century the differences of Indigenous societies in Australia were an important component of the development of sociology generally (e.g. in Durkheim's 1912 *The Elementary Forms of the Religious Life*), but by the post-World War Two period Australian sociology had become simply the application of metropolitan-developed theory and methodologies to Australian society, which was now seen as similar to the metropolitan societies of the Global North.

On this politics of research and representation, Linda Tuhiwai Smith (1999: 1) opens her *Decolonizing Methodologies*, a study of the relationship between research and Indigenous peoples and knowledges in New Zealand, with the statement, 'From the vantage point of the colonized, a position from which I write, and choose to privilege, the term "research" is inextricably linked to European imperialism and colonialism'. This is Said's (2003) point that even the most arcane theories, including, we would note, research methodologies, are distorted to some extent by relations of power and politics in both macro and individual relations senses. Postcolonial insights are important to the decolonizing and deparochializing strategies required.

Appadurai's call for the deparochialization of research is set against the effects of globalization after the Cold War and the presence of one global superpower operating unilaterally, with China rapidly emerging as a potential superpower. An important element of this context is the enhanced flows of students in the global market of higher education and the attraction of the USA as the place for graduate study to potential students around the globe, including students from China and the Global South. Here, there is the dangerous possibility for globalization to be synonymous with Americanization and a weak form of internationalization of research to occur, which simply means the inclusion of more people in the conversation of researchers without challenging its Western, metropolitan form, without enhancing and relocating the capacity to theorize. The disjunctions between the various human and cultural flows of globalization, however, also allow for some optimism for a stronger form of internationalization than this. There are, for example, other regional student flows, for example within South East Asia to Singapore and within the Caribbean to Cuba, which offer some challenge to the allure of the West in the global student market.

In rejecting a stance of epistemological innocence (Bourdieu *et al.* 1999), Appadurai suggests that some 'epistemological diffidence', and what Smith (1999) would see as 'epistemological openness', can help in a strong internationalization of research, and we would add theory, and thus move us beyond what we might see, *à la* Said, as an Orientalist approach to both research and theory. Such a project, according to Appadurai (2001a, 2001b), needs to be aligned with 'grassroots globalization' or 'globalization from below'. This is the question of whose globalization counts and how, and offers a challenge to globalization from above (in an economic policy sense in particular), as driven by some international organizations and US foreign policy and cultural industries.

In *Modernity at Large*, Appadurai (1996) spoke of 'vernacular globalization', the ways in which local sites and their histories, cultures, politics and pedagogies mediated to greater or lesser extent the effects of top-down globalization.[2] This is the outcome of relations and tensions between the context-productive and context-generative effects of globalization; some local sites are more able to be context generative and mediate global effects. The idea of globalization from below is about strengthening this mediation and enhancing global connections across non-governmental organizations (NGOs) and other groups of resisters to globalization from above, read simply as neo-liberal economics. Globalization from below could also be seen to be aligned with postcolonial aspirational politics.[3]

Gayatri Spivak (2003) has made some telling comments about the disjuncture at times between the local, educated elite in the Global South, who in human rights discourses are the 'righters of wrongs', and the rural poor within their nations. The former probably have more in common with the educated elite of the Global North. These are the epistemological disjunctures and exclusions of globalization about which Appadurai (2001b) speaks. As Spivak (2003: 173–74) argues, the sort of education required in the South is not that which would 'make the rural poor capable of drafting NGO grant proposals'! Importantly, echoing Said's observation about the elite universities in the USA being the last utopias for free and questioning thought,[4] she argues, rightly in our view, that globalization from below also requires an unmooring of such education from its elite location in both the North and the South. This would go well beyond Freire's banking conception of education towards conscientization, and 'beyond literacy and numeracy, and finds a home in an expanded definition of a 'humanities to come' (Spivak 2003: 173). We might think here of an educational research to come!

As noted already, Appadurai writes about the needs for research to examine its own 'taken for granteds' in the present globalizing context. These include 'systematicity, prior citational contexts, and specialized modes of inquiry', and replicability, along with 'an imagined world of specialized professional readers and researchers' (Appadurai 2001b: 12), which, taken together, work to inhibit the deparochialization of research, its theories and methodologies. The argument here is that a particular postcolonial politics is a useful starting point for a re-reading, re-examination, re-imagining, indeed deparochializing of re-search in the globalized context of ongoing American and Western neo-colonialism, a context often glossed over in talk about globalization, as Connell (2007) cogently argues.

Deparochialization of educational policy studies: narrative one

In Bob Lingard's educational policy research in Australia, he has shifted scalar focus from the national to the global. During the late 1980s and early 1990s under Labor governments, there was a move towards national policies in schooling in Australia, despite the federal political structure and the states being constitutionally responsible for schooling. This move towards national polices in schooling was researched through in-depth interviews with the policy and political elites. Through these interviews, Bob became aware of the emergence of global pressures on national policy and of what Bourdieu (1995) might have called an emergent 'world or global educational policy field' (Taylor *et al.* 1997; Lingard 2000; Henry *et al.* 2001; Lingard *et al.* 2005; Ozga and Lingard 2006; Lingard and Rawolle 2010). This suggested the need to deparochialize educational policy studies – the focus of this narrative.

The reality of trans- and supra-national processes labelled as globalization has challenged contemporary social theory as suggested in the Introduction to this chapter. In sociology, Urry (2000, 2002) has argued the need to refocus from the social as society to the social as mobilities, indicating the weakened connectivity between society and nation-state and the stretching of networks across the globe. While this might be an overstatement and only refer to certain segments of society in certain parts of the world, there is some veracity in the observation. The spatial turn in social theory has been another response. Massey (1994: 2) has noted that the 'spatial is social relations stretched out'. Related to this, Castells (2000) argues that today power is located in flows, while most people still live in the space of places; this disjunction, he suggests, results in political schizophrenia. Other theorists have demonstrated the implicit national space of much social theory and a complementary 'methodological nationalism' (Beck 2000). Bourdieu, for example, has observed how '[i]ntellectual life, like all other social spaces, is a home to nationalism and imperialism' (1999b: 220) and that 'a truly scientific internationalism' requires a concerted political project; this is another way of expressing the project in which Appadurai and Connell invite us to participate.

Bourdieu's theoretical stance and methodological disposition allow a way beyond such spatial and national constraints, a necessary position for analysing and understanding global effects in contemporary educational policy and the emergence of a global policy field in education. Globalization has had the phenomenological effect of enhanced awareness of the world as one place among (privileged) peoples across the globe, evidenced in, for example, talk of the 'world economy', 'world recession', 'global warming', 'world heritage sites', 'world policy', 'global educational indicators' and so on. Appadurai (1996) and Castells (2000) speak of the flows and networks across the globe, which render national boundaries more porous. Appadurai (1996: 33ff.), focusing on the cultural flows associated with globalization, speaks of ethnoscapes, mediascapes, technoscapes, financescapes and ideoscapes, and this is related to the emergence of a postnational era. Castells (2000: 442) also argues that society is now organized around flows, namely, 'flows of capital, flows of information, flows of technology, flows of organizational interaction, flows of images, sounds and symbols', with technology facilitating these flows via nubs and nodes located across the globe that are dominated by elites of various kinds. However, the postnational accounts proffered by Appadurai and Castells probably overstate the 'porousness' of national boundaries, and the extent of the postnationality of the present, particularly since 11 September 2001, and the bombings in Bali, Madrid and London, where such boundaries have become somewhat less porous in the so-called 'war on terror' (Gregory 2004; Rizvi 2004). And immobility has become a more salient element of contemporary social disadvantage.

Taking a relational approach to fields as a social space, following Bourdieu, rather than as a specific material, grounded space, also allows for the stretching of the concept of field in an elastic way across the social space of the globe, taking us beyond empirical investigation of only the local and the national to the nested regional, international, transnational and global spaces of educational policy production (cf. Lingard and Rawolle 2010). To elasticize Massey (1994), the global educational policy field sees the social relations of educational policy production stretched out.

Much writing about globalization, as Rizvi (2007) argues, has reified the concept, failing to historicize it and to recognize its hegemonic role, while neglecting the asymmetries of power between nations and colonial and neo-colonial histories, which see differential national effects of neo-liberal globalization. Connell (2007) offers a similar argument, also pointing out that such theory is Northern Theory. We are suggesting here that Bourdieu's work potentially offers a way beyond such reification of globalization and allows for an empirically grounded account of the constitution of a global policy field in education, an example of globalization from above and acknowledging national power differentials across this global field. In his later, more political work Bourdieu (1998a, 1999a, 2003) is concerned with the politics of globalization, read mainly as the dominance of a neo-liberal approach to the economy. Interestingly, this appears to argue against his earlier work on the various fields of social and cultural production, which suggested a relative autonomy of the logics of practice of each field. Instead, he seems to be suggesting ways in which global neo-liberal politics have dented somewhat the relative autonomy of the logics of practice of many social fields, including that of the educational policy field, which has become more heteronomous as a sub-set of economic policy. The media field and its logics have also affected the degree of autonomy of educational policy production (Lingard and Rawolle 2004).

While much talk about globalization has reified the concept, failing to locate agency in respect of its workings, Bourdieu's approach allows for an empirical investigation of the constitution of the global economic market. There is, however, another potential pitfall here, that of over-emphasizing collective agency in the process. This is why empirical investigation of these processes is needed. And of course there are the counter-hegemonic effects of anti-globalization movements and globalization from below.

In a homologous fashion, we would argue that the global field of educational policy is also a political project and yet another manifestation of the emergent politics in the age of flows and diasporas of people and ideas across the (more or less) porous boundaries of nation states in both embodied and cyber forms. Political imagination – a new social imaginary (Rizvi and Lingard 2010) – has been a central component in the creation of the global market and the global field of educational policy, just as political imagination is necessary to challenging their effects. Different nations now located in a post-Cold War world with one superpower seemingly committed to unilateralism are, of course, positioned differently in terms of power and the strength of national capital within these global fields of economy, governance and educational policy. The differing 'reference societies' (Schriewer and Martinez 2004) for different national educational systems within the global educational policy space also tell us something about political history and contemporary global politics. Policy making in education within the nation and at sub-national and local levels, nonetheless, still remains important but is now also affected by global discourses and pressures.

Drawing on Bourdieu (2003: 91), it can be argued that the amount of 'national capital' possessed by a given nation within these global fields is a determining factor in the spaces of resistance and degree of autonomy for policy development within the nation. Here the Global South is positioned very differently in relation to the educational policy effects of the World Bank and other international agencies from the Global North. National capital (education levels, democratic institutions, political stability, economic power, etc.) can be seen to mediate the extent to which nations are able to be context generative in respect of the global field. Under globalization and the emergence of global fields, the sovereignty of the different nation states is affected in different ways; as Jayasuriya (2001: 444) suggests, 'the focus should not be on the content or degree of sovereignty that the state possesses but the form that it assumes in a global economy'. Further, as an example of Appadurai's (1996) point about the disjunctions between the cultural flows of globalization, national capital in respect of the global educational policy space is not exactly homologous with economic capital. The iconic status of Singapore and Finland in this global educational policy space in terms of TIMSS (Trends in International Mathematics and Science Study) and PISA (Programme for International Student Assessment) results, respectively, is an illustrative case and also a clear example of the elision of contextual differences within this global educational space. In research on the OECD (Henry et al. 2001), for example, it was shown that OECD policy work had more salience in the policy culture of the more peripheral Australia and the Scandinavian countries than in Britain, while the USA played a hegemonic role in the creation of the educational indicators project, which was formulated against the policy inclinations of some OECD insiders (Henry et al. 2001). In work on the emergence of a European educational policy space, it was shown how a form of structural adjustment saw convergence effects in the educational policies of net benefactor countries within the EU, that is, in the least powerful and least developed countries of the Mediterranean rim such as Portugal and Greece, with talk of a supranational 'magistrature of influence' (Lawn and Lingard 2001). That research also demonstrated the awareness of policy-makers of this postnational policy and the lack of recognition of it by school-based practitioners: policy-globalized, practice-localized. In the developing countries of the world, the effects of the World Bank upon educational policy are palpable, though not necessarily taken up unconditionally, while not recognized or felt in Europe, North America or Australia.

Politics can also resist the global dominance of neo-liberalism as suggested by Bourdieu (2002) in his article on 'The politics of globalization' published in *Le Monde* the day after his death, where he observed that 'the construction of a Social Europe' would be a good bulwark for resistance against 'the dominant forces of our time'. The state is not powerless in the face of globalization, but different states have varying capacities to manage 'national interests', with the state needing to become more strategic in the face of globalization. This capacity is what Bourdieu refers to as 'national capital' and ought to be the focus of research on educational policy.

When combined with the argument about competing logics of practice, this offers another way of thinking about policy/implementation relationships across the contexts of policy text production and that of practice, both across and within national borders. The educational policy field today is multilayered, stretching from the local to the global. In terms of this multilayering, Mann (2000) speaks of five socio-spatial networks, namely local, national, international (relations between nations), transnational (passing through national boundaries) and global, which cover the globe as a whole. Theorization about and empirical investigation of educational policy fields today must recognize the growing global character of relations between national policy fields and international fields, re-emphasizing Bourdieu's conceptualization of fields as social rather than geographical spaces. Such an account needs to see the various networks, referred to by Mann as sitting within what we are calling a global educational policy field.

The educational policy field thus now demands an empirical and theoretical stretching beyond the nation. The argument here is that Bourdieu's approach enables us to do this in both theoretical and methodological senses. The model of adapting Bourdieu's notion of field to examine the relations between global, international and national educational policy fields offers a different way to locate the practices and products of policy. This global educational policy field encompasses the contexts of the policy cycle of which Ball (1994) writes, and offers some analytic gains in locating the effects of particular policies. That is, it caters for these matters and also offers a particular way of utilizing Bourdieu's concept of field to discuss issues around the impact of different fields on one another within national fields of power, and of different scalar levels of fields also affecting one another. All three contexts of the policy cycle – the context of policy text production, the context of influence and the context of practice –

are affected in different ways by globalization (Ball 1998), through both its policy mediation and more direct effects.

Bourdieu's conceptual apparatus allows for a deparochialization of educational policy studies by setting a frame for the theoretical and empirical study of the world educational policy field. What has been provided in this narrative is a skeletal outline of how and why the scalar focus of educational policy studies must be stretched and the contribution that Bourdieu's approach can make to that deparochializing project. What is needed now is much empirical investigation and new non-parochial theory development.

Deparochialization of theory and methodology in educational research: narrative two

> I've been teaching now for almost forty years. And I've always learnt during the actual class. There's something that eludes me when I read and think without the presence of students. So I've always thought of my classes as not a routine to go through but rather an experience of investigation and discovery.
>
> (Edward Said in Viswanathan 2001: 280)

Said's observation about learning through university teaching and his observation made elsewhere that 'displacement' can also be a productive source for considerations of knowledge reflect Bob Lingard's experiences as an Australian working in an English and then a Scottish university (2003–8) teaching international students located in Sheffield and students of the University of Sheffield located in the Caribbean, and teaching Masters students from China in Edinburgh. Two, somewhat cryptic, micro-narratives are provided below, drawn from this experience, to raise issues in relation to the need for strong internationalization of research and the globalization of knowledge.

Chinese international students at the University of Sheffield and University of Edinburgh

Bob worked with three cohorts of full-time MA students in educational policy and research at the University of Sheffield and one cohort at the University of Edinburgh. The majority of these students in each year of the programme were young women from China, self-sponsored, full fee-paying, who had been teachers of English, mostly in universities, but some in schools, in various parts of China. One Chinese male taught and supervised by Bob was in the international office of a large and important Chinese university. His research was about the meanings of internationalization for Chinese universities, but all framed by how, given language difficulties, China generally and his university in particular, could attract some of the full fee-paying students who now moved in flows towards the USA and to some extent the UK and Australia (Marginson 2004). He would joke that, when China became a world superpower, the flows of international students might be greater in China's direction, indicating the link between economic power, knowledge and language. He would also joke that in one hundred years the teaching of Chinese as a second language might be positioned in the way ESL (English as a second language) teaching is today.

What struck Bob about these students in teaching globalization and educational policy, as well as supervising dissertations, was their positive reading of globalization. Unlike much of the literature on globalization, which sees the dominant reading as that of neo-liberal economics, with all its attendant negative effects within and across nations, these international students regarded globalization as a positive phenomenon. We become aware here of the multi-faceted nature of globalization and the significance of positionality to reading it. In this respect, it is interesting to contemplate Tikly's (2001:152) observation about globalization and education theory:

> It has been a shortcoming of much of the existing literature on globalization and education that the specific *contexts* to which the theory is assumed to be applicable have not been specified. It is problematic to assume that there is one superior vantage point from which global forces can best be understood.

This is Connell's point about the Northern nature of much globalization theory.

Deng Xiaoping was seen as the centrally important figure for the Chinese students in relation to globalization, opening up China to the world in various ways after its inwardness (and, as some of the students interestingly suggested, 'backwardness') during the period of the Cultural Revolution. These students are, of course the beneficiaries of globalization; they are part of the ethno-scapes of globalization. They also make us aware of the centrality of English, along with ICT (information and communication technology), as the bearers of globalization and invite us to think of how a common language produces common ways of seeing, but also encourage us to think more closely about the role of English in contemporary globalization and what that means for aca-demic work in non-English-speaking parts of the globe and in relation to the matters being considered in this chapter. The question of language is a central one in the attempt to deparochialize research.

For some of these students, globalization was linked to aspirations for a more open political system in China, and their own desire for participation in global labour markets. They saw the possibilities for pressures from globalization and demands and contradictions, which stem from Chinese 'market socialism', for making things better. This was the case in particular with their still somewhat muted criticisms of the dual administrative structures within their own state-controlled work organizations of professionals and party officials. They saw this as meaning that their organizations were still sclerotic in relation to change, but global pressures and the embrace of the market would mean they would *have* to change, and this would be a good thing. Some change is evident in the principal responsibility system now extant in schools, where the school principal has authority over the party official. At the same time as desiring a new style, a more open and pluralistic polity, they feared a disastrous Soviet-type transition from command economy to market capitalism. They desired a new political way and see globalization as providing some pressure towards this, while profoundly recognizing that neo-liberal globalization manifested very differently within market socialism. They also seemed to support a 'hasten slowly' stance in respect of their desired political changes and realistically thought such change would take some time.

The question of criticality in content and pedagogy about globalization was very interesting. The students appeared able to be critical to a point, within certain parameters: always critical of the USA and, at the time, very critical of the Bush regime, for example. In terms of the research topics the students pursued, these were in many ways accounts of their own experiences, as beneficiaries of one of the central flows associated with globalization, but utilizing Western research methodologies and theories. In terms of the citational contexts in which their research was located, they tended to be very limited, or about similar issues in other contexts, rather than their own. This is certainly the case in respect of methodological issues as well. There is also the interesting issue of translation in respect of much of their interview data and all the complexities that entails. Further, the students were resistant to the use of the personal in their writing, and perhaps research and write within an academic tradition of smaller citational frames and where researchers take research problems in terms of the infidelities of the implementation of government-determined policy.

Some of the students were very open to the type of argument proffered by Appadurai and Connell, seeing the need to include Chinese research and theorizing within their work and thus seeking to deparochialize educational research and theory. Others rejected this approach, arguing that they were studying in a Western university to learn Western, Global North theories and methodologies. Some even suggested that it was this, at a personal level, that would give them an advantage in labour markets when they returned to China. Here a higher degree was linked to future advantages that it might bestow, rather than seen as contributing to the deparochializing of educational research and theory. There were quite heated debates in the classes between groups of students on this very point of difference.

Teaching and supervising Caribbean students

For a short period, Bob Lingard was Chair of the University of Sheffield's Caribbean programme, which has been functioning since 1989. The political frame for this programme was postcolonial, taking the local and national civic missions of the University of Sheffield onto a global and postcolonial stage. However, we need to recognize as well the old colonial relation as backdrop to the involvement of an English university in the Caribbean, even though the programme was seen at the time more as part of the globalization of the University's civic mission, rather than as part of a revenue-raising market.

While recognizing the multi-meanings of 'post' when attached to colonialism (Shohat 2000) – after, beyond, neo, building upon, aspirational etc. – and indeed its ambivalence (Radhakrishnan 2000), the programme was framed by a reading of post as aspirational, in terms of the pedagogies, methodologies, topics and intellectual resources utilized in the teaching and research and in terms of the desired outcomes: research capacity building in the Caribbean linked to postcolonial politics. In this respect it was significant that the programme worked with Caribbean-based tutors and through a local Caribbean consultancy firm. The programme's underpinning aspirational definition recognized the differences between postcolonialism and postmodernism, particularly in relation to provisional commitments to the Enlightenment project in respect of equality and democracy. As Said (in the Afterword of *Orientalism*) put it:

> Yet whereas post-modernism in one of its famous programmatic statements (by Jean-Francois Lyotard) stresses the disappearance of grand narratives of emancipation and enlightenment, the emphasis behind much of the work done by the first generation of post-colonial artists and scholars is exactly the opposite: the grand narratives remain, even though their implementation and realization are at present in abeyance, deferred, or circumvented.
>
> (Said 2003: 351)

Specifically in the Caribbean, Bob worked with course work Masters students and in dissertation supervision. The thing he noticed was the impact of Freire's (1972) 'banking education' on these students. Criticality and the capacity and right to express one's own voice had not been encouraged. In early writings, the student's voice was usually missing. Quotations from others sometimes substituted for an argument. On querying this, many of the students said they were not allowed to express their argument and voice in their undergraduate degrees in the Caribbean. Often the literature reviews, which the students prepared as part of their dissertation work, dealt only with US literature without a mention of its specificity or, more accurately, its specificity having segued as universal. The presence of one citational context has effects, as does the absence of another, that is, an extensive literature about their research topics in the Caribbean. These research students were out of place, as it were. Further, in the early stages of the programme, many students held a narrow conception of what research in the social sciences ought to look like. Their dependency discouraged, even disallowed, experimentation and creativity. It is from reflection upon these matters, through what we might tentatively call 'post-colonial pedagogies' and 'conscientization', that all those working in the Caribbean programme sought to encourage a disposition of criticality and a postcolonial attitude. (See also Dimitriadis and McCarthy (2001) for an account of postcolonial pedagogies useful in the West.) Postcolonial histories of education in the Caribbean were provided as a contribution towards streng-thening public memory of colonialism and its residual legacies and as a way of challenging the amnesia resulting from the colonial experience. This post-colonial pedagogy worked against the silencing of the local and of the past; such silencing and forgetfulness are effects of colonialism. Said (2001: 502) describes this desired disposition this way: 'a sense of critical awareness, a sense of scepticism, that you don't take what's given to you uncritically'.

Bob's work with Caribbean doctoral students was of a different order, in the professional doctoral programme taught in the Caribbean, as well as in supervision of Caribbean PhD students in Sheffield. Teaching about educa-tional policy to the doctoral students in the Caribbean, Bob was always struck by their deep awareness of their political location in the contemporary globalized world. Of all the educational policy students whom Bob has taught over the years in Australia, the UK, the Caribbean and Singapore, they are the ones who immediately raise issues to do with globalization, global geopolitics, the World Bank and other donor agencies and their effects on educational policy production, the globalized policy discourses in education, which they ventriloquize, and their very real effects on policy implementation and peda-gogies. They were very aware of a global educational policy field, the focus of the first narrative. They articulated the negative effects of running to policy tunes set elsewhere in terms of timing of policy agendas and implementa-tion. They talked at length about the effects of WTO decisions on the banana industry in the Caribbean; they knew about the creation of new regional blocs and markets in the Caribbean, as both an expression of and response to globalization. They were also patently aware of their colonial and neo-colonial legacies and at the same time they had deep postcolonial aspirations for themselves, for their families, for the young people of the Caribbean, for Caribbean education, for their research work and for their nations. They wanted to speak back contrapuntally to the metropolitan centre (Said 1993) to which they are connected historically and through flows of people, of culture and of theory and research methodologies. Some of their research involved the prod-ding of 'public memory' about colonial histories and their neo-colonial present and what this meant for postcolonial aspirations. They were also aware of the gap that Spivak (2003) pointed to between their intellectual and material locations within the Caribbean and those of the less privileged, but they also saw themselves in some ways distanced from the agentive capacity of doctoral researchers working in the academic centres of the Global North.

These doctoral students were very politically aware of the impact of US cultural industries on culture, politics, young people and schooling in the Caribbean; they were aware of Western metaculture. They understood the ways in which globalization has spawned a neo-liberal individualism and aspirations among the young in the Caribbean to be like rich young black Americans. These aspirations have partially replaced the independence and nationalist movements and their collectivity in the national habitus. But the students want to work with and against these matters, politically and in research terms. And for some, Cuba and Venezuela provided political alternatives. Their major aspiration for their own doctoral research was to build research capacity in the Caribbean, developing the capacity to research, rather than simply being researched, both individually and collectively. They desired for the Caribbean to be more than a site for research and the application of theories and method- ologies developed elsewhere. Here they talked of the ways in which donor agencies have to this point defined who were regarded as researchers in the Caribbean. They also saw the heavy research *for* policy character of most of the research that has been conducted. They saw their enhanced capacity to do research as potentially strengthening national capital in the face of globalization and demands and conditionalities of international agencies. Some of the students were involved in policy-making inside the state and others in the political process involving teacher unions and other political organizations. They were close to government and wanted educational policy research to be *for* policy as well as *of* policy.

Despite all of this and the awareness that some Caribbean concepts such as 'creole' were vernacular versions of the concept of 'hybridity' central to postcolonial theory, the Western, metropolitan character of citational contexts, theories and methodologies restricted possibilities and was itself reflective of past and present geopolitics. The Caribbean students Bob worked with were very aware of the need to deparochialize educational research and its sustaining theories and methodologies. Central to their postcolonial aspirations in research terms was a demand for the right to theorize.

Journal rankings in Australia and the geopolitics of knowledge production, reception and circulation: narrative three

Over recent years, many governments in the Global North have become increasingly involved in measuring and managing university research output as a new form of accountability for researchers, including educational researchers, who work in universities. The most recent instantiation in Australia is Excellence in Research Australia (ERA), created for the government by the Australian

Research Council (ARC). A large-scale ranking of academic journals has been integral to ERA processes. The Australian Research Council, a government statutory authority, has responsibility for ERA and has created rankings for all journals in all disciplinary fields, covering more than 20,000 journals, including all journals publishing educational research (at least in the English language).

Technologies such as journal ranking that are used for collecting and collating information about research processes are potentially powerful instruments, helping to constitute that which they seek to measure. They serve as technologies of governmentality within the hegemony of neo-liberalism globally. These specific technologies constitute only one aspect of the 'grid' that specifies and measures educational outputs of many kinds. Governments are able to use this information in order to represent a version of accountability of public expenditure, and from this representation allocate resources for research. The allocation of these resources is not insignificant, as research agendas are promoted and particular forms of research are favoured, which leads to particular forms of outcomes. One such is that, rather than research evidence informing policy, the reverse becomes true. Policy informs research. In the extreme versions of this, there is no longer field-specific research that provides discipline-specific knowledge about ways in which, in the case here, educational research might and perhaps should be undertaken. Rather, government decides the forms that education may take and allows research that informs and supports these possibilities. We are not suggesting that this is happening in Australia, but such tendencies are evident in the logics underpinning the journal rankings.

Such metrics for the measurement of research productivity are also intimately linked to the globalized policy discourse of the centrality of research and innovation to globally competitive national knowledge-economies. Indeed, just as student performance scores on international tests such as PISA serve as a surrogate measure of the effectiveness of national education systems and the potential global competitiveness of a national economy, so thus too do measures of research productivity to which systems of journal rankings contribute. These surrogate measures reflect the centrality of education policy as economic policy in the context of reduced national economic sovereignty in the face of globalization (Rizvi and Lingard 2010). There is also a way in which the journal ranking metric created and used by the ARC might potentially be another knowledge commodity to be sold or at least circulated in the international higher education marketplace, or in the cultural circuits of global capitalism as Thrift (2005) would put it. Further, a section of what Apple (2006) has called the new middle-class technical intelligentsia will benefit from these developments as the creation of such metrics requires technical expertise.

Although academics engage in an informed but informal process of journal 'ranking' when determining the 'best' outlet for their research, formal journal ranking is new to educational research in Australia. It needs to be noted that, for the ERA exercise of measuring research quality, all journals in all disciplines have been classified by the ARC. This represents a huge bibliometric exercise and is seen by the ARC as a contribution that it is making globally to research assessment exercises and research accountability (Yates 2010).

In this third narrative, the data set comprises a breakdown of educational research journals, according to the latest, finalized ERA rankings list. This breakdown broadly reflects ERA's expectation that 5% of journals within any given academic field will be categorized as 'A*', the next 15% 'A', the following 30% 'B', and the remaining 50% will be allocated a 'C' ranking.

The ranking descriptors for each journal category are significant because of the specificity of the research they imply, including that much of the research in this category will be undertaken in particular types of institutions:

> Typically an A* journal would be one of the best in its field or subfield in which to publish and would typically cover the entire field/subfield. Virtually all papers they publish will be of a very high quality. These are journals where most of the work is important (it will really shape the field) and where researchers boast about getting accepted. Acceptance rates would typically be low and the editorial board would be dominated by field leaders, including many from top institutions.
>
> (ARC 2010)

Such criteria serve to constitute the educational research field, while also legitimating power differentials within contemporary academic geopolitics. Presumably, the 'top institutions' being referred to are synonymous with the Global North, rather than the Global South. It is interesting to note the assessment criteria contained within this description. As with all criterion-referenced assessment, the validity of the assessment depends crucially on the clarity of the interpretability of the criteria and the expertise (and impartiality) of those making the assessments. Descriptors such as 'virtually all', 'best', 'very high quality', 'important' and 'top' make it difficult for assessors to account for their decisions in an impartial way. Criteria related to academic 'boasting' about publication outlets seem incongruous with supposedly impartial assessment criteria. We also note the *reductio ad absurdum* that the highest quality journal would be that which had a zero acceptance rate or, to be fair, 1%; reputedly the *American Educational Research Journal* has an acceptance rate of 4%.

One of the problems with the five-band scale (A* to unranked) is that it implicitly assumes that 'research quality works with simple hierarchies in which the top stratum is always more global and universal than those under it' (Yates 2010: 9–10). This assumption, Yates argues, will produce biases against non-English journals, and will 'work against research which has specificity to a location' (Yates 2010: 10), for example with educational research conducted in Australia. (As an aside, we note that the Australian Association for Research in Education's journal, *The Australian Educational Researcher*, is ranked a B.) Further, as Yates also observes, the rankings will 'reproduce historical status differentials and prejudices' (2010: 10), thus reinforcing, rather than challenging, extant geopolitics of educational research production and circulation. It seems that this ranking list will result in the reification of current hierarchies of prestige across type of research, type of journal and where it is produced and as such will not assist in the deparochialization of educational research, as we have been arguing for throughout this chapter. All of these observations have significant implications for the field of educational research and the work of educational researchers, particularly for research students, younger academics, those in tenuous employment circumstances, those working in the periphery of the Global North, and all those in the Global South. For example, the highest ranked New Zealand journal is B-ranked.

An aggregation of educational research journals on the ARC ranking reveals that, out of approximately 1,010 education journals, 32 were ranked A*, 128 ranked A, 325 ranked B, 510 ranked C, and 15 were unranked. That is, about 3.2% occupy the highest ranking, 12.8% are classified as A-rated journals, 32% are identified as a B, 51% are C-rated, with 1.5% unclassified. In short, 16% of educational journals are classified as either A or A*, and 32% as B, with the remaining 52.5% classified as C or ungraded. The figures indicate slightly fewer journals in education allocated to A* or A rankings than indicated in ERA guidelines.

Interestingly, of A* journals titles, none were recognizably Australian. Only one, the *Asia-Pacific Journal of Teacher Education*, was recognisable as associated with the general geographic region in which Australia is located, although this journal did have an Australian editor. There are interesting issues here regarding how one classifies the national location of a given journal: through its intellectual focus, through its location of production, through the geographical location of its authors, through the nationality of its editors, through the national location of its publisher? At the same time, some A* journals were titularly American or British, or had titles that were readily associated with either Britain or the USA. Two journals' titles reflected this national status – the *American Educational Research Journal*, and the *British Educational Research Journal* and these journals are associated respectively with AERA and BERA. A further three journals took their names from the iconic American and English universities from which they originated, and as such, were recognisably either English or North American – *Harvard Educational Review, Cambridge Journal of Education, Oxford Review of Education*. It is interesting and linked to the dominance of theory and research of the high-status universities of the Global North that journals from single institutions meet the criteria for an A* classification. In total, 16% of journals were 'recognizably' American or British, while no other nationality or region was obviously represented (except the Asia-Pacific region through the single journal, *Asia-Pacific Journal of Teacher Education*).

At the same time, the institutional affiliation of editors of A* journals clearly reflects a North American and British bias. Across 32 A* journals, a total of 42 editors are identified (some journals having more than one editor). Of these 42 editors, 22 are affiliated with universities from the USA, 10 with British institutions and 1 with an Australian academy, and 9 are working in institutions with other national affiliations. That is, more than half of the universities in which A* editors are located are American (approx. 52%), a quarter are British (approx. 24%) and the remaining quarter (approx. 24%) are from the rest of the world. Similarly, from a total of 128 editors of A journals, 47 are from the USA, 37 are British, 23 are Australian and 21 are from other countries. For A-ranked journals, a slightly lower proportion of editors are affiliated with US institutions (approx. 37%), slightly more with British universities (29%), and the remainder (34%) are from the rest of the world, with about half of these (18%) associated with Australian institutions. Therefore, for both A and A* journals combined, about 40% of editors are affiliated with US institutions, 28% with Britain, 14% with Australia and 18% with universities located throughout the rest of the world.

In relation to publishing houses, there is also a clear bias towards international publishing houses, often based either in New York or London, or elsewhere in the USA. A third of A* journals are published by one publisher – Routledge/Taylor and Francis (34%), with almost another third published by another two publishers – Sage (19%) and Wiley (13%). The remaining third of A* journals are published by other major international publishing houses, including Springer, Blackwell, Elsevier or Emerald (13%), by an American university (7%) or by an American society (14%) – the latter including such groups as the National Council of Teachers of Mathematics, National Council for Social Studies, the American Psychological Association, and the American Society for Engineering Education.

This narrative clearly demonstrates the way in which the field of educational research, while having national variances, is becoming global, but with the USA and Britain holding dominant positions within this global field. This legitimates rather than challenges the extant geopolitics of knowledge production and circulation that this chapter has been arguing for. There is little incentive to deparochialize educational research in the ways argued for here.

Connell (2007: 83) has written about the impact on sociology in Australia of academics writing for high-status journals coming out of the powerful nations of the Global North and commented, 'to publish in those forums, Australians had to write in forms familiar to metropolitan editors: to use metropolitan concepts, address metropolitan literatures, and offer credible interventions in metropolitan debates'. As a consequence, he argues, Australian sociology provided professional sociological accounts of Australian life 'as seen through metropolitan eyes'. The same is the case with Australian educational research and will not be challenged by the journal rankings introduced by the ARC as a form of research accountability. It was such a reality – viewing Caribbean education through Northern metropolitan eyes – that the Caribbean doctoral students referred to in the previous narrative were also challenging from a postcolonial perspective. And we note here that Australia is part of the Global North and in a stronger position here than those researching education in the Global South.

Conclusion

The argument has been proffered that Bourdieu's theoretical work and research disposition, in conjunction with Appadurai's notion of globalization from below, and, to a lesser extent, Connell's conception of Southern Theory, allow for the deparochializing of educational research in terms of the global stretching of the research gaze and for the challenging of the elision of society with the national in social theory. Narrative one has shown how this work can enable such a global gaze within the field of educational policy research. Bourdieu's approach also encourages epistemological diffidence, as called for by Appadurai, in its overt rejection of an epistemological state of perfect innocence in research and its demand for reflexivity as central to the (deparochialized) research habitus. Bourdieu's work also allows us to deal with globalization in a non-reified way by suggesting that it is a political project reflecting past and present (colonial, neo-colonial and postcolonial) politics and resultant asymmetries of power between nations. This is in alignment with the argument also offered by Connell (2007).

The pedagogical anecdotes of narrative two demonstrated the desperate need for, as well as difficulties of, deparochializing educational research, but also suggested some hope in the concept of 'creolization'. Young (2003: 142) has picked up on the politics of hope in creolization, commenting:

> As the word 'creole' implies, here translation involves displacement, the carrying over and transformation of the dominant culture into new identities that take on material elements from the culture of their new location. Both sides of the equation get creolized, transformed, as a result.

Didacus Jules (1998), former permanent secretary of education in the Caribbean nation of St Lucia and with a doctorate in education from a prestigious North American university, talks of the tensions between the current state of educational research in the Caribbean and that aspired for under a postcolonial politics. He observes that the Caribbean is located precariously within the possibilities of simply being a 'scavenger of civilization' or 'the inheritor of rainbow possibilities' and 'new sensibilities'. There are echoes here of both Appadurai's and Connell's calls for more Global North/Global South dialogues around theory and knowledge production. This is the project that this chapter is aligned with.

There have been some serious challenges to the research canon from within the Western academy itself. The research edifice is perhaps not as impermeable as Appadurai's account might imply, yet there is no denying the multiple ways in which contemporary public policy about research and universities in the West at least have somewhat constrained research possibilities in terms of disciplines and topics and the intellectual resources brought to bear upon them (Ozga, Seddon and Popkewitz 2006). There have been challenges nonetheless from several directions to the research ethic as defined by Appadurai, including feminist, neo-Marxist, critical theory, poststructural, postmodern, narrative, queer theory, life-history and more lately postcolonial theories and methodologies (Robinson-Pant 2005; Mutua and Swadener 2004). The work of Smith (1999) on decolonizing methodologies was a boon to the Caribbean doctoral students, allowing a view of how things might be done and thought otherwise, epistemologically and methodologically.

Appadurai argues that progressive globalization requires a destabilization of the research ethic and its paradigmatic approach. This requires a new mix that would include ideas and perspectives from the Global South, from 'pre' research paradigm thinkers, from student and academic flows, from NGOs, from activists, from public intellectuals, from state workers and policy makers, from humanities and social science scholars, from the 'post' literatures, and so on. This chapter has sought to demonstrate that Bourdieu's work, inflected by postcolonialism, creolization of research, and theory as a two-way process of re-translation, and challenges to the dominant research ethic from post-positivist epistemologies of many sorts, together offer an important contribution to deparochializing research in education. But asymmetrical power realities on the world political stage also make the globalization of knowledge and the deparochialization of research a difficult but continuing and necessary task to continue to struggle towards, as our account of the new journal ranking system in Australia so clearly demonstrates. Destabilizing hegemonic research relations involves constantly critiquing the nature of extant power relations and how these sanction the research considered of most worth. How these relations continue to reconstitute power, and how they may be rearticulated towards more progressive ends, matter for what educational research is and what it can become.

Notes

1   As an aside, we need to recognize how deeply parochial are the neo-liberal political and economic agendas. Further, there is also often a deeply parochial character to US academic literature reviews, where the world and the USA are taken to be synonymous, not unlike the the concept of the World Series in baseball.
2   For an account of vernacular globalization in educational policy production and implementation see Lingard (2000).
3   Young (2003: 1–8) sees four elements of what we see as aspirational postcolonial politics: i. the right of all people to the same levels of material and cultural well-being; ii. contesting the reality that the nations of Africa, South America and parts

of Asia are in multiple positions of subordination to the USA and Europe; iii. creating theoretical approaches that challenge dominant Western ways of seeing; and iv. a reorientation towards 'the perspectives of knowledge, as well as needs, developed outside of the West'.

4   Said (2001: 6) in his essay, 'On defiance and taking positions', sees as central to the role of the public intellectual a functioning as a public memory. This is even more the case in respect of public intellectuals in postcolonial nations and is also a central element of postcolonial pedagogies. Theory development also demands recognition of power/knowledge relations on a global scale.

References

Appadurai, A. (1996) *Modernity at Large*, Minneapolis: University of Minnesota Press.
—— (2001a) (ed.) *Globalization*, Durham: Duke University Press.
—— (2001b) 'Grassroots globalization and the research imagination', in A. Appadurai (ed.) *Globalization*, Durham: Duke University Press, pp. 1–21.
Apple, Michael W. (2006) *Educating the 'Right' Way: Markets, Standards, God, and Inequality*, 2nd edition, New York: Routledge.
ARC (2010) 'Tiers for the Australian ranking of journals'. Online, available: www. arc.gov.au/era/tiers_ranking.htm (accessed 9 November 2010).
Ball, S. (1994) *Education Reform: a critical and poststructural approach*, Buckingham: Open University Press.
—— (1998) 'Big policies/small world: an introduction to international perspectives in education policy', *Comparative Education*, 34 (2): 119–30.
Beck, U. (2000) 'The cosmopolitan perspective', *British Journal of Sociology*, 51 (1): 79–105.
Bourdieu, P. (1990) *In Other Words*, Stanford: Stanford University Press.
—— (1995) 'Foreword', in Y. Dezalay and D. Sugarman (eds) *Professional Competition and Professional Power: lawyers, accountants and the social construction of markets*, London: Routledge.
—— (1996) *The Rules of Art: genesis and structure of the literary field*, Cambridge: Polity Press.
—— (1998a) *Acts of Resistance: against the new myths of our time*, Cambridge: Polity Press.
—— (1999a) 'The abdication of the state', in P. Bourdieu, *et al.* (eds.) (1999) *The Weight of the World: social suffering in contemporary society*, Cambridge: Polity Press, pp. 181–88 (originally 1993).
—— (1999b) 'The social conditions of the international circulation of ideas', in R. Shusterman (ed.) *Bourdieu: a critical reader*, Oxford: Blackwell.
—— (2002) 'The politics of globalization', *Le Monde*, January.
—— (2003) *Firing Back: against the tyranny of the market 2*, London: Verso (originally 2001, translated by Loic Wacquant).
Bourdieu, P. *et al.* (1999) *The Weight of the World: social suffering in contemporary society*, Cambridge: Polity Press.
Castells, M. (2000) (2nd edn) *The Rise of the Network Society*, Oxford: Blackwells.
Connell, R. (2007) *Southern Theory: the global dynamics of knowledge in social science*, Sydney: Allen & Unwin.
Dimitriadis, G. and McCarthy, C. (2001) *Reading and Teaching the Postcolonial from Baldwin to Basquiat*, New York: Teachers College Press.

Durkheim, É. (1915 [1912]) *The Elementary Forms of the Religious Life*, trans. Joseph Ward Swain, London: Allen and Unwin.

Fisher, J. and Mosquera, G. (2004) 'Introduction', in G. Mosquera and J. Fisher (eds) *Over Here: international perspectives on art and culture*, Cambridge, Massachusetts: The MIT Press.

Freire, P. (1972) *Pedagogy of the Oppressed*, Harmondsworth: Penguin.

Gregory, D. (2004) *The Colonial Present*, Oxford: Blackwell Publishing.

Hardy, I., Heimans, S. and Lingard, B. (forthcoming) *Power and Education*.

Henry, M., Lingard, B., Rizvi, F. and Taylor, S. (2001) *The OECD, Globalization and Education Policy*, Oxford: Pergamon Press.

Jayasuriya, K. (2001) 'From political to economic constitutionalism', *Constellations*, 8 (4): 442–60.

Jules, D. (1998) 'Kweyol culture: cultural differentiation in a globalized context', address delivered at the International Symposium on Creole Cultures, 28 October, Roseau, Dominica.

Lawn, M. and Lingard, B. (2001) 'Constructing a European policy space in educational governance: the role of transnational policy actors', *European Educational Research Journal*, 1 (2): 290–307.

Lingard, B. (2000) 'It is and it isn't: vernacular globalization, educational policy and restructuring', in N. Burbules and C. Torres (2000) (eds) *Globalization and Education*, New York: Routledge.

Lingard, B. and Gale, T. (2010) 'Defining educational research: a perspective of/on presidential addresses and the Australian Association for Research in Education', *The Australian Educational Researcher*, 37 (1): 21–49.

Lingard, B. and Rawolle, S. (2004) 'Mediatizing educational policy: the journalistic field, science policy and cross field effects', *Journal of Education Policy*, 19 (3): 361–80.

—— (2010) 'Globalization and the rescaling of education politics and policy: implications for comparative education', in M. Larsen (ed.) *New Thinking in Comparative Education*, Rotterdam: Sense Publishers.

Lingard, B., Rawolle, S. and Taylor, S. (2005) 'Globalizing policy sociology in education: working with Bourdieu', *Journal of Education Policy*, 20 (6): 759–77.

Mann, M. (2000) 'Has globalization ended the rise and rise of the nation state?', in D. Held and A. McGrew (eds) *The Global Transformation Reader*, Cambridge, UK: Polity Press.

Marginson, S. (2004) 'National and global competition in higher education', *Australian Educational Researcher*, 31 (1): 1–28.

Massey, D. (1994) *Space, Place and Gender*, Cambridge: Polity Press.

Mutua, K. and Swadener, B. B. (eds) (2004) *Decolonising Research in Cross-Cultural Contexts*, New York: State University of New York Press.

Ozga, J. and Lingard, B. (2006) 'Globalization, education policy and politics', in B. Lingard and J. Ozga (eds) *The RoutledgeFalmer Reader in Educational Policy and Politics*, London: RoutledgeFalmer.

Ozga, J., Seddon, T. and Popkewitz, T. (eds) (2006) *Education Research and Policy: Steering the Knowledge-based Economy*, London: Routledge.

Power, M. (1997) *The Audit Society: Rituals of Verification*, Oxford: Oxford University Press.

Radhakrishnan, R. (2000) 'Postmodernism and the rest of the world', in F. Afzal-Khan and K. Seshadri-Crooks (2000) (eds) *The Pre-occupation of Postcolonial Studies*, Durham: Duke University Press, 37–70.

Rizvi, F. (2004) 'Debating globalization and education after September 11', *Comparative Education*, 40 (2): 151–71.

—— (2007) 'Postcolonialism and Globalization in Education', *Cultural Studies, Critical Methodologies*, 7 (3): 256–63.

Rizvi, F. and Lingard, B. (2010) *Globalizing Education Policy*, London: Routledge.

Robinson-Pant, A. (2005) *Cross-Cultural Perspectives on Educational Research*, Maidenhead: Open University Press.

Said, E. (1993) *Culture and Imperialism*, London: Chatto & Windus.

—— (2001) *Reflections on Exile and Other Literary and Cultural Essays*, London: Granta Books.

—— (2003) *Orientalism*, London: Penguin.

Schriewer, J. and Martinez, C. (2004) 'Constructions of internationality in education', in G. Steiner-Khamsi (ed.) *The Global Politics of Educational Borrowing and Lending*, New York: Teachers' College Press.

Shohat, E. (2000) 'Notes on the "postcolonial"', in F. Afzal-Khan and K. Seshadri-Crooks (2000) (eds) *The Pre-occupation of Postcolonial Studies*, Durham: Duke University Press, pp. 126–39.

Smith, L. Tuhiwai (1999) *Decolonizing Methodologies: research and Indigenous peoples*, London: Zed Books.

Spivak, G. C. (2003) 'Righting wrongs', in N. Owen (ed.) *Human Rights, Human Wrongs*, Oxford: Oxford University Press.

Taylor, S., Rizvi, F., Lingard, B. and Henry, M. (1997) *Educational Policy and the Politics of Change*, London: Routledge.

Thrift, N. (2005) *Knowing Capitalism (Theory, Culture and Society)*, London: Sage.

Tikly, L. (2001) 'Globalization and education in the postcolonial world: towards a conceptual framework', *Comparative Education*, 37 (2): 151–71.

Urry, J. (2000) *Sociology beyond Societies: mobilities for the twenty-first century*, London: Routledge.

—— (2002) *Global Complexity*, Cambridge: Polity Press.

Viswanathan, G. (ed.) (2001) *Power, Politics, and Culture: Interviews with Edward W. Said*, New York: Pantheon Books.

Yates, L. (2010) Research building versus research auditing: the ERA intervention in Australia, European Council of Education Research Conference, Helsinki, August, 2010.

Young, R. (2003) *Postcolonialism: a very short introduction*, Oxford: Oxford University Press.

Index